PB
301.1
All   Allen, Bem P

$8.95

35886

Social behavior: Facts & falsehoods

FEB. 1 7 1992

35886

Claysburg Area Public Library
Claysburg, Pennsylvania

Y0-DWL-793

SOCIAL BEHAVIOR

Facts and Falsehoods
about Common Sense, Hypnotism,
Obedience, Altruism, Beauty, Racism,
and Sexism

Bem P. Allen

Illustrations by

Matt Zumbo

Nelson Hall nh Chicago

"Wish You Were Here," written by Harold Rome. Copyright © 1952 by Harold Rome. Chappell and Co., Inc., owner of publication and allied rights throughout the world. International copyright secured. All rights reserved. Used by permission.

"Eve of Destruction," written by P.F. Sloan. Copyright © 1965 by American Broadcasting Music, Inc. Used by permission only. All rights reserved.

"Back When My Hair Was Short," written by Glen Leopold. Copyright © 1972 by Gun Hill Road Music. Used by permission of Paul Colby, Ltd.

"American Pie," written by Don McLean. Published by Mayday Music and Yahwey Tunes, Inc. Copyright 1971.

"Apolitical Intellectuals," from *Let's Go* by Otto Rene Castillo. English translation copyright © 1971 by Margaret Randall. Reprinted by permission of Grossman Publishing.

LIBRARY OF CONGRESS CATALOGING IN PUBLICATION DATA

Allen, Bem P., 1940–
    Social behavior.

    Bibliography: p.
    Includes index.
    1. Social psychology.   I.   Title.
HM251.A528   301.1   77–28709
ISBN 0–088229–393–1 (*cloth*)
ISBN 0–088229–611–6 (*paper*)

Copyright © 1978 by Bem P. Allen

All rights reserved. No part of this book may be reproduced
in any form without permission in writing from the publisher,
except by a reviewer who wishes to quote brief passages in connection
with a review written for broadcast or for inclusion in a magazine
or newspaper. For information address Nelson-Hall Inc.,
325 W. Jackson Blvd., Chicago, Illinois 60606.

Manufactured in the United States of America

10   9   8   7   6   5   4   3   2   1

To Paula, Margaret, Kathleen, Bem, Bem, Margaret, Margaret, Sarah, Sarah, Bob, Benny, Kay, Mike, Danny, Mary Jane, Benita, Stella, Chuck, Chuckie, Todd, Jennie, and the Honeas

Contents

Acknowledgments

Yes folks, I will thank Mom and Dad, and not just because most writers do. Mom and Dad provided me with some very needed encouragement. And I'll also thank my wife Paula whose patience in the face of my compulsiveness was laudable. More important, Paula's thinking influenced my own in ways too numerous and subtle to relate.

Karen Nelson deserves thanks for help in preparation of the book. I want also to thank Janet Wade for the fine job she did in typing the first draft of the book. I thank my boss, Paul Weller, not just because one should take every opportunity to thank one's boss. Paul supplied typing time and materials when these "commodities" were particularly scarce.

I wish to thank the following individuals for the helpful and encouraging comments they made after reading parts or all of the first draft: M. K. Ellis, Bibb Latané, T. X. Barber, Elaine Walster, Eric Ward, Stanley Milgram, Karen Dion, and Harry Triandis.

Last but most important, I want to thank my good friend and

colleague, Charles Potkay. Charlie spent many hours perusing the rough draft of the book and persuading me to write more clearly. On many occasions Charlie provided a better way to make a point. Our debates on several of the controversies considered in the book helped to keep my mind open.

Introduction

Hold it! Don't turn to the first chapter. This is one introduction that you should read. It contains some information which should help in understanding the chapters which follow. I hope that it also contains some information that might prove interesting in and of itself.

WHAT IS THE BOOK ABOUT?

Before presenting the information which is needed for understanding the content of the book, let me describe the content and its purpose. The book is broken up into six chapters each focusing on a different socially relevant topic. Racism, physical attractiveness (beauty), the effects of sexism on women, obedience to authority, hypnotism, and helping in a crisis are considered in separate chapters. These topics were chosen because in each case there is an apparent discrepancy between common beliefs about the topic and evidence produced by scientific research in social psychology. As will be supported in subsequent chapters, Americans have tended to believe that racism is not a serious problem in this country, that whether a person is "beautiful" or "handsome" makes little difference in how other people react to her or to him, and that sexism has affected women very little. Americans also have tended to believe that people would not commit an immoral act at the behest of an authority figure, that hypnotism is a kind of magic, and that when someone is suffering a terrible calamity, people who witness the person's plight will not care enough to come to his or her aid.

The purpose of this book is to show that these beliefs are contradicted by some research in social psychology. In a sense, this book represents an attack on some commonly held beliefs. Beliefs that a large number of people share in common may be very important to them. Wouldn't an attack on such beliefs create psychological discomfort and disillusionment?

WHY ATTACK COMMON BELIEFS?

The purpose of this book is not to make people uncomfortable and disillusioned, but to propose that the beliefs described above can be harmful both to the individuals who hold them and to others. Thus, these beliefs should be challenged. It is my contention that the most effective way to challenge possibly harmful beliefs is by the presentation of evidence produced by scientific research rather than by merely engaging in polemics. In the pages of this book the evidence of research in social psychology is presented as a challenge to the beliefs noted above.

I don't mean to communicate that the book is depressing or frightening. It is neither. To the contrary, I hope that the book is enlightening and uplifting. I believe that the reader will find that the information contained in the book is relevant to his or her everyday life. I have made every effort to enhance the natural relevance to everyday life of information about social psychological research by using real-life examples to illustrate research results. It is also my hope that a consideration of such evidence will help the reader to better understand his or her own behavior vis-á-vis other people's. Finally, this book is, in a sense, a definition of "social psychology." After reading the book one should have a good idea of what the discipline of social psychology is all about. In the meantime the following definition may be helpful: social psychology is the study of how an individual's behavior is both determined by and determines the behavior of other individuals.

DOES COMMON SENSE MAKE ANY SENSE?

Everybody is a social psychologist. This is true because everybody has some "common-sense" notions about social behavior which he believes to be true. Unfortunately many of these notions are probably worse than useless for understanding social behavior. Very often common-sense notions come in contradictory pairs. No matter how an event turns out, the event can be "explained" after it has occurred by invoking whichever member of an applicable pair seems to fit the outcome. Although common-sense "explanations" may provide intellectual satisfaction and make one feel that he or she understands, the "understanding" is a delusion. "Explanations" involving common-sense notions are not explanations at all. "Explanation" implies the ability to predict events before they occur. Common-sense notions merely *describe* events after they occur. Let's take some examples.

Imagine two lovers who are forced to part because of circumstances beyond their control. Perhaps one went away to college and the other had to stay home. Suppose it is noticed that the one who had to stay home became remorseful and proclaimed his or her love even more frequently than he or she did while the lover was present. How would the behavior of the lover who was left behind be explained? "Absence makes the heart grow fonder," of course. Easy, wasn't it?

However, suppose that the outcome was different. Instead of showing remorse, let's assume that the lover who was left behind never mentions the absent sweetheart even though he or she used to talk incessantly about the now absent lover. How might this different outcome be explained? "Out of sight, out of mind," right? No matter what the behavior of the lover who is left behind, it could be explained by invoking one of the members of a contradictory pair of common-sense notions. Common sense can always provide a description of an outcome after it has occurred. However, what would one who used common sense *predict* the next time that he hears about a couple of lovers who are about to part?

Imagine two people who are strongly socially attracted to each other. Let's suppose that these two people spend a great deal of time together. Why are they attracted to one another? Let's suppose further that the characteristics of these two people are investigated and they happen to have very similar characteristics. Ah ha! "Birds of a feather flock together." However, what if the investigation had revealed that these two people were very dissimilar in characteristics? Would "opposites attract" then be invoked? What "explains" social attraction—"birds of a feather flock together" or "opposites attract"? Common sense leaves us confused as to what determines social attraction.

Imagine that you know someone who uses common sense to "explain" social behavior. Pretty easy, isn't it? Everyone knows someone who uses common-sense notions to explain social behavior.

Let's suppose that you are trying to understand the behavior of someone that you know whose name is Joe Blow and who is fifty-four years old and busily spending every dime he has to his name. Because you don't understand Joe's behavior, you tell your acquaintance who uses common sense everything about the case *including how Joe Blow has already behaved.* He now knows the outcome (spending money) and he can invoke a common-sense notion and thus appear to understand where you failed to understand. He would probably say to you something like the following: "That's easy to explain. 'You can't take it with you.' "

The mistake was to reveal the outcome. If a person who operates on common sense is asked to make a prediction he can be exposed as not so smart after all. You could tell him about Joe Blow and then ask him how Joe would treat his money. If you're lucky he will think "a penny saved is a penny earned" and "predict" (actually guess) that Joe will save his money. Now you can show him that his common sense has failed him. However, he might be lucky and think "you can't take it with you" which would yield the "prediction" that the man would spend his money. Don't despair. Pretend he has made a mistake. Tell him that the man "actually" saved his money. The person who uses common sense, having equal reverence for the contrary common-sense notion, will probably say, "Oh I know, 'a penny saved is a penny earned.' " Now reveal the actual outcome. Anyone who gives two different and contradictory answers to the same question doesn't understand what the question is about.

Snow White and Cinderella

Sometimes it is difficult to locate a contradictory notion for a given common-sense notion. However, common-sense notions which have no apparent contradictory correspondent also are invoked after a behavioral outcome is known in order to create the illusion of understanding. Common-sense notions about "beauty," or, more generally, physical attractiveness, fit into this category. One example is "Beauty is skin deep." This notion implies that being beautiful or handsome is irrelevant for most purposes. That is, people are assumed to react to attractive and unattractive individuals in the same way.

Other common-sense notions about beauty emerge from fairy tales. Snow White was "the fairest in the land." She was also gentle and kind and innocent. Most important of all, "everybody" reacted positively to Snow White. The woodsman who was to kill Snow White came under her spell instead. Of course the dwarfs accepted Snow White immediately. Even the animals of the forest were drawn to Snow White. This fairy tale teaches children (and adults) that "beautiful is good" and that beautiful people receive especially positive attention.

The tale of Snow White provides another lesson as well. What did the queen have to do in order to get really mean—mean enough to poison Snow White? She had to "put on a powerful ugly," of course. As the ugly old witch, the queen was able to do her foul deed. People also learn from the tale of Snow White that "ugly is bad."

The Cinderella fairy tale yields still another common-sense notion about "beauty." Cinderella's beauty was obvious despite the fact that she was covered with filth and clothed in rags. Cinderella's ordinary-looking stepsisters were jealous of her beauty and treated Cinderella badly. One of the lessons of the Cinderella fairy tale is that a "beautiful person" may be subject to negative reactions due to the jealousy of less endowed persons. The queen's attempts to kill Snow White may be interpreted similarly.

Now let's suppose that reactions to beautiful or handsome people actually were investigated. A person who used common sense to "explain" social behavior could not predict the outcome of this investigation. Such a person could make a guess by choosing one of the several available common-sense notions about beauty. However, if the actual outcome of the investigation proved his or her guess to be incorrect, the common-sensical person would readily switch to another common-sense notion. No matter what the outcome of the investigation, common sense could "explain" it (i.e., describe it after the fact). If it was found that people reacted in the same way to both beautiful and ugly people, "Beauty is skin deep" would be invoked. If, on the other hand, it turned out that the reaction to beautiful people was positive, "Beautiful is good" would be invoked. Finally, if it turned out that the reaction to beautiful people was negative, "jealousy" would be invoked. In the course of reading this book, the reader will encounter some evidence concerning how people actually reacted to beauty.

Common Sense vs. Scientific Theory

If a child is told that he can't play with a desirable toy, how will he regard that toy? Will he regard it as more or less desirable than before? This example is a good one for comparing the value of common sense and the value of a scientific theory for understanding social behavior.

Common sense offers two notions which are relevant to playing with a prohibited toy. One, "forbidden fruit," implies that a prohibition pertaining to a desirable object makes the prohibited object more desirable. Another, "sour grapes," implies that if a desirable object is prohibited, one decides that it's not very desirable after all. But which is to be chosen for predicting the liking of a prohibited object? Of course, it is impossible to say which is to be chosen because common-sense notions do not include specifications of the circumstances to which they apply.

Cognitive Dissonance

However, there is a scientific theory that can predict desirability of an object after it has been prohibited. The theory consists of statements about social behavior that *do include* specifications of the circumstances to which the different statements apply. It is called the "cognitive dissonance theory."

Cognitive dissonance theory was developed by Leon Festinger (1957). This theory states that if possession of a desired object is prohibited and there would be only a weak punishment resulting from breaking the prohibition, the object would be regarded as less desirable than before the prohibition was instituted. This is because there would be conflict or "dissonance" between the belief that the object was desirable and the knowledge that a weak threat of punishment was enough to cause the person to refrain from possessing the object. Because "dissonance" is uncomfortable, a person would be motivated to get rid of it. The easiest way to eliminate "dissonance" is for a person to change his beliefs about the desirability of the object, so that its desirability is lowered. There is no conflict between believing that an object is not very desirable and knowing that one is refraining from breaking a prohibition to possess it due to a weak threat of punishment.

On the other hand, the theory states that if strong punishment would result from breaking a prohibition to possess a desirable object, the object would be liked as much as before the prohibition was instituted. This is because the belief that an object is desirable is not dissonant with the knowledge that one is refraining from possessing the object due to a strong threat of punishment. In this case a person who desires the object has sufficient justification for refraining from possessing the object. Thus he may maintain this belief that the object is desirable.

A study by Elliot Aronson and James Carlsmith (1963) shows how cognitive dissonance theory can predict the behavioral outcome in the case of prohibition of a desirable toy. The subjects in the experiment were children who were about four years old. The experimenter escorted the children one at a time to a large playroom. After arriving at the playroom, the child's attention was directed to five toys which were displayed on a table. After an opportunity to play with the toys had been given, the experimenter asked the child to rank the toys in order of desirability or attractiveness. The toy that the child liked second best was left on the table while the other toys were spread out on the floor. The experimenter then told the child that he had to leave for a few minutes to run an errand. After leaving the room, the experimenter went to an adjoining room where he observed the child through a one-way mirror (the experimenter could see the child, but the child could not see the experimenter).

In one condition the experimenter told the child to play with any of the toys except the one on the table. Children in this condition also were told that they would receive a mild punishment if they violated the prohibition. The threatened punishment was a statement that the experimenter would be annoyed if the child played with the toy. The second most liked toy was chosen for the prohibition, because, although it was desirable, it was not maximally desirable, and thus its desirability could increase.

In a second condition, children also were told that they could play with all of the toys except the second most desirable toy. However, these children were told that they would receive a strong punishment if they played with the prohibited toy. In this case the threatened punishment was a statement that the experimenter would be very angry with the child, would think badly of the child, and would never again play with the child if the child played with the toy. None of the children in this condition or the other condition actually played with the prohibited toy.

After a lapse of ten minutes, the experimenter returned from the adjoining room and asked all subjects in both conditions to rerank the toys. Each child again decided which toy was the most desirable, which was second most desirable, which was third most desirable, and so on. As predicted by cognitive dissonance theory, children in the strong-threat condition regarded the prohibited toy to be just as desirable after it had been prohibited as they did before the prohibition was instituted. For them there was no dissonance between the belief that the toy was desirable and the knowledge that they had refrained from playing with it due to a strong threat of punishment. Because there was no dissonance there was no reason to devalue the toy.

Children in the mild-threat condition also exhibited behavior which was predicted by cognitive dissonance theory. These children regarded the prohibited toy as less desirable than it had been before the prohibition had been instituted. They had to change their beliefs about the desirability of the toy in order to get rid of the conflict between the belief that the toy was desirable and the knowledge that only a mild threat was sufficient to cause them to refrain from playing with the toy. The new belief that the toy was not very desirable after all was not dissonant with the knowledge that a mild threat had been enough to deter the children from playing with the toy.

To sum it up, scientific theory allows for the prediction of social behavior in advance of its occurrence. If one can predict behavior, one can legitimately claim to understand it. Common sense doesn't allow for prediction of social behavior and thus can't provide genuine understanding of behavior. Common sense can only describe behavior after it has occurred.

"Common sense" has more than one meaning. If "common sense" refers to logical thinking rather than to the application of the simple notions discussed above, then all to the good. However, I believe that when simple notions like "sour grapes" or "out of sight, out of mind" are applied to social behavior and the claim is made that the behavior is "explained," more confusion than understanding is likely to result.

GOOD CRITICS AND BAD CRITICS

The preceding section may sound like a claim that it is never legitimate to criticize a research project after its outcomes have occurred. No such claim is being made. If such a claim had been made it would be like saying that one can't criticize a behavioral research project after the results of the project are known. Certainly it is legitimate to criticize a research project after its outcomes are known. However, such criticisms can be valuable or worthless, depending on how they are made.

It can be easy to be a critic. It is always possible to imagine a number of factors which might have generated the results of an experiment other than those factors which the experimenter considered to be the determinants of his results. Let's take an experiment by Festinger and Carlsmith (1959) as an example.

The "Money-for-Telling-a-Lie" Experiment

The subjects of this experiment were male college students. They had been told in advance that they would be in an experiment and that they would be asked some questions about the experiment after it was completed. The questions supposedly were to be used to evaluate psychology experiments in general and were to be asked by some individuals who were not associated with the particular experiment in which a given subject participated. Actually, the answers to the questions were the critical outcome of the experiment by Festinger and Carlsmith. The reason for the deception was that subjects would not associate the questions with the experiment. If the subjects had made such an association, they might not have given frank and honest answers to the questions.

When subjects appeared for the experiment, the first thing the experimenter did was to remind them of the postexperiment interview to evaluate psychology experiments. The experimenter then told the subjects that they were to participate in an experiment about "measures of performance." Each subject first was presented with some spools and a tray. He was to put the spools onto the tray one at a time. After the tray was full the subject was told to empty the tray and start all over again. Each subject performed this task for thirty minutes. The next task was to turn forty-eight pegs on a pegboard one-quarter of a turn each. The peg-turning task also was performed for a half-hour. Sound like fun? Actually, unbeknownst to the subjects, the tasks were purposely designed to be exceedingly boring. The reason will become apparent.

After both tasks had been performed, the experimenter "debriefed" subjects by explaining the "purpose" of the experiment. However, subjects were not told the actual purpose of the experiment. The information that they received set the stage for the main part of the experiment. Each subject was told that there were two groups in the experiment, an experimental group and a control group. *All* subjects were told that they were in the "control group," because they had been given no information about the experiment before performing in it, except what tasks they were supposed to do. "Control subjects" were informed further than an "experimental group" had been told that participation was very enjoyable before this group had a chance to participate in the experiment.

This pre-participation input was supposedly provided by a collaborator who posed as a subject who had just completed the experiment. It supposedly was the collaborator who lied to potential "experimental group" subjects, telling them that the boring experiment really was a lot of fun.

Up to the "debriefing" point in the experiment, all subjects were treated the same. However, after this point three different conditions were created. A real control group condition was created by terminating the experiment for some subjects after the "debriefing." These actual control subjects went directly to the interview and were asked some questions about the experiment. The most important question was, "How enjoyable was the experiment?" The responses of control subjects to this and other questions were to be a baseline or standard against which reactions to the experiment on the part of other subjects were to be compared.

Other subjects were to be in one of two real experimental conditions. In both of these two additional conditions, the experiment continued beyond the "debriefing." The experimenter began to hem and haw, exclaiming that the "collaborator" who normally talked to potential subjects would not be able to come in that day. According to the experimenter this was a serious problem that required an immediate solution, because the next subject was waiting to be in the "experimental condition." With some hesitation and embarrassment, the experimenter revealed that the project director had authorized him to recruit actual subjects to talk to the "potential subjects." Each real experimental subject was then offered either $1 or $20 to take the collaborator's place and tell the "potential subject" who was waiting that the experiment had been very enjoyable. Hereafter, the two conditions will be called the "$1-condition" and the "$20-condition."

If the real subjects accepted the money, they went immediately to the waiting room to tell the potential subject what fun they had just had. The real subject who was male told the "potential subject" who was female that the experiment was very interesting and enjoyable. Unbeknownst to subjects, the "potential subject" was really a collaborator of the experimenter. The "Oh how much fun it was" spiel of the subject was tape-recorded, for reasons to be explained below. After the session, subjects in both the $1- and the $20-condition went to the interview to be asked, among other things, "How enjoyable was the experiment?"

The major question that interested Festinger and Carlsmith was whether the $1- or the $20-subjects would, as a result of "lying," become the most convinced that the boring experiment really had been enjoyable. The researchers reasoned that only those subjects who had insufficient justification for lying would suffer from "dissonance," and therefore be motivated to change their belief that the experiment had been boring. They predicted that for the $1-subjects the belief that the experiment had been boring would be dissonant with or in conflict with the knowledge that for a $1-payment, they had been willing to say that it was interesting and enjoyable. In order to eliminate the dissonance between their belief about the experiment and knowledge of their behavior with regard to it, $1-subjects were expected to decide that the experiment was enjoyable after all. The knowledge that one had taken a dollar to tell someone else that an experiment was enjoyable would not be dissonant with the new belief that the experiment *was enjoyable.*

However, the situation was different for the $20-subjects. They had sufficient justification for lying. There is not much dissonance between the belief that an experiment is boring and the knowledge that one had accepted $20 to tell the little white lie that it was enjoyable. Thus $20-subjects were not expected to change beliefs about the experiment.

According to Festinger and Carlsmith, the results of the experiment were as predicted. Relative to the control group, $1-subjects saw the experiment as much more enjoyable than did the $20-subjects. That is, ratings of the experiment by the $20-subjects were the same as those of control subjects, but ratings of the $1-subjects indicated much more enjoyment of the experiment than the ratings of control subjects.

Enter the "Bad Critic"

Now let's imagine all of the factors that might have accounted for the results other than the factor of cognitive dissonance. How about the $20-payment? Wasn't that amount implausibly large for telling a little white lie? Perhaps $20-subjects became suspicious that the experimenter was trying to get them to see the boring experiment as enjoyable. If so, maybe they felt coerced and refused to show the change they thought the experimenter expected of them. Maybe many subjects interpreted the payoff as a "bribe" and refused to take it, leaving the experimenter with people who "can be bought off." Perhaps then, their results apply only to people who can be bought off.

Wasn't it peculiar that male subjects were required to lie to a female collaborator? Can males lie to females more easily than they can lie to other males? If so, Festinger and Carlsmith's results might not hold in a case where subjects lie to someone of their own sex. Also, maybe these results can be obtained only in the case of saying something that is untrue about a consideration that is rather unimportant to subjects, like a "one-time-only" psychology experiment. Would the results be the same if subjects had to say something that they actually didn't believe about a consideration that really was important to them?

The reader probably can think of other such criticisms. But why should these criticisms be believed instead of Festinger's and Carlsmith's explanation of their experimental results based on cognitive dissonance? Festinger and Carlsmith had support for their "cognitive dissonance" interpretation because they had predicted the outcome of the experiment and obtained evidence to confirm their prediction. However, our hypothetical critics only have speculations about what *might* have caused the outcome of the experiment. A "bad critic" is a *post hoc* speculator. A bad critic waits until he sees the outcome of an experiment and then imagines all sorts of things. "Bad critics" are not to be believed, because it is just as necessary for critics to support their criticisms with evidence as it is for an experimenter to support his hypothesis with evidence. If you wouldn't believe an experimenter who says "dissonance causes change in beliefs" without evidence, why believe a critic who presents no evidence to support his criticisms? But what would a "good critic" do?

Enter the "Good Critic"

A good critic supports his criticisms with evidence rather than speculating on what might have determined the outcome of the experiment
without reference to supportive evidence. One of the most devilishly
clever ways to criticize an experiment is to use some part of an experimenter's results or some incidental part of his procedure against
him. This strategy is quite different from that of the speculative critic
who does not clearly refer to evidence produced by either the experimenter being criticized or by others. Let's take some examples.

Festinger and Carlsmith tape-recorded the "talk to the potential
subject," because a rival theory states that people who do the best job
of talking against their own belief are most likely to persuade themselves to change in the direction of their talk. To rule out the explanation of this rival theory, Festinger and Carlsmith had some raters read
transcripts of the recorded sessions with the "potential subject." The
raters judged how good a job $1- and $20-subjects did in arguing that
the experiment was enjoyable. There was no observed difference between how good a job was done by $1- and $20-subjects. Thus
Festinger and Carlsmith concluded that "dissonance" rather than
"self-persuasion" accounted for the changed belief of the $1-subjects.

The good critic would examine Festinger and Carlsmith's written report of their experimental procedure very carefully. In the process the critic might discover that the session with the "potential subject" *in fact* lasted only two minutes. Based on this fact taken from
the experimenters' own account of their procedure, the good critic
could reasonably argue that self-persuasion might have played a role
in producing results. This would be reasonable because two minutes
of talk which included some responses by the collaborator probably
provided insufficient information for determining whether the $1- and
$20-subjects had differed in self-persuasion.

A good critic might examine results to determine whether the
experimenters' basic assumptions were met. One important basic assumption of the Festinger and Carlsmith experiment was that the
tasks were boring. However, an examination of the results indicated
that the control subjects had rated the experimental tasks as neutral
with regard to enjoyment. Doesn't this undermine Festinger and Carlsmith's claim that the $1-subjects felt dissonance because they ac-

cepted a little money to say the task was enjoyable *when they believed it was boring*? Maybe, they didn't believe it was boring.

Remember, subjects were asked more than one question about the experiment. A good critic would wonder about the other questions. An examination of Festinger and Carlsmith's results reveals that there were three other questions asked of subjects. On none of these other three questions was there a difference between the $1, $20, and control groups. What should one pay attention to, the one question on which there was a difference or the three on which there was no difference? There is some appreciable probability of getting one out of four by chance. Maybe Festinger and Carlsmith's finding that only $1-subjects changed their beliefs was due to chance.

A second major strategy adopted by good critics is to produce their own experimental results to support their criticisms. A critic could replicate the Festinger and Carlsmith experiment. In the replication an amount much less than $20, but more than $1, might be used. Then it would be possible to see if the same results are obtained when a large but plausible reward for lying is given to subjects. A replication might include a condition in which subjects tell someone of their own sex something that they don't believe. The effect of cross-sex lying then could be examined. Also in the replications special care could be taken to see that subjects don't quit the experiment before it is completed and that there is sufficient information available to determine whether self-persuasion has an effect. A critic is on especially firm ground when he replicates an experiment that he has criticized and shows that when the factors that he claimed actually accounted for results of the original experiment are eliminated, results which are different from those obtained in the original experiment are observed.

As a matter of fact, all of the replications suggested above as well as many others have been done (see Cohen, 1962, Linder et al., 1967, McGuire, 1969). It is now fair to say that the Festinger and Carlsmith (1959) results have been reproduced in a wide variety of circumstances. Apparently, the above *post hoc* speculations were not worthwhile. Even the good critics' criticisms may not have been valid. Although there continue to be questions about Festinger's "dissonance theory" there can be no question that the original results of the "money-for-telling-a-lie" experiment were genuine.

Replication speaks louder than all the *post hoc* criticism one can imagine. With each replication, some of those "other factors" that critics might point to as actually generating the original results will be absent or represented differently than in the original experiment. If the original results can be reproduced in spite of the absence or different operation of those "other factors," then those "other factors" must have been rather unimportant in determining the original results. With many successful replications of an experiment, such as the "money-for-telling-a-lie" experiment, one can be sure that a wide variety of "other factors" are unimportant for determining the results for that experiment. This is why replication is so important to the science of social psychology or to any other science for that matter.

In sum, a "bad critic" criticizes an experiment by speculating about "other factors" not considered by the experimenter that might account for the results of an experiment, but doesn't support his criticisms with evidence. A "good critic" produces evidence of some sort to support his criticism that "other factors" may have accounted for the results of an experiment. However, the final judge is replication. If a result can be reproduced over and over again, it may be considered genuine in spite of the criticisms of "good" and of "bad" critics.

It is important to be critical in examining the social psychology experiments which are described in this book, but remember to be a good critic. And don't forget the importance of replication. Also, be aware of my own criticisms of experiments in the pages that follow. In any case where I might criticize an experiment, the degree of trust that you put in my criticism should depend on how "good a critic" I am in that case.

JOKERS IN THE LABORATORY?

"Deceptions" frequently are used in the social psychology laboratory. That is, in a social psychology experiment, the experimenter may not tell his subjects the whole truth about the purpose of the experiment or he may even tell his subjects something that is false. Remember in the Festinger and Carlsmith (1959) experiment, subjects were led to believe that the questions that they were asked at the end of the experiment had nothing to do with that particular experiment. It was believed that more "frank and honest" answers might be obtained if subjects saw no connection between the questions and the experiment. Festinger and Carlsmith were afraid that if subjects had seen a connection, they might have become suspicious, hypothesized about what answers the experimenter wanted, and then given what they thought was wanted. In this case the researchers could have been "right for the wrong reasons." If the subjects saw no connection, they would probably not be suspicious and they might not form hypotheses about what the experimenter wanted. Even if they hypothesized without seeing a connection, they probably wouldn't have invoked their hypotheses while answering questions which they assumed were unassociated with the experiment.

However, I will not dwell on reasons for deceptions here, as the chapter on obedience to authority contains a general discussion of deception and why it is sometimes necessary in research. In that chapter the reader can see why the alternative to deception, telling the experimental subjects exactly what social circumstances the experimenter is interested in investigating and asking them to pretend that they are in those circumstances, would very often lead to invalid observations of human behavior.

There are two other purposes for this section on deception. First, given that an experimenter has scientific and practical reasons for deceptions, does the experimenter also seek to make fools of his subjects or play tricks on them? Recently a social psychologist accused his colleagues of being "jokers in the laboratory." This accusation implies that social psychology experimenters are trying to play tricks on subjects and may enjoy "fooling" subjects. Second, there is the related question about the effects of deception on subjects. Are subjects "fooled" by deceptions so that they might have reason to feel gullible, naive, and even stupid? I believe that the answer to both of these questions is no. Let me explain why.

Seeing What You're Supposed to See
Even if It's "Really Out There"

In 1955 James J. Gibson and his colleagues Jean Purdy and Lois Lawrence did a very clever and elegant experiment. Like most clever and elegant experiments, the experiment of Gibson and colleagues was quite simple. They hung nineteen identical, rectangular pieces of plastic from an overhead metal track. The pieces of plastic resembled dominos placed one in front of the other in a straight line as if they were arranged for a chain reaction. Although half of the pieces of plastic were black like dominos, the rest were white. All were arranged so that every other one in the lineup was white. Just like dominos arranged for a chain reaction, the pieces of plastic were spaced so that there was exactly the same distance between one and the next. Right in the middle of each piece of plastic, at exactly the same point on each piece, Gibson and colleagues cut a large perfectly circular hole. Beneath the pieces of plastic, overlapping fluorescent lamps were arranged so that almost exactly the same amount of light fell on each piece of plastic.

Gibson and colleagues simply brought their subjects individually into the room where the pieces were hung, situated them in front of the hole in the first piece of plastic in the line, lifted a panel which obscured the holes, and asked the subjects what they saw. Subjects reported that they saw a solid three-dimensional tunnel down which they could roll a ball!

Was this an illusion? Did Gibson and colleagues "fool" their subjects? Their answer would be emphatically no. Subjects were not fooled, they saw what they were supposed to see. Gibson and his colleagues had studied the physical-stimulus components which give rise to the perception of a whole tunnel. They then duplicated those components in their laboratory. As a result, subjects "saw" a tunnel even though an actual, solid, three dimensional tunnel was not present.

Social psychologists try to do research in a way that is analogous to what Gibson and colleagues did. We try to create a "slice of life" in the laboratory (or sometimes outside the laboratory). As closely as possible we try to duplicate reality in the absence of reality. The "slice of life" that we duplicate is more simple than its corresponding reality. This makes it easier to study extremely complex social behavior. But if we didn't duplicate reality, how could we believe that our subjects would behave in the real world as they did in the laboratory? After all, in the last analysis it is real world behavior in which we are interested.

Thus we do not try to "fool" our subjects. We recreate reality for them. If we do a good job of setting up an experiment so that a life situation is accurately duplicated, subjects should act as they would if they actually were in the real-life situation. If they then act as if the real-life situation actually existed for them, they are being reasonable people rather than fools.

Debriefing

Most social psychologists debrief their subjects after an experiment. Subjects are told what the experiment was all about and why the deception occurred, if any. When I use a deception, I also try to tell my subjects that they *should have seen* what they saw and that they should have acted as they did. They were told of the life situation I attempted to duplicate experimentally and why their behavior in the duplicated situation was reasonable. I find that subjects are interested and fascinated by the reasoning behind the deception rather than put down and humiliated because they were deceived. The whole debriefing process seems to communicate a genuine interest in the subject and his or her behavior rather than a desire to fool the subject.

Don't get me wrong. I'm not saying that deceptions are good for subjects. Deceptions should be avoided when they are not necessary. However, it is possible to use deceptions without perverting oneself or risking psychological damage to subjects.

Despite this discussion on deception, as the reader peruses this book, it may occur to him or her that subjects of social psychological experiments seem downright gullible. It may seem to the reader that he or she could never have fallen for an experimenter's deception. The problem is that once one has read all about an experiment and thereby gets a good deal of information that the real subject didn't have (including that there was a deception), it becomes honestly impossible to believe that one would fall for the deception.

Suppose a good magician told you how one of his best tricks works. Also, suppose that the trick was really very simple. After knowing how the simple trick worked, could you ever believe that you *would have been fooled* by the trick had the magician shown you the trick without telling you how it works? Most people could honestly answer no. Once one knows about a deception, it is difficult to imagine that one would have fallen for it.

HOW TO FIND OUT HOW PEOPLE FEEL
ABOUT SOMETHING OR SOMEONE:
RATING SCALES

In social psychology we often have a need to know what people believe about a topic of social relevance, or about someone or sometimes even what people believe about themselves. What is the best way to find out how people feel about something, someone, or themselves? It seems that the most valid information concerning what a person believes about a target such as another person is what that person would say about the target. Thus, if we want to know what people believe about a target, we usually ask them to indicate their beliefs about the target. Sometimes we ask them orally, but usually we ask them with the use of a written method called a "rating scale." Below are some examples of rating scales which have been used in social psychological research.

A bipolar adjective scale would look like the following.

```
                         "myself"
        good    __ __ __ __ X __ __ bad
        pleasant __ X __ __ __ __ __ unpleasant
        valuable __ __ __ X __ __ __ worthless
```

This scale might be used for people's ratings of themselves. The rating is quantified by assigning a "7" to the most extreme blank at the favorable or positive end of the scale and a "1" to the most extreme blank at the unfavorable or negative end of the scale. If a subject in an experiment had responded to the scales as indicated by the "Xs" on the blanks in the example above, his score on the "good-bad" scale would be "3." His scores on the other two scales would be "6" and "4" respectively. Very often an experimenter would be able to assume that all three scales are measures of the same dimension and he would sum over all three scales. This procedure would give the hypothetical subject a score of "13." Since the highest total score in the case of the above example is "21" and the lowest possible score is "3," it would be assumed that the hypothetical subject was rather neutral about himself.

It should be noted that in the case of ratings with bipolar adjectives, one or many scales might be used and an experimenter might consider the scores separately, or might sum over all of the scales and consider a total score, or both. Bipolar adjectives also can be used to rate nonhuman targets as well as human targets.

A different kind of scale which is often used is shown below.

"It's important to take a tetanus shot in order to prevent tetanus."

agree __ __ X __ __ __ __ __ __ __ __ disagree

In this case subjects would be given a statement in written form and asked to indicate the degree to which they agree with it by placing an "X" on one of the blanks. A hypothetical subject's score for the above example would be "3" if it was decided that the blank closest to "agree" would be assigned "1" and the blank closest to "disagree" would be assigned "11." The hypothetical subject in this case would be assumed to believe that one should take a tetanus shot in order to prevent tetanus. This form of rating scale could be used to rate a person. For example, the agree-disagree format could be used with the statement "The nation's president is doing a good job."

With still another kind of rating scale, the subject may be asked to imagine the target person (which could be himself) or object, may be shown a picture of the target, or may have the target described to him orally. An example is given below.

attractive X __ __ __ __ __ __ unattractive

In this case assume that a picture of someone is shown to a hypothetical subject and that the subject finds that someone very attractive (i.e., the target receives a score of "7" on a seven-point scale).

These rating scales are very simple, of course. Their complexity and sensitivity as measurement instruments don't compare to that of a thermometer. However, in most cases rating scales are as good as or better than more complex instruments such as physiological equipment. Furthermore, very often rating scales are the only means available for quantifying a psychological phenomenon.

It is remarkable how different subjects interpret the same rating scale in the same way, and how the same subject interprets the same rating scale in the same way on different occasions. It is also true that rating scales have allowed for the confirmation of hypotheses in many, many experiments. Of course, there are situations in which these kinds of scales are not valid. Some of these situations are encountered in the chapters which follow in which the strengths and weaknesses of rating scales are considered in more detail.

HOW BIG A DIFFERENCE
MAKES A SIGNIFICANT DIFFERENCE?

Consider the following experiment. Howard Leventhal and his colleagues, Robert Singer and Susan Jones (1965), wanted to know whether a strong dose of fear or a weak dose of fear was better for inducing college students to believe that it is important to take a tetanus shot in order to prevent tetanus. Their final goal was to induce the students to actually take a tetanus shot. One group of subjects was presented with a booklet which described the case history of a patient who had died of tetanus. Color photographs of the patient accompanied the booklet. The booklet contained vivid language to describe the suffering of the patient. The photographs graphically depicted the painful treatment received by the patient. This group was called the "high fear" group. A "low fear" group was given the same booklet except that the language was toned down. They also received photographs, but their photographs were black and white and, therefore, less frightening.

After reading the booklet and looking at the photos, all subjects responded to some rating scales and were instructed to get a tetanus shot. Among the rating scales was one which measured subjects' beliefs about the importance of preventing tetanus by getting a tetanus shot. The rating scale used by Leventhal and colleagues was similar to the "tetanus shot" scale described in the previous section.

What Leventhal and colleagues wanted to know was whether the high-fear information was more effective than the low-fear information for inducing subjects to believe in the importance of tetanus shots. On a more concrete level they wanted to know whether the average scores of the high-fear subjects on the tetanus shot scale reflected a greater belief in the importance of tetanus shots than the average scores of the low-fear subjects.

But how different should the average scale scores for the two groups be in order for Leventhal and colleagues to conclude that the difference is significant? Is any difference great enough to be considered significant? For example, what if the average score of the high-fear group was 3.23 and the low-fear average was 3.24? That's a difference, but does it really "make a difference"? How about average scores of 1.53 for the high-fear group and 5.87 for the low-fear group? Or would the average scores have to fall at opposite ends of the scale in order for these researchers to conclude that the average scale scores were different (e.g., high-fear average = 1.05 and low-fear average = 10.92)?

The best answer to this question seems to be that a probability statement about the magnitude of an acceptable difference must be made before an experiment is done. Some researchers decide before they do their experiments that to be regarded as significant, the difference between their critical groups' average scores must be so large that it would occur only five times in a hundred by chance. Other researchers require that the difference would occur only one time in a hundred. If the difference between the average scores of the critical groups actually turns out to be as large as or larger than the predetermined difference which would occur only five times in a hundred by chance (or one time in a hundred), then the obtained difference is considered "statistically significant." Notice that this use of the word "significant" when applied to statistics is somewhat different from its common use. In common use, "significant" means "important" or "meaningful." The reader would do well to remember this distinction when he or she is confronted with television commercials. "Excipient" pain reliever may be "significantly (statistically) more effective" than aspirin for relieving pain, but is the difference between "excipient" and aspirin "meaningful" or "important"? What's "meaningful" or "important" is a matter of interpretation. As indicated in the next section, an absolutely small difference can be "statistically significant."

In the chapters that follow, the reader can assume that all of the experimental outcomes reported are "statistically significant" according to the "probability statement" criterion described in the above paragraph. Sometimes I shall use the words "statistically significant" and sometimes I shall just use the word "significant." For various reasons I occasionally may not use either "statistically significant" or "significant." Nevertheless, unless I indicate otherwise, every experimental outcome that I refer to is "significant." I have taken care to see that this is in fact the case.

Incidentally, Leventhal, Singer, and Jones did observe a significant difference between the average score of their two groups. Subjects in the high-fear group showed stronger beliefs in the importance of taking a tetanus shot than subjects in the low-fear group. However, results revealed that high-fear and low-fear information didn't differ in effectiveness for inducing subjects to actually take a shot. Subjects who received a dose of fear, regardless of whether it was strong or weak, and who also received some specific instructions telling them exactly how to go about getting a shot, took significantly more shots than subjects who only received a dose of fear. Thus high fear was not better than low fear for inducing subjects to take a shot.

IS BIGGER ALWAYS BETTER?

Sometimes when I report the results of an experiment to my introductory social psychology class, some of my students tell me that they don't believe the results because there are too few subjects in the experiment. Somehow results of experiments are not maximally believable unless there are a great number of subjects in the experiment.

Actually there is one sense in which having few subjects in an experiment leads to stronger conclusions based on results than having many subjects in the experiment. With a large number of subjects in an experiment, an experimenter can detect "a sneeze in a hurricane." No matter how trivial the relationship between factors such as level of fear information and beliefs in tetanus shots, the relationship can be detected as statistically significant if one has enough subjects in the experiment. Conversely, a relationship must be quite strong if it is to be detected as significant when there are relatively few subjects in an experiment. If a researcher reports a significant relationship between the factors that he is investigating and that researcher has used only a few subjects, one can assume that the researcher is reporting a relatively strong relationship.

Of course there is a sense in which a large sample of subjects helps in drawing conclusions from results. Everything else being equal, the more subjects that one has sampled for an experiment the more certain one can be that his sample is representative of the population from which it was drawn. Recruiting a large number of college students for an experiment increases the likelihood that the sample will be representative of college students. If one does an experiment to find out the effect of different kinds of sex education on high school students' sexual attitudes, a large sample of subjects will put one on firmer ground in generalizing results to the population of the high school from which the sample was drawn or to the entire population of high school students.

Selecting a large sample is not the only way to arrange for "representativeness." Careful selection of subjects can insure that one's sample, regardless of its size, represents its population. For example, the political poll and the TV-program evaluations often entail samples of the U.S. population of only about 1,500 persons. And yet the reader will recognize that these polls often are extremely accurate. The reason they are so accurate is because extraordinary care is taken to insure that the sample includes proportional representation of all factions of the U.S. population. A researcher can also make his sample representative of its population if he randomly samples his subjects carefully and also randomly assigns them to experimental conditions, even though he actually uses only a small sample of subjects.

Large numbers of subjects also may be important if a researcher wishes to show that two factors are *unrelated,* or to put it another way, that two groups do not differ significantly in average scores. Use of many subjects gives the researcher a lot of power to detect a relationship, if it exists at all. If a researcher uses a large number of subjects to investigate a relationship and then fails to detect a statistically significant relationship (or, alternatively, a significant difference between his critical groups), he or she can be reasonably sure that the relationship doesn't exist or is quite trivial.

Just as readers may find it useful to refer back to the rating scales given in this chapter as they read the book, they may wish to refer back to the section on statistical significance and number of subjects in the experiment when these matters arise in the pages that follow. I also hope that readers will remain aware of the sections on common sense, deception, and critiquing experiments. Finally, I would be happy to receive comments about the book from readers.

Hypnotism

Magic, hoax or ordinary phenomenon

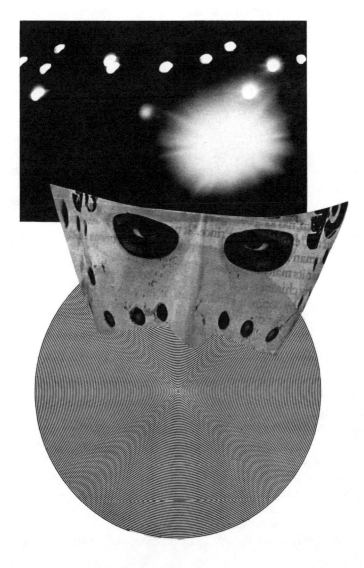

In the 1770s a physician named Friedrich Anton Mesmer popularized what was to become known as hypnotism. Mesmer spoke of a power called "animal magnetism." Supposedly the universe and all its inhabitants were controlled by the stars. The control was exercised by stellar influence on animal magnetic fluids which filled the universe. Harmony and balance of these fluids were associated with good health, and imbalance with illnesses of various sorts. Mesmer presented himself as a "magnetizer" who could restore the magnetic fluid balance.

In Paris near the end of the 1770s, Mesmer unveiled his famous *baquet,* an oak chest filled with chemicals and adorned with appendages of iron. Mesmer "magnetized" this device and used it to cure all those who sought his special brand of medicine. Sometimes he formed his patients into a circle about the *baquet,* binding them together with cords or by hand clasp. The room which contained the *baquet* was dimly lighted and permeated with soft music. Numerous mirrors were hung about the room. Mesmer often entered this scene dressed in magician's clothes. He would swirl around the room, touching some of his proselytes, making a pass over others, and fixing some with a penetrating stare. On occasion he approached one of his patients and uttered the word "Dormez." Immediately the believer would seem to go to sleep. Many cures were effected by these methods. However, investigations failed to reveal the scientific nature of his techniques and he was roundly rebuked.

It was said that the French government offered Mesmer 20,000 francs to reveal his secret (Boring, 1957), but Mesmer refused and was thereafter branded a charlatan. However, his discovery was not forgotten. In the 1830s, another physician, John Elloitson, revived what was by then called Mesmerism. When the technique was again questioned, Elloitson engaged the scientific community of his day in an attempt to gain respectability for Mesmerism. It seemed that he would succeed when in 1842 an Englishman named W. S. Ward successfully amputated a leg with no analgesic agent save Mesmerism. The response to this feat was less than encouraging. Most physicians doubted the truth of Ward's claim, and pronounced the method without benefit, even if it was valid. It was deemed better to have patients suffer pain while their physicians operated. Pain was considered to be a wise provision of nature.

In 1845, James Esdaile read of Elloitson's work. Esdaile who was also a physician immediately tried Mesmerism on a patient who was suffering intractable pain. When the patient was "cured," Esdaile became a convert. Fortunately he was located in India at the time where opposition to Mesmerism was much less than in Europe. An investigative commission appointed by the Indian government examined more than one-hundred of Esdaile's cases involving Mesmerism. The commission's report was favorable, thus giving Esdaile the green light to use Mesmerism for a variety of purposes, including surgery. He responded by using Mesmerism in more than three-hundred major operations, each apparently performed without pain. It is little wonder that when the United States Congress bestowed an award on an American dentist for the discovery of a chemical analgesic agent, Esdaile wrote a letter of protest, claiming prior discovery of a method for eliminating pain.

By the 1840s Mesmerism was recognized as possibly useful, but condemned as unscientific. Scientific respectability came when James Braid threw out the term Mesmerism in favor of "hypnotism" ("nervous sleep"). Braid at first fostered the belief that hypnotism was the result of sensory fixation on some discrete object which paralyzed the muscles of the eyelids and thus induced sleep. Now hypnotism had a "scientific" explanation. Thereafter, it became acceptable to the scientific community to use the technique in medicine and in research.

Nobody seemed to notice when in 1866 the Frenchman, A. A. Liebeault, adopted still another explanation of hypnotism (Allport, 1954). Hypnotism was merely a form of suggestion according to Liebeault. Suggestibility was considered to be a human instinct at the time and thus it was hardly radical to claim that hypnosis was a kind of suggestion. Hypnosis involved the arousal of the suggestion instinct under conditions of unusual rapport between suggestor and suggestee. The result of these conditions was limited attention on the part of the suggestee which allowed for the implantation of an idea. The idea was then simply acted out. On the surface there seemed to be nothing mystical about this point of view. This is probably why the "suggestion" interpretation of hypnosis has become widely accepted many years after being first advanced. Thus, Boring (1957), an experimental psychologist, was able to conclude that hypnosis had become a part of the body of scientific knowledge. What escaped everyone, until recently, was that the induction of the trance-like state associated with hypnosis was the method assumed to be responsible for gaining the "unusual rapport." It was assumed that only in a trance could people take suggestions which would lead to extraordinary outcomes like analgesia.

ENTER THE HERETIC, THEODORE XENOPHON BARBER

Since Liebeault, few modern researchers who have concerned themselves with hypnosis have questioned the assumption that hypnosis is a form of suggestion. However, it has been assumed that the suggestion continuum is anchored at one end by ordinary, everyday suggestions, and at the other end by the extraordinary suggestions associated with hypnosis. It was further assumed that there is a great deal of space in between. Ordinary suggestions like 'let's go get a hamburger" aimed at a person who is vaguely hungry at the noon hour are assumed to be far removed from hypnotic suggestions. Although everyday suggestions may be kin to hypnotic suggestions, the latter are thought to be possible only when the suggestee is in the trance state implied by the word "hypnosis." One may "go get a hamburger," "go to the movies," or "take a coffee break," as a result of a suggestion given under ordinary wakeful conditions, but one will "feel no pain while a physician operates," "regress to the age of six," or "become blind" only when given suggestions while in a hypnotic trance. In other words, the trance state is believed necessary in order to impart suggestions resulting in extraordinary behaviors like age regression, blindness, and analgesia.

These assumptions about hypnosis have been so engrained that T. X. Barber (1969) was regarded as a sort of heretic when he began to challenge them. Barber's contention was simple: people do perform extraordinary behaviors under suggestion, but they need not be in a trance in order to produce such behaviors. According to Barber, the trance state of hypnosis is not unique, not really different from a wakeful state, and therefore not a necessary condition for producing extraordinary behaviors.

Barber (1969) has attacked the assumptions about trance state in two different ways. First, he has argued that if trance is a unique state, different from the wakeful state, it should be accompanied by physiological responses which are different from those associated with the wakeful state. Numerous researchers have attempted to differentiate the physiological responses of persons who are said to be in a trance from the responses of those who are not in a trance. These attempts have involved such diverse measurements as EEG (brain waves), pulse rate, and GSR (electrical resistance in the palm of the hand). None of these attempts has succeeded in demonstrating that "hypnotized" people differ in responses from people who are wide awake.

A more dramatic source of evidence that the trance state is not physiologically unique comes from a demonstration of hypnotic analgesia employed during abdominal surgery. I witnessed the demonstration via motion picture (see reference list). The patient required a cesarean section because normal birth was dangerous for her. Hypnosis seemed the best available means of eliminating pain. The woman's regular physician was the hypnotist, and he had developed strong rapport with her as a result of being acquainted with her for a long period of time. The physician was able to put his patient into a trance with ease, apparently due to many practice sessions which occurred prior to the actual surgery.

Aside from the usual techniques of hypnosis, this particular physician induced a tranquil and pleasant feeling in his patient by having her sing while in a trance. It was remarkable to watch her sing happily while the surgeon cut through successive layers of muscle until he reached the uterus. She remained calm and immobile throughout the entire process. The hypnotist-physician noted that his patient was connected to an instrument which measured a physiological response. He proudly indicated that her response pattern was quite normal! After the baby was withdrawn and the incision stitched, the woman was taken to her room where the trance was ended. The woman was alert, cheerful, and immediately ready to care for her baby. The aftereffects seemed very positive compared to those of chemical anesthetics. However, if the trance state accounted for the elimination of pain, why was her physiological response pattern the same during surgery and after? It appears that, at least in part, something besides "trance" accounted for the remarkable behavior of this person.

Barber's first point, then, would be supported in this case. The second strategy used by Barber (1969) to discount trance was to examine common hypnotic induction procedures in order to determine whether components other than trance instructions might account for suggested behaviors. These procedures usually require the hypnotic subject to fixate on a small but distinctive object, such as a blinking light or a swinging pendulum. Subjects are also typically instructed to relax completely and to allow their muscles to become limp. There are normally many assurances that hypnosis is harmless and cannot cause a person to embarrass himself. Usually the subject is told that his arms and legs are becoming heavy, as these limbs do when sleep approaches. Almost all induction procedures involve repeating the statements that the subject's eyelids are becoming heavier and heavier, that his eyes are becoming very tired, and that he is becoming more and more drowsy.

A typical sleep or trance instruction might also take the following form: "You are becoming more and more sleepy. Don't fight your feeling of drowsiness. Sleep will be pleasant. As you go to sleep you will continue to hear my voice. You will respond only to my voice. Now I will begin to count backwards from ten. By the time I get to one you will be in a deep, deep sleep, but you will still hear my voice and you will do the pleasant things that I will ask you to do. Ten— you are going into a deep sleep. Nine—deeper and deeper into sleep. Eight—you are sinking into deep sleep. Nothing can disturb you. . . . One—you are now completely asleep. You are ready to have some wonderful experiences that you have never had before." Alternatively, the subject may be given a posthypnotic suggestion. Posthypnotic suggestions involve telling the subject that he will soon be asked to wake up and shortly after he awakes he will be given a cue to perform some behavior or another. The cue usually involves the hypnotist snapping his fingers or clapping his hands.

These elaborate trance instructions seem to constitute most of typical induction procedures, but Barber has discovered by examining many procedures that there are other more subtle components. Most prominent among these additional components are "it's easy to do" instructions and "cooperative-try" instructions. The subjects are told that it is easy to respond to suggestions, that anyone can take suggestions if there is the desire, and that others have found it easy to do the tasks that the hypnotist would impose. The subjects are also admonished to cooperate with the hypnotist and try hard. They are told that if they will cooperate and concentrate on what they are to do, they will have beautiful experiences, but if they refuse to cooperate, they will make the hypnotist look foolish and waste their own time. Together these two instructions will be referred to as "motivational instructions." The purpose of these instructions is to motivate the subjects to accept suggestions.

Having thus dissected typical induction procedures, Barber and P. S. Calverley (1965) sought to show that motivational instructions were at least as important as trance instructions for generating suggested behaviors. To this end they designed an experiment in which one group of subjects was given cooperative-try and easy-to-do instructions while fully awake while other groups of subjects were given only trance instructions. The subjects in the latter groups were told that they were in a hypnosis experiment, and then were given "go-to-sleep" instructions. All subjects were given a standard set of suggestions. These standard suggestions included "your hands are stuck together and you can't get them apart," "your throat muscles are paralyzed and you can't talk," "you are stuck to your chair and can't move," and "you'll not be able to remember one of the tests that we have done here today." Subjects who were given motivational instructions did as well in accepting the standard suggestions as subjects who were given trance instructions.

In a second experiment (Barber and Calverley, 1963) one group of subjects received trance instructions plus motivational instructions, while another group received only motivational instructions. The motivational-instruction group did as well in taking the standard suggestions as did the trance-plus motivational-instruction group. In some of his other experiments (e.g., one involving suggested deafness) Barber (1969) has shown that motivational instructions can be superior to trance instructions. However, the bulk of his research has shown no difference between trance instructions and motivational instructions in producing suggested behaviors.

Other research has shown that trance instructions are better than no instructions. For example, Barber and Calverley (1965) compared the suggestion-taking performance of subjects who were given trance instructions with the performance of subjects who were given no instructions, but were told that they were in a hypnosis experiment. Trance-group subjects did better in this case. Research outside of Barber's laboratory confirms that trance can induce suggestion-taking (Wickramasekera, 1971). In sum, trance is sufficient but not necessary for accepting suggestions normally expected only in a trance state. One can observe the same suggested behaviors when subjects are wide awake, if they are given proper motivational instructions.

But why does trance play any role at all for inducing people to accept suggestions if it is not a unique state? Barber (1969) indicates that trance instructions may be of some importance for inducing sug-gestion-acceptance because these instructions *imply* motivational instructions. Most people assume that when one is in a trance or, more generally, being hypnotized, one is supposed to be especially pliable and willing to accept the suggestions: i.e., to cooperate. Also, being in a trance implies that accepting suggestions will be especially easy. Implicitly if not explicitly, trance may imply that cooperative-ness is appropriate and suggestion-acceptance is easy. If so, it is un-derstandable that trance yields suggestion-acceptance even though it is apparently not different from a wakeful state.

The best conclusion concerning the comparison between the im-portance of trance and the importance of motivational instructions for inducing suggestion is that motivational instructions are just as important as trance. This conclusion is consistent with the con-clusion that trance is not physiologically unique because both con-clusions imply that trance is not a necessary condition for obtaining suggested behaviors which may be extraordinary. Trance state is not physiologically different from a wakeful state and motivational in-structions are as effective as trance instructions for yielding sug-gestion. Therefore, putting persons in a trance as opposed to allow-ing them to be in a normal, wakeful state is unnecessary for im-parting suggestions that will be acted upon. This means that we may close the gap between ordinary, everyday suggestions and unusual or extraordinary suggestions. The same processes must underlie both. The difference between the everyday suggested behavior "going to get a cup of coffee" and the extraordinary suggested behavior "showing no pain when a painful stimulus is applied" is not that the trance state is required only for extraordinary behavior. Rather, it is that motivational instructions are required for extraordinary suggested behavior but not for everyday suggested behavior.

In spite of all of this evidence it is probably true that most persons who attempt to obtain extraordinary behaviors cling to the notion that trance is necessary. Most of them would expect embarrassment and failure should they attempt to obtain extraordinary behavior without using trance. However, there is an outstanding exception.

THE GREAT KRESKIN

One of the best known and successful of performing suggestors, The Great Kreskin, has been convinced by Barber that trance is unnecessary for obtaining extraordinary behaviors. Kreskin typically commits heresy from the point of view of hypnotists by beginning his act with an argument that trance is unnecessary. Most hypnotists would believe that this refutation of trance would inhibit trance induction and guarantee failure of suggestion acceptance. Further, if trance instruction implies motivational instructions, it would seem that Kreskin would be stacking the cards against himself by denouncing the importance of trance. However, if Kreskin has handicapped himself, it is not evidenced by witnessing his performance. He is able to obtain extraordinary suggested behaviors from people *who are told to remain fully awake* by simply presenting motivational instructions. One particularly good example was provided by a college student during one of Kreskin's campus performances. After motivational instructions were given, a young university man was told to turn his shirt inside-out. He also was told that he would no longer remember his name. Both name and shirt reversal were to be forgotten until Kreskin removed the suggestion. Kreskin then left the student for a few minutes while he made other demonstrations. Upon returning his attention to the young man, Kreskin asked various routine questions such as "where do you live?" and "what's your college major?" The young man reacted quite normally. But when asked his name, he became confused, turned red in the face, and began to stutter and stammer. He looked exactly as a person would be expected to look if he forgot his name. The audience's response was spontaneous and uproarious. Members of the audience recognized the authenticity of the young man's behavior. Upon being asked why his shirt was inside-out, the young man became totally flustered, much to the delight of the audience. Unless Kreskin had by chance happened upon an Academy Award actor, he had indeed produced some extraordinary behavior in an unextraordinary college student. Except under suggestion, most people could not convincingly look as if they could not recall their name.

HEADS I WIN AND TAILS YOU LOSE
OR AROUND AND AROUND WE GO

It is remarkable that in the two-hundred years since Mesmer popularized hypnosis, few people have questioned the necessity of trance for eliciting extraordinary suggested behaviors. There are two basic reasons why this has been the case. First, research done in this century has appeared to support trance, because of certain methodological errors. These errors will be discussed in the next section. This section will be devoted to discussion of a logical error which has helped to propagate the belief that trance is necessary for inducing extraordinary behaviors. The logical error is found in the definition of hypnosis.

Hypnosis is defined as a special trance state in which extraordinary suggested behaviors can be obtained. Therefore, "trance" is explained or verified by invoking observed behaviors that have been suggested to the subject, and these behaviors are explained by invoking "trance." To put it another way, if one were to ask a hypnotist why people take suggestions, he would reply "because they are in a trance." Then if the hypnotist is asked, "How do you know that people are in a trance?" he would respond "because they take suggestions." Thus if the event "suggestions accepted" is observed, trance is inferred, but if the event is not observed, trance is not inferred. The definition of trance is therefore tautological or circular. Such definitions are logical errors because they purport to provide "explanations" of events when, in fact, they merely provide descriptions of events after they occur, rather than predictions of them before they occur. A statement which does not yield predictions cannot be confirmed or disconfirmed and, therefore, has little scientific merit.

But why would anyone embrace a circular definition? Because a circular definition provides those who accept it with an unbeatable position. No one knows this better than Barber. In effect hypnotists and researchers who accept the necessity of trance have said to Barber, "Heads I win, tails you lose."

For example, when Barber reported that his subjects took more suggestions when told that it would be easy to take suggestions than when told that it would be difficult, those who accept trance replied that the instruction "it will be easy" must have produced a deeper trance (Barber, 1970). But if the results had turned out the other way, these people would have argued that "it will be difficult" produced a deeper trance. When Barber reported that motivational instructions produced the same level of suggestion-taking as trance instructions, the trance people said that, unbeknownst to Barber, his motivation group had slipped into a trance! No matter what happens, those who embrace the circular definition of trance can "explain" it after it has happened. Such hindsight may allow a feeling of satisfaction but it does not constitute an "explanation." In a scientific sense, and for that matter in a practical sense, a genuine "explanation"—commonly referred to as a theory—provides predictions of events in advance of their occurrence. As indicated in the introductory chapter, theories can be confirmed or disconfirmed, because they make predictions. However, because circular definitions allow only hindsight "explanations," they cannot be confirmed or disconfirmed. That is, we can determine whether or not a theory is correct by testing its predictions, but we cannot say anything about the correctness of a circular definition, because it yields no predictions.

OUR SACROSANCT BASIC ASSSUMPTIONS

It remains to be explained why the logical error of trance definition has escaped everyone until Barber revealed it in 1964 (Barber, 1969). Sometimes we take our basic assumptions about something important to us as givens. These assumptions become premises upon which we build our logic. We may question our logic, but it may not occur to us to question our premises. This state of affairs may exist because our basic assumptions date so far back in time that the original reasons for adopting them have been forgotten. Assumptions that have been around so long that the reasons for adopting them have

been forgotten may be so strongly held that to question them becomes
heresy. That which goes unquestioned may become unquestionable.
The earth was assumed to be flat for so many years that the unscientific reasons for the assumption were forgotten. When the "flatness
of the earth" was questioned, the questioners were considered to be
heretics.

A modern-day parallel existed in the assumption that it was necessary to defeat the communists in Viet Nam in order to avoid communist domination of Asia (*The Pentagon Papers*, 1971). Franklin
Roosevelt was the first president to consider involvement in Viet
Nam. Harry Truman apparently thought that Viet Nam was a critical
area for containment of the communists. Eisenhower translated beliefs into behavior by supplying the French with massive support for
their effort to defeat the communists. It was Kennedy who committed
himself and us to "victory" in Viet Nam when he decided that we
would not accept a communist takeover in that country. By the time
that Lyndon Johnson became president, the Pentagon report revealed
that it was a basic assumption that "victory in Viet Nam" was necessary to the security of the United States. Debates among Johnson's
associates were concerned with *how to win,* not whether winning was
essential. The original "domino theory" of involvement in Viet Nam
was never seriously questioned.

A similar process may have occurred in the assumption that
trance is necessary for the acceptance of extraordinary suggestions.
Mesmer had made hypnosis seem like magic. To many of those who
followed Mesmer, the "magic" of the hypnotic trance was what
caused subjects to take suggestions resulting in extraordinary behaviors. After Mesmer, others such as Braid debated about how trance
determined suggestion-taking, not whether it was essential to suggestion-taking. By the beginning of this century even Braid's level of
analysis was abandoned and questions about hypnosis centered on
how it might be used in research and in psychotherapy (Boring,
1957). It is little wonder then that it didn't occur to anyone to question the necessity of trance until the early 1960s (Barber, 1969).
The post-Mesmer original reason for assuming the necessity of trance
—magic is needed to obtain extraordinary behaviors—had been forgotten. Perhaps people could prevent their own errors of thought and
behavior if occasionally they would suspend concern with their logic
and, instead, reconsider their premises.

SLEIGHT OF HAND IN THE LABORATORY

The second reason why the belief in the necessity of trance has gone unquestioned for so long is that research on hypnosis has appeared to support the necessity of trance due to the commission of certain methodological errors. These errors and how they led to incorrect conclusions concerning trance are the focus of the present section. Also, the relevance of the methodological errors committed by researchers in hypnosis to research in social psychology will be noted. Hypnosis research provides particularly clear examples of the kinds of error which have plagued social psychological research and other forms of research involving human subjects.

Control Groups

Anyone who has had a course in research design knows that if one wants to know whether some factor A has had an effect on subjects' responses, one must compare the responses of subjects "treated" with A (experimental group) with the responses of subjects not treated with A (control group). A common illustrative example is the case of A being a dosage of some drug. To conclude that a drug dosage has influenced subjects' responses, the responses of subjects who are given the drug must be compared with the responses of subjects not given the drug. The "not drugged" group must be treated exactly the same as the "drugged" group, so that the only difference between the groups is that one group actually is administered the drug. If these conditions are met, differences in responding between "drugged" and "not drugged" subjects may be attributed to the drug, *rather than to one of the several other "treatments" that subjects receive* in the course of administering the drug. Let's suppose that a drug is administered by the use of a large hypodermic needle. Needles scare people and thus may make them display the symptoms of anxiety. Let's suppose that some subjects who are injected with a drug subsequently are observed to be highly anxious. Was the anxiety due to the "drug treatment" or to the "needle treatment"? One could conclude that "the drug treatment was responsible for the anxiety" only if control subjects who received a non-drug injection showed less anxiety than the "drugged" subjects.

By the same token, if a hypnotist "hypnotizes" some subjects,

gives them some suggestions and then notes that they take the suggestions, can he conclude that the hypnotic trance caused the suggestion-
acceptance? Of course he cannot draw such a conclusion unless he
has given the same instructions and suggestions to a group of subjects
who are comparable to his hypnotic subjects, omitting only the trance
instructions, and noted that this second group of subjects didn't take
suggestions. We have already seen that when these conditions are
met, the nontrance group does as well at suggestion-acceptance as the
trance group.

Controlling the Control Group

Although nonresearchers (e.g., professional entertainers who use
hypnotism) who believe in trance may have been guilty of not using
a control group, this generally has not been true of researchers who
believe in trance. Researchers in every discipline of science are aware
of the need for control groups. Thus researchers seeking to support
the necessity of trance have used control groups, but, according to
Barber (1969), they generally have employed inappropriate control
groups. For example, the "hypnotic group" is typically composed of
individuals who have shown high suggestibility, usually by easily
"falling into a trance" Control supjects, on the other hand, have
been randomly selected without regard to their level of suggestibility.
Under these conditions hypnotic subjects are almost always observed
to take more suggestions. Little wonder since they were more suggestible to begin with! The proper way to proceed, according to
Barber (1969), is to assign highly suggestible people to *both* the
hypnotic group and to the control group, or to assign randomly chosen
people to both the control group and to the hypnotic trance group.
Barber (1969) generally has adopted these latter strategies for conducting his experiments in which he finds no difference between
trance and control groups (motivational instructions only).

There is another kind of inappropriate control group which
bears mentioning. Martin Orne (1971) has developed a special type
of control group in order to test some assumptions which are beyond
the scope of this book. However, in his studies, differences between
responses of the control group and the hypnotic group might be taken
as evidence for the necessity of trance, because the control group is
"awake." Orne's control group, called "simulator group," receives

instructions to "act as if you are hypnotized." Sometimes such groups display less suggestion-acceptance than hypnotic subjects (Levitt and Overly, 1971).

There are two reasons why such results cannot be taken as evidence of the necessity of trance. First, usually experiments involving the use of the simulator control entail assigning low-suggestible subjects to the simulator group and high-suggestible subjects to the hypnosis group (see Orne, 1971, and Barber, 1969). Second, the simulator instructions strongly imply that subjects are to *pretend* that they are hypnotized and thus are *not* to be susceptible to suggestions. In short, the simulator group against the hypnotic group comparison does not meet the criterion of holding everything constant across control and hypnotic groups except trance instructions (see drug example above). For these reasons such comparisons cannot be taken as evidence of the necessity of trance for suggestion-acceptance.

It is interesting that even though in simulator-group/hypnotic-group experiments the cards are stacked in favor of suggestion-acceptance being greater for hypnotic group subjects, there is in many cases no difference between suggestion-acceptance for the simulator group as compared to the hypnotic group (e.g., McDonald and Smith 1975). These results are quite embarrassing for those who support the position of necessity of trance.

Leaking Bias into Instructions Given to Subjects

In any research discipline in which human subjects are employed, there is always the danger that experimenters will leak their personal bias into the experimental procedure. For example, an experimenter may, through subtle behaviors or unintended additions to planned experimental manipulations, cue subjects as to what he or she wishes to find. Of course, such cues could affect the behavior of subjects and possibly cause them to manifest behaviors which confirm the experimenter's hypothesis. An experimental hypothesis is genuinely confirmed only if subjects display behaviors which they would normally perform in their own lives. Behaviors born of the motivation to please the experimenter, to display knowledge of the "real" purpose of the experiment or other motivations peculiar to the experimental context can produce false confirmations (and sometimes false disconfirmations).

Some confirmations of the "trance is necessary" hypothesis appear to have been produced by bias introduced into instructions to subjects. It is almost always necessary to instruct subjects concerning what they are to do in an experiment. Because instructions are often long and complex, it is sometimes possible to unwittingly create differences between experimental and control groups which are not a part of the intended manipulations, but which tend to create bias in favor of the experimental hypothesis. Barber (1969) asserts that bias in favor of the "trance hypothesis" may be created by subtle, unplanned variations in instructions to trance and control groups. For example, an experimenter who believes in the necessity of trance may "prove himself right" by delivering trance group instructions in an enthusiastic tone of voice and control group instructions in a lackadaisical tone of voice, without any awareness of what he is doing. Obviously, the trance group would be expected to take more suggestions than the control group, quite aside from possible differences in suggestion-acceptance which might be expected on the basis of intended differences between groups. To support this possibility, Barber and Calverley (1964a) gave the same instructions concerning the performance of some standard suggestions to two different groups of subjects. Although the content of the instructions did not vary across the two groups, one group was given the instructions in an enthusiastic tone of voice while the other group was given the instructions in a lackadaisical tone of voice. The "enthusiastic group" was much better at accepting suggestions than the "lackadaisical group."

In addition, if instructions to subjects are long and complex and often repeated, it is possible for an experimenter to unwittingly use slightly different wording when addressing experimental group subjects than when addressing control group subjects. The difference in wording may constitute only a few words out of the many spoken to subjects and thus may go unnoticed by the experimenter. Such a "little difference in wording" may make a world of difference in the experimental outcome. The "little difference" can be a subtle addition to planned instructions or a subtle variation of planned instructions. For example, an experimenter who believes in the necessity of trance can, without awareness, add something to control group instructions which may imply to control subjects that they are not expected, or it is inappropriate for them to accept suggestions. Barber and Calverley (1964b) supported this possibility by giving the exact same instructions to two different groups concerning the performance of some standard suggestions. However, one group was told that the experiment was to test "imagination" while the other group was told that it was to test "gullibility." The "imagination group" accepted more suggestions. One likes to show "imagination," but one does not like to display behaviors which will depict him as "gullible."

Inquiry Bias

It is very usual in experiments employing human subjects for the target behavior to consist of answers to questions asked after experimental procedures have been completed. In persuasive-communication research, subjects are presented with a persuasive communication and then asked some questions to determine whether they have been persuaded. In hypnosis research, subjects typically are asked whether or not they were in a trance and their answers are accepted as primary evidence of whether the trance state existed for them. Also, such subjects may be asked "did you take the suggestions" and if they answer yes, it is assumed (in circular fashion) that they were in a trance. The "bias problem" is that the answer obtained may be determined by the way the question was asked. A person who believes in trance may "obtain evidence" that subjects who took suggestions were in a trance by phrasing the trance inquiry so as to elicit affirmative replies. Barber (1969) reports a study in which "hypnotized" subjects were asked some questions after they were "awakened." Only 17 percent answered that they had experienced the trance state as different from the waking state when asked, "Did you experience the hypnotic state as basically *similar* to the waking state?" However, 72 percent said the two states were different when asked, "Did you experience the hypnotic state as basically *different* from the waking state?" The latter question may have implied to subjects that they were expected to perceive a difference in trance and waking states (i.e., they were in a trance) while the former question may have implied that subjects were not to perceive the states as different. Also, only 22 percent of the subjects replied that they could *not* resist suggestions when asked, "Do you feel that you *could* resist?," but 83 percent said that they could *not* resist suggestions when asked, "Do you feel that you *could not* resist?" This second result strongly indicates that Barber (1969) is correct in calling for more objective criteria for assessing suggestion-acceptance. Subjective reports of suggestion-acceptance may be influenced by the phrasing of the questions used to elicit the reports. This is an important point to bear in mind when one encounters "public opinion polls." It may be as important to look at the questions asked of respondents as it is to look at the answers that respondents provide.

Barber (1969) indicates that instruction bias may be minimized by having instructions tape-recorded. For example, bias in instructions for the performance of suggested behaviors can be minimized by playing taped instruction to both experimental and control groups which vary only as is necessary to create different group conditions. With this method, subtle variations in tone of voice and wording may be minimized relative to the method of having instructions read or recited by an experimenter who may be privy to the experimental hypothesis. Bias in the inquiry phase may also be minimized by presenting questions in written form. When it is appropriate to ask subjects in different group conditions the same questions, using the same written form will guarantee that the phrasing of the questions will not vary.

SUGGESTED BEHAVIORS: REAL OR BOGUS?

So far this chapter has focused on the *methods* of obtaining suggested behavior. Principally, the belief in the necessity of trance for accepting suggestion has been challenged. This section is devoted to the suggested behaviors rather than to the methods for obtaining suggested behaviors. For the sake of convenience, and to avoid redundancy, I would like the reader to make an assumption about the several suggested behaviors which will be considered. For each and every suggested behavior to be discussed, the behavior can be obtained from subjects who are fully awake and who are given motivational instructions as well as from hypnotized subjects. I will mention evidence to support this assumption only in the case of a few suggested behaviors. If the reader should wish to check the assumption in the case of a particular suggested behavior, Barber's (1969) excellent book contains the evidence. Henceforth, I will discuss the extraordinary behaviors that people are able to perform under the influence of suggestion as opposed to normal circumstances, but I will not generally distinguish between suggestions given under trance instructions and suggestions given under motivational instructions only. Instead of continuing to worry about how extraordinary behaviors are obtained, this section will center on another problem. Are these extraordinary behaviors real or bogus? By "real" I mean that the subject is actually doing what he claims to be doing. For example, suggested analgesia is real if a subject who claims to be feeling no pain actually experiences no pain as opposed to showing pain tolerance. By "bogus" I mean that the subject is not doing what he claims to be doing. As we shall see, a few extraordinary suggested behaviors are "real" by virtue of their basic nature, while the remainder are bogus.

In reading what follows, please do not forget that neither Barber nor I deny that suggestion allows for the performance of behaviors which would normally be difficult or impossible for individuals. We agree that suggestion is a powerful controller of behavior. Also, I don't think that Barber sees people who accept extraordinary suggestions as being fakers. I certainly don't see them as fakers. For example, a "good hypnotic" subject is one who believes that trance is a special state which allows him or her to do certain things that he or she couldn't do otherwise. He believes that he is under the control of the hypnotist and that the *hypnotist makes him* behave in extraordinary ways.

Further, I find the "role-playing" explanation of suggested behaviors to be misleading (Barber agrees on this point: personal communication). "Role-playing" implies that suggestees become actors who mimic some stereotyped behaviors that are supposed to occur under "suggestion," but which are not a part of their actual repertoire of behavioral capabilities. Under suggestion people perform behaviors drawn from their repertoire of behavioral capabilities rather than from their capacity to mimic. These behaviors may be extraordinary in that individuals would not or could not perform them without the supports provided by the suggestor and all that surrounds him. On the other hand, this position is also quite different from that of Orne (1971) who sees individuals as performing behaviors under suggestion which are beyond their "normal volitional capacity" (i.e., novel behaviors which are produced by suggestion rather than being a part of individuals' repertoire of behavioral capabilities). We all have the potential for performing many behaviors which we have never displayed because circumstances have not drawn them from us. Suggestion is a means of making these potential behaviors actual, but not the only means. A person who never has lifted three-hundred pounds may be able to do so under suggestion or if he must in order to save his own life. In sum, suggestion may allow individuals to perform remarkable behaviors which they have never before performed, but suggestion will not impart capabilities not already present in individuals. Barber (personal communication) has indicated that just because "role-playing" may be misleading does not mean that all variations of the "role" concept are of no value. In fact, he has asserted that Sarbin's "role-taking" theory has merit as an explanation of suggestion. (Interested readers should see Sarbin & Farberow, 1952.)

Suggested Analgesia

Under suggestion, people may appear to feel no pain. Typical demonstrations involve driving a sterile needle into the fleshy part of a finger, immersing a foot in ice-cold water, and having surgery under suggestion. But does the fact that people are able to unflinchingly accept such stimulation indicate that they feel no pain, or is it an indication of extraordinary pain tolerance? The most dramatic example of "suggested analgesia" is surgery performed under suggestion, without chemical anesthetics. Barber (1969) examined written reports of Esdaile's many cases of surgery performed under suggestion. In most cases it was apparent that patients were experiencing pain, even though they were able to undergo the surgery. For example, there were reports of patients "crying out" periodically, twitching, moaning, or "coming out of the trance." Esdaile's cases are remarkable in that he was able to impart such a high level of pain tolerance, but these cases do not stand as evidence that suggestion eliminates pain in the same way as does an anesthetic. In the case of the woman who underwent the cesarean section described above, there was also evidence of remarkable pain tolerance, as opposed to lack of pain sensation. As the woman sang during surgery, there was a noticeable change of pitch of her voice when the cutting began and when it became more critical. It sounded almost as if she had adapted a high-pitched scream to music.

All the cases of surgery considered so far have been performed under hypnotic suggestion. There is at least some evidence that nonhypnotic suggestion can allow for tolerance of surgery. Barber (1969) recounts the experiences of surgeons in a prisoner-of-war camp who, having no chemical anesthetics, resorted to hypnosis. However, in some cases they reported that patients "would not go into a trance." Since surgery had to be performed anyway, the surgeons in desperation told the wakeful patients "trust us and you will feel no pain." To their surprise, the surgeons found that the patients were able to tolerate surgery.

There are some possible reasons why subjects are able to show such remarkable tolerance during surgery. Among the most noxious concomitants of pain are fear and anxiety. Barber and a colleague John Chaves (Chaves & Barber, 1976) have contended that suggestion lessens fear and anxiety. Chaves and Barber also point out that the parts of the body which are frequently involved in surgery (e.g., internal organs) may occasion little or no pain upon being cut. In addition, "knowing what to expect" because of extensive preparation, careful selection of only those who believe that suggestion eliminates pain, faith in the surgeon-suggestor, and distraction such as the singing of the cesarean-section patient all may contribute to high tolerance of surgical pain (Chaves & Barber, 1976).

Suggested Amnesia

The claim of suggestees who have been told to forget events filling an entire block of time is that they have forgotten completely, as if the events had never occurred. The evidence indicates that suggested amnesia is bogus. Patten (1932) reports an experiment in which subjects who were placed under hypnotic suggestion claimed to forget a practice session in which they had worked some arithmetic problems. If they truly had forgotten they should have shown no improvement in performance when subsequent to the suggestion they were given a second opportunity to work on the same kinds of problems. Subjects under suggestion did show improvement which indicated that they had not forgotten.

Age Regression

Age regression involves the claim on the part of suggestees that they have entered a time machine and have gone back into time to become themselves at an earlier age. Age regression is to the believing suggestee similar to reincarnation, except that he becomes himself at an earlier time, rather than someone else who lived at an earlier time. I saw a remarkable performance of age regression elicited by my colleague James Garrett. The subject was a twenty-one-year-old woman who performed in front of a large audience in a dimly lighted auditorium. She was successively "taken back" to previous birthdays. With great confidence and spontaneity she was able to cite who was present at her birthday parties, what gifts she had received, and the day of the week of each birthday. Of course, the chances of guessing the latter are one in seven, but she answered without hesitation and proved to be correct when we later consulted calendars. (Incidentally, Barber (1969) has discovered that college students who are wide awake can employ a self-developed formula to quickly derive the day of the week for any previous day.)

As she passed back to her teens, pre-adolescence, and childhood, the subject showed other noteworthy behavior. She was able to be accurate and spontaneous in reporting who was president of the country, governor of her state, mayor of her city, and which rock groups were popular at the time of each of her previous birthdays. As she "passed back" in time she displayed behaviors, emotions, voice tone, and cognitive functioning appropriate to the suggested age she had assumed. For example, when she was "taken back" to an early elementary school year, she began to swing one leg which she had crossed over the other. Later when we queried her about this behavior, she related that it was a nervous habit which her parents had eliminated through scolding.

In fact, her portrayal of childhood behaviors was so accurate that I bet that she could, *under suggestion,* pass the proficiency test for our introductory child psychology course. She apparently had buried in her memory the remnants of many observations of her own and other children's behaviors, emotions, and cognitive functioning which were released from memory by suggestion. Later when we interviewed her after the age regression suggestion had been removed, she showed none of the understanding of children that she had under age regression. Apparently suggestion facilitated recall!

This observation indicates that suggestion might help students (or nonstudents for that matter) to do better than usual in recalling previously learned materials. This possibility, if verified, might prove to be due to greater concentration and/or elimination of distractions under suggestion as opposed to normal circumstances. This proposed heightened concentration also might allow for greater efficiency of recording information into memory as well as recalling it, once it is recorded. Barber (1969) cites some evidence to support these possibilities.

However, is suggested age regression real or bogus? On the face of it, one would have to accept reincarnation of self in order to accept age regression as real. However, there is concrete evidence to indicate that age regression is bogus. First, age regression often involves taking people back to age two or less. Subjects may then report in baby talk—could you talk at two?—or report as if observing themselves at age two. These reports may relate complex events which could not have been recorded into memory at age two due to lack of sufficient cognitive ability! For example, an age-regressed person who reports what his parents said to one another during an argument which took place when he was two years old must be considered suspect. A two-year-old usually hasn't the ability to record complex adult language into memory. Further, Barber (1969) reports that college students who were "regressed" to the elementary school years did better on intelligence tests than children at the age to which the students were regressed. If these students had actually become schoolboys and schoolgirls, they should have performed cognitively like schoolboys and schoolgirls.

Assuming an Unusual or Inappropriate Role

An individual who under suggestion assumes an unusual role (e.g., the role of politician by a nonpolitician) or inappropriate role (acting like a dog) is fully informed that he is to act like something or someone rather than to become that something or someone. Individuals also will report that they acted like something or someone under suggestion. In other words, people who assume an unusual or inappropriate role claim to be acting or role-playing under suggestion and in fact they are. Therefore, this section deals with a suggested behavior which is real. The remarkable aspect of assuming an unusual or inappropriate role under suggestion is that people do a much better job of acting than they do if they were attempting to assume the role under normal conditions. A couple of examples will suffice to make the point. I once witnessed a stage hypnotist transform a rather in-articulate and shy young man into a convincing public office seeker. The young man, after barely being coaxed onto the stage, scurried to a corner in the apparent hope of escaping the spotlight. When he was dragged to the center of the stage for a personal interview preliminary to the administration of hypnosis, his verbal responses were almost inaudible. Under suggestion he was told to take the microphone on cue and convince the audience that he should be elected city dog-catcher. When the cue was given, the young man suddenly bounded from his chair, strode confidently across the stage, and grabbed the mike from the hypnotist's hands. He then delivered a most forceful and persuasive campaign speech including many plausible and logical arguments concerning why he would be a fine dog-catcher. In the course of his speech, the young man mentioned many "problems as-sociated with the office of dog-catcher" which had probably not oc-curred to members of the audience. The hypnotist induced an equally reserved young man to act if he were Paul Revere being pursued by the British. On cue the man leaped astride a chair and hopped across the floor as if he were on a galloping horse. The terror in his eyes suggested that the British were getting very close.

Suggested Blindness

A person who indicates that he has become blind under suggestion is claiming that he cannot see what is going on around him. Persons who accept the suggestion that they are blind can be very convincing. They give every appearance of being blind. For example, they will not flinch when a hand is moved rapidly toward their face and will not respond to amusing or embarrassing events which are occurring within their field of vision. However, Barber (1969) has indicated that suggested blindness is bogus: people who appear to be blind un-der suggestion actually do see what's happening around them. To prove the point, Barber referred to an experiment in which the sug-gestion "you're blind in one eye" was given to individuals who were unaware of how a stereoscope works (Pattie, 1935). A stereoscope is a device which requires vision in both eyes in order to produce its perceptional effects. When exposed to the stereoscope, these sub-jects reported perceptual effects which could occur only if they had vision in both eyes.

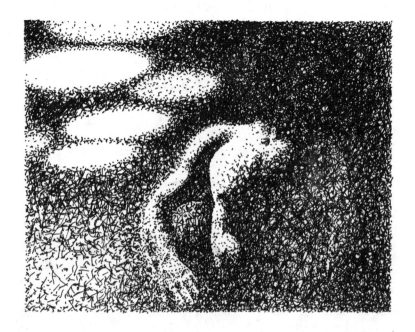

Suggested Deafness

Persons who accept the suggestion "to be deaf" are claiming that they have no auditory sensations and cannot react to auditory input. Suggestees can look convincingly deaf. Under suggested deafness, suggestees will not react to the presentation of jokes which have other people who are present "rolling on the floor." They also will not react to insults which normally would result in a fist fight. However, Barber (1969) reports that this kind of suggested behavior also is bogus. The demonstration (Barber and Calverley, 1964c) involved a delayed auditory feedback device. Normally we coordinate our speech by hearing ourselves talk. Obviously, it takes some interval of time for sounds emerging from our mouths to arrive at our ears. The apparatus for delayed auditory feedback increases the amount of time usually taken for speech to arrive at the ears by a small portion of a second. The result of receiving delayed auditory feedback for normal individuals is stuttering and stammering. Subjects who had accepted the suggestion "to be deaf" showed the same level of stuttering and stammering as subjects who had not been given the suggestion, indicating that the former group could actually hear, in spite of their claims to the contrary.

Suggested Auditory and Visual Hallucinations

A person who claims to be hallucinating under suggestion is in fact hallucinating. Hallucination is seeing or hearing something which is not actually present and thus those who say under suggestion that they are seeing or hearing something which is not there are doing what they claim to be doing; i.e., suggested hallucination is "real." What's remarkable about suggested hallucination is that people do a better job of hallucinating under suggestion than they do under normal circumstances (awake, rested, and not under the influence of any drug or psychotic episode). Anyone can hallucinate, if everyday imagination is accepted as hallucination, but suggested hallucinations are more vivid than everyday hallucinations. For example, under suggestion a person can sit for an hour "seeing all those things in life that are beautiful" and thoroughly enjoy the experience. Also, suggestees may report that hallucinating their favorite music is as enjoyable as actually listening to it on a good stereo set. The most dramatic example of suggested hallucination that I have seen was produced by a stage hypnotist. The hypnotist told some male suggestees that, on cue, their glasses would take on a magic X-ray quality which would allow them to see female members of the audience in the nude. When the cue was delivered the men looked rapidly about the room as if they were vitally interested in what they were seeing. I suspect that if they had been hooked up to the appropriate physiological equipment, they would have shown responses consistent with their hallucinations. In fact, the process was so convincing that several male members of the audience attempted to shield their dates.

Warts

How great is the power of suggestion? It appears that suggestion can even influence bodily processes. Barber (1969) reports that warts which are caused by a virus are degenerated by an actual physiological process, and that suggestion may speed up that process. To support this assumption, some subjects who had warts were told under suggestion that the warts would disappear from one half of their body. Subsequently it was established that the warts had degenerated more rapidly on the side of the body that was the target of the suggestion. Thus there is truth to the old wives tale that consultation with the seventh son of a seventh son will cause warts to drop off! Such consultation actually may cause warts to drop off, but the seventh son of a seventh son is not a magician; he just imparts a powerful suggestion. Swabbing warts with an innocuous dye described as a "new medicine" also may cause degeneration, but it's not the dye that does the trick (Barber, 1970). Rather it is a bodily process which has been influenced by suggestion.

Hysteria as Self-Suggestion

The observation that suggestion can influence bodily processes raises the possibility that hysterical disorders might be thought of as produced by self-suggestion. A hysterical disorder traditionally has been defined as one in which a person converts anxiety into actual symptoms of physical disease or condition without there being any actual physical basis for the symptoms. This is different from psychosomatic disorders in which psychological stress and anxiety create a real physical disorder. One can imagine that if an individual believes that he is losing his ability to walk, he may suggest to himself that his leg muscles are losing their strength. This self-suggestion could actually lead to a state of paralysis, in the absence of any actual physical disorder.

 False pregnancy may also be seen as a result of self-suggestion. In one case, a woman somehow was able to pump up her abdomen to give the appearance of pregnancy, and then, over a period of an hour, pump it back down again in the process of mimicking labor and childbirth. This extraordinary feat of muscular control may be thought of as accomplished through self-suggestion. A woman who wants very badly to become pregnant, or greatly fears pregnancy, may so strongly suggest the state of pregnancy to herself that her abdominal muscles are influenced to create the appearance of pregnancy. Thinking of hysterical disorders as a form of self-suggestion may, in some cases, allow therapists who are charged with the elimination of the hysteria a short cut to understanding its etiology.

SOME CONTINUING MISCONCEPTIONS ABOUT HYPNOSIS AND SUGGESTION

Because of the ever present hypnotist on stage, it is likely that certain misconceptions about hypnosis and suggestion in general will be perpetrated indefinitely. The present section is devoted to exposing these misconceptions so that the reader may be able to confront them when they are encountered. An understanding of these misconceptions is especially important, because some of them have strong ethical implications.

Some Can and Some Can't?

A typical hypnotist will assure potential suggestees that some of them can be hypnotized—which means to him going into a trance and doing wonderful things—while others can't. Now why do you suppose a hypnotist would make this seemingly self-defeating statement before attempting to hypnotize people? Because he knows that many people will not assume the appearance of "trance," and that some of those who do appear to "go into a trance" will do poorly at taking suggestions. Thus he makes his excuses for failure in advance!

The hypnotist's excuse perpetuates an unfortunate misconception. It is true that some people stubbornly refuse to take on the appearance of being in a trance, but it is not true that only a "lucky" few are able to perform extraordinary behaviors under suggestion. There are, of course, individual differences in suggestibility. For example, a stage hypnotist once bet that he could go to the business district of Anytown, USA, tap shoppers on the shoulder and say "sleep" and observe a small portion of them collapse to the sidewalk. Such behavior would represent the maximum level of susceptibility to trance. Others might not go into a trance at all or be willing or able to display extraordinary suggested behaviors even under the most ideal laboratory conditions. Most of us are somewhere between these two extremes, and it is reasonable to assume that given the proper motivational circumstances and, more important, the proper suggestor, we might take suggestions leading to extraordinary performances. Think for a moment of someone that you trust and respect a great deal. If in an emergency he or she suggested that you do something that you have never done before and that you thought was impossible for you, can you imagine that you might do that something? If you adopt the assumption that accepting suggestions to perform extraordinary behaviors is determined by perfectly understandable motivational conditions rather than by "magic" trance, you probably answered the above question in the affirmative. If you did answer in the affirmative, you probably realize that you might, at the behest of a suggestor, perform some behaviors that would be unacceptable to you. On the other hand, a person who believes that extraordinary behaviors—including socially unacceptable behaviors—can be induced only while in the highly unusual "trance state" may fail to monitor his or her behavior to avoid the rare but possible occasion when a nonhypnotic suggestor attempts malevolent influence.

God Made Only a Few Hypnotists

Hypnotists are those who are able to induce others to perform extraordinary behaviors, and they tend to be self-flattering. They would have you believe that only a gifted few have the mystic power to put people in a trance which, for them, is tantamount to having the power to induce extraordinary behaviors. While it may be true that some people are better than others in getting people to "go into a trance" and that some people are better than others in getting people to perform extraordinary behaviors, it is not true that only a few could influence others in this way. There is a stereotype of hypnotists: middle-aged, graying, possessing a deep voice, and male. People who fit this stereotype probably will do better as suggestors than people who don't fit the stereotype. However, I will bet that almost anyone could walk into my introductory psychology class of two-hundred students, and after having had a few minutes' practice, recite a typical hypnotic induction procedure with the result that at least two or three "tranced" persons would display extraordinary suggested behaviors. For every individual there probably is someone who would take suggestions from the individual to perform extraordinary behaviors, given the proper motivational circumstances. It is true that the "proper motivational circumstances" might rarely occur, but as an example, a rare opportunity for a successful theft might become an occasion for a teenager to induce a normally law-abiding friend to become a thief.

This should be a sobering thought to those who assume that they
could never influence another person to perform behaviors which
would be unacceptable to him or her.

Snakes and Acid

The preceding section implies another misconception. Will a person
perform behaviors under hypnosis that he normally would consider
to be unacceptable or even immoral? Anyone who has ever watched
a stage hypnotist knows that it is part of the act to make a claim to
the contrary. The hypnotist typically begins his presentation by assuring the audience that he will not cause potential suggestees to do
anything that would be embarrassing, degrading, or dangerous. If he
didn't say this, no one would step forward to help him with his act!
This "reassurance statement," uttered for purely practical reasons,
sometimes borders on the unethical. In particular a stage hypnotist
entertains by humor which is often obtained by making fools of suggestees. Suggestees are sometimes reduced to being a drunk, an
animal, or reduced to some other state which involves humiliating
themselves. That the audience is laughing at, rather than with suggestees often is apparent.

The seriousness of this misconception is manifested in the observation that people will, in fact, perform immoral and dangerous
behaviors at the behest of a suggestor. Martin Orne and Frederick
Evans (1965) reported an experiment in which it was suggested to
subjects who were wide awake and to hypnotic subjects that they
could touch a poisonous snake and throw acid into the experimenter's
face with impunity. Unbeknowst to the subjects, the snake was behind
an invisible plate glass screen and the acid had been exchanged for
a harmless substance. Several hypnotized and several nonhypnotized
subjects reached for the snake and threw the "acid." It was true that
most subjects who took suggestions had assumed that no harm would
result from their behavior, even though they weren't aware of the
safety precautions which had been taken. However, under everyday
circumstances, without the influence of suggestion, would people perform such dangerous behaviors based on the *belief* rather than *certain
knowledge* that no harm would result? A moment's reflection should
produce a no answer. Further, Barber (1969) has shown that sub-

jects will take suggestions leading to harmful outcomes, even if they do *believe* that actual harm will result.

Incidentally, the reader might see a good deal of similarity between the snake-and-acid experiment and Milgram's research which is considered in the next chapter of this book. If so, the perceptions are accurate. In both cases, individuals are suspending their own thought processes and passively accepting the dictates of another person.

Obedience

2

Theirs not to reason why, theirs but to do or die

270   285   300   **DANGER**

After his remarkably easy victories in the West, Hitler's thoughts turned to the East. In March of 1941 Hitler instructed his generals concerning their duties for Barbarossa, the imminent life and death struggle with Russia. They were to act under different assumptions from those which guided their behavior in the West. After all, the western operation had been only to insure a one-front war; a main task of Nazism was to crush the hated Slavs and to steal their lands. For Barbarossa, accepted conventions of war were to be suspended. Not only prisoners-of-war, but also civilians were to be starved to death, and influential civilians and army personnel were to be shot without court martial. German soldiers guilty of breaking international law were to be excused upon direct order of the Fuehrer. Hitler concluded, "I insist absolutely that my order be executed without contradiction." And, indeed, Hitler was obeyed.

Russia was to be Lebensraum for the German people, and its resources were to sustain the Aryan race. Thus Hermann Goering and the muddled-headed Nazi philosopher Alfred Rosenberg plotted to remove food and other life supporting materials from Russia. Both knew that this action would mean the starvation of millions. But this outcome was not considered regrettable—not even to Rosenberg who was Russian-born—because the Slavs were subhumans. Only those Russians who could survive at a primitive agrarian level were to be allowed to live.

Not all of the killing was to be a passive, incidental outcome of Barbarossa. Hitler had decided that certain of the large Russian cities were not needed. They would be replaced by German-built cities. Leningrad was to be razed to the ground and its people crushed beneath the rubble. Here was a case where Hitler's orders suffered no contradiction. Leningrad was besieged for nine hundred days. During this time the city was completely surrounded and bombarded daily. The only outside source of food for the Leningrad population was by transit across Lake Lodoga, by boat or by truck across the ice. Otherwise, food grown in tiny plots here and there about the city provided sustenance.

These sources of food and supplies were insufficient. Fully one half of the three-million population died by starvation, disease, or bomb-blast. The beautiful city itself was reduced to rubble. But Leningrad's citizens fought on, for they knew what would happen if they surrendered. Hitler's army had accepted orders to regard the people of the city as subhumans to be exterminated. Most of the slaughtered were combatants, many of whom starved to death in German prison camps. Examples of treatment of prisoners will suffice to illustrate how willingly Hitler's generals obeyed. German generals readily abdicated their soldierly duty to treat prisoners humanely, not only by direct neglect, but also by releasing them to SS-boss Heinrich Himmler, who they knew would subject the prisoners to extraordinary barbarism. In fact, the SS lined up Russian prisoners by the thousands and shot them in the head. Himmler also ordered that Russian prisoners be used in certain "scientific experiments." In one case two Russian officers were immersed in water at just above 32° F and allowed to slowly freeze to death while their physiological responses were monitored.

In all, some twenty million Russians died at the hands of the Nazis. This number was more than the total deaths for all other participants of World War II. It is more than the total populations of New York City, Chicago, and Los Angeles combined. Surely, in the entire history of mankind, there have never been more tragic consequences of blind obedience.

OBEDIENCE IN THESE UNITED STATES

An American psychologist, Stanley Milgram (1974), became interested in the kind of obedience described above. He believed initially that obedience resulting in death and torture was so extraordinary that it was probably specific to cultures like Germany's, where, historically, militarism had prevailed. His goal was to develop an experimental procedure for studying obedience, and then take it to Germany where it would allow him to discover the essential nature of submission to authority. The data he collected here in the United States was to be of interest mainly as a means of validating his method for studying obedience. After many tries, Milgram finally developed the following method which might be regarded as the prototype for studying obedience.

Advertisements were placed in local newspapers to recruit subjects to participate in a psychology experiment at prestigious Yale University. This same method of recruitment was used not only for the prototype experiment described just below, but also for all the other experiments done by Milgram. As a result of this public announcement, all sorts of people were recruited: professionals (engineers, business managers), unskilled workers (construction workers, factory workers), persons who possessed advanced degrees (beyond the B.S. or B.A.), and persons with less than a high school education. All subjects were male for the prototype experiment and for almost all of the experiments conducted by Milgram. Otherwise the subjects used by Milgram seemed representative of the United States population. The only remuneration received by subjects was $4.50 and a chance to participate in the advancement of the behavioral sciences.

The prototype experiment, as well as the others done by Milgram, was completed during the 1960s. In order to explain procedures of the prototype experiment, a description of a composite of experimental sessions will be given. There were forty experimental sessions. One actual subject served in each session.

When subjects arrived at Yale's social-interaction laboratories they encountered a young man dressed in a laboratory coat, and a middle-aged man dressed in a business suit. The young man who was the experimenter explained that the purpose of the experiment was to study "learning processes." Specifically, the experimenter said that he was interested in a neglected determinant of learning, *punishment*. For this reason, one of the participants was to be a "teacher" in the experiment and the other was to be a "learner." Since the teacher was to administer electric shock to the learner as punishment for failure to learn, the experimenter suggested that a lottery be conducted so that each participant would have an equal chance to be the learner.

Actually the lottery was rigged so that the middle-aged man (who was the experimenter's confederate) drew the "learner's" lot, and the real subject drew the "teacher's" lot. Of course the real subject was not told that the middle-aged man was a confederate of the experimenter rather than a fellow subject. After the drawing, both the "teacher" and "learner" were led into an adjoining room which was filled with sophisticated-looking electronic equipment. Most prominent in the room was a long console of metal construction. The console had numerous switches arranged horizontally across its front panel. Each switch was labeled with an electrical voltage designation ranging from 15 volts to 450 volts, in 15-volt increments. In addition, numerous lights and other labels were displayed on the panel.

Included among these were verbal descriptions of shock placed above the switches, evenly spaced across the face of the console. Beginning at the low-voltage end of the console "slight shock" was indicated, followed from left to right by "moderate shock," "strong shock," "very strong shock," "intense shock," "extreme intensity shock," "danger: severe shock," and finally "XXX." The equipment was so impressive in appearance that it once inspired some words of admiration from an experienced electronics salesman who visited Milgram's laboratory.

After allowing participants a moment to inspect the equipment, the experimenter led both learner and teacher to an adjoining compartment. Here the "learner" was strapped to a chair and an electrode placed on his wrist. The experimenter then asked the learner if he had any questions. The learner's reply was that he had a heart condition and was concerned that the shocks might harm him. The experimenter responded in a rather businesslike manner that although the shocks could be extremely painful, they wouldn't cause any permanent damage.

Next the teacher was returned to the room containing the large console where he was given a sample shock so that he could better appreciate the situation of the learner. The task of the teacher was to present pairs of words to the learner. First, word pairs such as dog-cat and bird-house were read over a microphone to the learner. The first word of each pair was to be the stimulus word and second word was to be the response word. The learner's job was to learn the response to each stimulus so that when given each stimulus word he could provide the response word from memory.

After all of the pairs had been presented to the learner one time, the main part of the experiment began. The teacher then read each stimulus word and following it, provided four alternative words. Only one of the alternatives was the correct response word. The learner chose one of the alternatives by pressing a key which activated a digital monitor situated in front of the teacher. The monitor indicated the number of the alternative chosen by the learner. If the feedback number corresponded to the correct response word, the teacher simply announced to the learner that he was "correct." The teacher then proceeded to the next stimulus word. However, if the learner's choice was incorrect, the teacher administered an electric shock to the learner by operating one of the panel switches. The teacher was told that he was to increase the shock level 15 volts after each incorrect answer. The teacher was also instructed to repeat the presentation of the stimulus word list until the learner made no errors in reporting response words.

The learner provided many incorrect answers according to a prearranged schedule, and received increasingly stronger shocks. At first, neither the teacher nor the learner showed any strong reaction. However, at 75 volts the learner began to react with audible sounds of pain which became louder with each increase in shock intensity. At this point, each of the teachers would frequently display strange behavior. Some of them responded to these early cries of pain with giggling and nervous laughter. At 150 volts, the learner shouted that his heart was bothering him and that he wanted to quit. At 180 volts he shouted that he couldn't stand the pain anymore. Thereafter, he repeatedly demanded to be let out and protested he was having heart trouble.

At this high-voltage phase of the experiment, the teachers' behavior tended to change radically. The nervous laughter sometimes lapsed into noticeable sobbing. Also at this point some of the teachers slipped down into their chairs, bowing their heads and covering their faces as if they were trying to shield themselves from the consequences of their behavior. Typically, in this phase the teacher turned to the experimenter to ask if he should continue, or to declare that he did not wish to continue. In each case the experimenter responded in a firm voice "Please continue," or "The experiment requires that you continue." In the face of teachers' persistent demands to discontinue the experiment, the experimenter announced "You must go on, you have no choice," or "While the shocks are painful, they are not dangerous."

If a teacher continued to obey the experimenter's orders and thus increased the shock level with each incorrect answer, he was confronted with the learner's agonized screams and desperate demands to be let out. At 300 volts, the learner shouted that he would no longer provide answers. At 330 volts, the learner screamed hysterically that his heart was bothering him and that he wanted out. Thereafter the learner provided no further answers.

If a teacher was still obedient at this point he typically turned to the experimenter to ask what to do when the learner did not respond. The experimenter's reply was "Treat the absence of a response as a wrong answer." Teachers who continued after this command appeared to have lost control over their own behavior. They acted as if they somehow had been beaten into submission and therefore had no choice but to do as they were told. Reduced to this state, teachers typically continued on to the last switch, the label of which implied that they would either seriously harm the learner or possibly even kill him, if they had not already done so. The experimenter's instruction at this point was for the teacher to continue to use the 450-volt switch. After a few uses of this last switch, it was assumed that the teacher was fully obedient and the experiment was terminated.

Obviously, the learner was not actually receiving shocks. The experiment was contrived to create the appearance of someone being "shocked to death." In order to standardize the learner's responses to the shock, the screams and protests were tape recorded. At the end of the experiment, the "learner" emerged to assure the "teacher" that no harm had been done. Additionally, the teachers were debriefed at length to reduce any anxiety and guilt which may have accompanied their participation.

Did the subjects actually "fall for" Milgram's elaborate deception? That is, did they actually think during the course of the experiment that they were harming or killing the learner? All the evidence indicates that the subjects did accept the experiment as it was presented to them. Extensive interview and questionnaire data collected both immediately after the experiment and on later occasions indicated that subjects believed that they were actually delivering intense shocks to another human being. Even more convincing, however, was the evidence provided by the reactions of subjects, graphically recorded on motion picture film (see reference list). The laughter which turned to sobbing, the trembling hands, the contrite posture, the pleas to be allowed to stop all were profound evidence that subjects believed that they were hurting the learner. If the reader is still skeptical, he only needs to see Milgram's film and witness the reactions.

I have shown the film to my social psychology classes some twenty times and never cease to be amazed at the consistency of audience reaction. Upon the first cry of the learner, the audience laughs right along with the subject. Derisive comments directed at the film and the subject are typically made by members of the audience. However, as the subject's reaction changes so does the reaction of the audience. As the film progresses the implications of the "teacher's" behavior—and the audience's laughter in the face of the learner's suffering—become apparent. The audience also begins to slip down into their chairs and their faces begin to reflect embarrassment and chagrin. By the end of the film, the audience is typically stone silent.

WOULD YOU BEHAVE AS MILGRAM'S SUBJECTS DID?

Each time that I have shown Milgram's film, I have asked the audience, "How many would behave as did Milgram's subjects?" No one ever raises a hand, partly due to the social pressure present in a large audience. Milgram, however, asked the question more formally. Psychiatrists, college students, and middle-class adults were asked essentially the same question. First, the experiment was explained to them in detail, omitting the results, of course. Then each member of each of three groups was asked to indicate privately how far they would go in obeying orders. No member of any of the groups indicated that he would obey fully and go all the way to the end of the shock panel, thereby delivering possibly lethal shock.

How Many Typical Americans Would Be Expected to Obey?

Milgram asked groups comparable to those listed above to indicate what proportion of one-hundred representative Americans would obey fully. No more than 2 percent was projected to obey fully by any group. The psychiatrists projected that only .1 of a percent would obey. Obviously, these people thought that only the rare psychopath would obey an experimenter's commands to shock someone to death.

How many persons actually did obey fully in the prototype experiment described above? An astounding 26 out of 40 subjects or 65 percent obeyed fully, going all the way to the end of the shock panel. This result has been replicated many times by Milgram and others, as we shall see. Over all, Milgram used about 1,000 subjects in the long series of experiments that he performed at Yale. In variations of the prototype experiment he found that full obedience ranged as high as 93 percent. Thus a typical person, like you and me, would find it difficult to justify a negative answer to the question posed as a title to this section. It seems fair to say that most people drawn at random from the United States population would probably behave like Milgram's obedient subjects if placed in his experiment, given only that they had no prior knowledge of the experiment.

WHY CAN'T WE PREDICT OUR OWN BEHAVIOR?

Why do people fail to see themselves or others as behaving like Milgram's subjects? Are they lying? I think not, and Milgram would agree. The problem is that people have a great deal of difficulty projecting themselves into situations that have strong social-desirability implications. A situation which has strong social-desirability implications is one for which there is clearly a behavior that would be performed by a "good" or "moral" person. Most people see themselves as good and moral (with justification in most cases), and cannot imagine that they would behave in other than the acceptable or desirable manner. However, if they found themselves in a situation like that defined by Milgram's experiments, their sense of morality would likely be overwhelmed by the powerful social forces which exist in the situation. One can easily recognize what is the desirable way to behave, but it is often impossible to appreciate the subtle but strong social forces that exist in a complex social setting. Even the psychiatrists were "fooled." In fact, Milgram admitted that he did not anticipate such a high level of obedience, nor did his colleagues. The level of obedience that he observed in his early experiments was so high that he was faced with the difficulty of refining his procedure so that he could obtain enough variation in obedience to study the phenomenon.

Perhaps understanding why the psychiatrists failed to predict accurately will help to understand why most people fail in their predictions. Psychiatrists commonly work on a one-to-one basis in their psychotherapy. At the most they theorize about and encounter human behavior in small groups. This is probably the reason that they couldn't anticipate the effect of social forces which existed in the more complex situation represented by Milgram's experiment. Their prediction that only .1 of a percent of the population would obey fully then was probably based on the relatively small number of psychopaths or sadists that they have encountered in their professional work. To sum it up, if one understands what behavior is considered socially desirable for a situation, but fails to understand the power of the social forces which dictate socially undesirable behavior in the situation, he is likely to predict the display of the socially desirable behavior. The above reasoning also indicates why *experiments* are performed in social psychology, rather than investigating social behavior by simply asking persons how they would behave in a given social situation. If social psychologists merely defined a situation for subjects and then asked them how they would behave in the situation, the answers could not be trusted. Instead, a real-life situation is re-created in an experiment, and subjects are placed in the situation so that their actual behavior can be observed directly. The re-creation generally involves a deception, but perhaps now it can be seen why the deception is necessary (see Introduction).

WHAT ARE THE "SOCIAL FORCES" WHICH DETERMINE OBEDIENCE?

In the course of his experiments, Milgram was able to show that several factors controlled the amount or level of obedience displayed by subjects. By varying these factors, he was able to obtain obedience ranging from 0 percent fully obeying to 93 percent fully obeying. In this section, the factors investigated by Milgram which most clearly affected obedience levels will be discussed.

Psychological Distance of the Victim

Psychological distance is correlated with physical distance, but the two factors do not correspond in a one-to-one fashion. Thus it is easier to blast an "enemy" into oblivion from 30,000 feet than it is to kill him in hand-to-hand combat. The humanity of the "enemy" cannot be fully appreciated in the first case compared to the second. However, an enemy can be as easily bombed from just above the jungle tree tops as from 30,000 feet. The victim cannot be seen in either case. Psychological distance dehumanizes the victim.

To systematically demonstrate this point, Milgram (1974)

varied the psychological distance of the learner across several experiments. One of these experiments used the same procedure as did the prototype experiment, except that there was no mention of a heart condition and, more important, the learner made no protest except to pound on the wall at 300 volts. Sixty-six percent of the subjects obeyed fully in this experiment. When voice feedback was added to the above method (without mention of the heart condition), 62 percent obeyed. Obviously the difference between the two percentages was small, and in fact, it was nonsignificant. However, a significant decrease in obedience was obtained when the "learner" was moved into the same room as the "teacher" and placed only one-and-a-half feet from the teacher. In this case, only 40 percent obeyed fully. In a further experiment, teachers were required to place the victim's hand on a shock plate when he refused to cooperate at the 150-volt level. It is remarkable that 30 percent of the subjects obeyed fully. These experiments indicate that the less the psychological distance, the less the obedience. It is important to note that the type of feedback made little difference in these experiments. Pounding on the wall yielded as much obedience as did agonized screams. Also, attributing a heart condition to the victim made little difference.

Perhaps now it is easier to understand how people can kill at the behest of authority. Hitler's soldiers had little difficulty killing Russians once they accepted the Fuehrer's proclamation that Russians were subhuman.

"I'll Do What You Say Until You Turn Your Back"

The degree of surveillance exercised by authority is an important determinant of level of obedience obtained. A series of experiments were designed by Milgram to support this hypothesis. One of these experiments suggested that the authority figure is the most important "force" in the obedience situation. Whereas 65 percent obeyed in the prototype experiment, only 23 percent obeyed when the experimenter left the room and gave commands by telephone.

This experiment provided an interesting sidelight. Milgram automatically recorded the levels of shock used by teachers, but the teachers were unaware of this fact. Some teachers told the experimenter over the phone that they were increasing the shock level, although the automatic recorder indicated that they were not increasing shock. Ob-

viously these teachers found the delivery of shocks to the learner repugnant, but they still could not bring themselves to openly defy
authority. Instead, they lied. The power of authority is great indeed.

In another experiment (Milgram, 1965), the experimenter was
never physically present. Orders were given by tape recorder. Obedience dropped even further, although Milgram doesn't say how much
further. These experiments showed that when an authority figure is
not present to observe whether or not his orders are being obeyed, he
loses much of his power.

"The Larger Institutional Context"

Milgram reasoned that the fame and prestige of Yale University in
part accounted for the high levels of obedience that he obtained. The
official sanction of a well-known and respected institution such as
Yale probably adds to an authority figure's "power." One can imagine that a private citizen trying to direct rescue operations at the
scene of a natural disaster is going to have less success than a person
in a civil defense helmet. To test the importance of institutional back-
ing, Milgram moved his prototype experiment to a nondescript office
building in the business section of a moderate-sized Eastern city. The
sponsoring organization was simply called "Research Associates."
In this less prestigious setting 48 percent of the subjects fully obeyed,
as compared to 65 percent when the experiment was performed at
Yale. Although the absolute difference between percentages seems
large, the difference actually was not statistically significant. Since
the statistical power to detect a difference was not great, here may be
a case where a nonsignificant result might be given some credence
(see Introduction).

Effects of Group Pressure and Control over the Circumstances

As is obvious from a great deal of research on conformity, if a person
is a member of a group and the group members demand some "X"
behavior from him, he is more likely to perform "X" than if he were
acting alone. Milgram (1974) investigated the effects of group pressure using an experimental procedure which was like that of the
prototype experiment, but with the inclusion of two confederates who
were introduced to the real subject as fellow subjects. In these experi-

ments the real subject sometimes was the one to control the actual administration of the shock to the learner, and sometimes one of the confederates delivered the shock while the real subject played a subsidiary role. In one such experiment, the confederates obeyed fully, showed no sympathy for the learner, and chided the subject to continue. Since the subject was the one to throw the switch and thus bore the greatest responsibility for the consequences of shock administration, the experimenter's power was increased very little by group pressure. Seventy-three percent obeyed fully as compared to 65 percent in the prototype experiment.

In a second experiment, the procedure was the same except that the confederates were disobedient. As in the first experiment the subject was the one to deliver the shock. Thus he was left "holding the bag" when his "fellow subjects" "defied" the experimenter and discontinued their participation. The subject's feelings of responsibility must have been very great under these circumstances, because he had control of the situation and the persons with whom he had shared responsibility deserted him. Under these circumstances, only 10 percent of the subjects obeyed fully.

In another experiment, the subjects again had control of shock administration. The subject's responsibility was increased by the fact that he could make the final decision as to whether the shock level was to be raised. In spite of pressure by obedient confederates to raise the shock level, only 18 percent of the subjects went all the way to the end of the shock panel. Here the subject's great control placed great responsibility on him. Here, for most subjects, the personal responsibility for the learner's well-being outweighed the need to obey.

Finally, an experiment was done in which the subject's control was minimized and thus his responsibility was greatly diminished. In this case the subject was faced with fully obedient confederates, but was not the one to "pull the switch." Here the subject was still morally responsible for the learner's well-being, because he was a member of the group, but his obvious and practical responsibility was greatly reduced. Under these circumstances, 93 percent of the subjects obeyed fully.

Because Milgram's procedure failed to separate group pressure from amount of control exercised by the subject, it is difficult to make generalizations about the influence of these two factors on obedience. However, when subjects had control of shock administration, the presence of obedient confederates increased the subject's level of obedience only a little. This result implies that group pressure effects themselves are not very great.

The effects of personal responsibility on shock administration do seem very great. Responsibility increases as subjects' control over shock administration increased. When the subject's control was maximal, because he delivered the shock and decided on the shock levels, "obedient" confederates influenced very few subjects to obey fully (7 out of 40). That the amount of control was critical was supported by an experiment in which the subject could decide on shock level when no confederates were present (Milgram, 1974). In this case only one out of 40 subjects obeyed fully. Because subjects exercised the same maximal degree of control in these last two experiments, it can be seen that group pressure added little. Only six additional subjects were pressured into obedience by the group. By contrast, when control was minimal and its accompanying responsibility was minimal, because an obedient confederate rather than the subject was the one to "pull the switch," almost all subjects obeyed fully. It seems that in Milgram's "group experiments," the subject's degree of responsibility for the well-being of the learner was a more important determinant of level of obedience than group pressure.

When Authority Is Undermined

There are probably many ways to undermine the power of an authority figure. Among the most apparent is the contradiction of an authority figure's orders by a figure of equal authority. In an experiment patterned after the prototype experiment, Milgram (1974) employed two authority figures instead of just one. The experiment proceeded as usual up to the point of the first strong protest by the learner. At this point, using the same language as the experimenter used in the prototype experiment, one experimenter told the subject to continue. However, the other experimenter urged the subject to stop shocking the learner. Not a single subject went to the end of the shock panel under these circumstances. It seems that authority can undermine authority.

Incidentally, the above experiment was not the only one reported by Milgram in which no subject obeyed fully. If these zero-cases are counted in averaging obedience over the twenty-two experiments done and reported by Milgram, the average percentage of subjects who obeyed fully is closer to 30 percent than to the 50 percent claimed by Milgram in his film.

Another experiment conducted by Milgram (1974) shows that authority can be undermined if the authority figure is removed from the context in which he usually issues orders. In this experiment, after the subject has arrived, the would-be learner phoned to say that he could not keep his appointment. The two experimenters, ostensibly wishing not to waste a session, flipped a coin to see who would serve as the other "subject." In the subsequent rigged drawing, the experimenter who lost the coin toss drew the "learner" lot and the real subject drew the "teacher" lot. At 150 volts the experimenter-become-victim demanded to be let out, but the experimenter who was commanding the subject instructed the subject to continue delivering shocks. Just as in the prototype experiment, 65 percent of the subjects obeyed fully. Real-life authority figures may also lose their power to command once they are removed from the context of their authority. A general of the army can expect to find his orders fully obeyed when he is at the army post, but may find his orders ignored by his family when he returns home.

A King Divested of his Crown and Robes Is a King No More

We are all aware that there are certain stereotypes of authority figures. An authority figure affects a certain style and manner of speaking. An authority figure also often adopts a particular type of dress which is appropriate to the context in which he issues commands. For example, in Milgram's experiments the experimenters wore laboratory coats. Finally, an authority figure often is expected to exhibit more expertise than others in regard to the operations and procedures of the setting he commands. A person who attempts to command, but lacks these attributes, may be said to lack the quality of authority.

Two of Milgram's (1974) experiments illustrate the effects of attempting to command without authoritative quality. In one of these experiments, the experimenter initially greeted a subject and two confederates as if all were subjects. As usual, one of the confederates was given the role of the learner and the subject was given the role of administering the word-pairs task and administering the shocks. The other confederate was given an ancillary role. After the experiment had begun, the experimenter received a rigged phone request to leave the experimental area. As the experimenter left he reminded the "subjects" that they could continue in his absence, as the data were recorded automatically. Immediately upon the experimenter's departure, the confederate who had the ancillary task assumed command. He "decided" that the subject should increase the shock level with each error on the part of the learner, and he began to demand that the subject raise the shock level. Only 20 percent of the subjects obeyed fully. Commands tend not to be obeyed if the commander lacks the accouterments of an authority figure.

There was an interesting sidelight to this experiment. Sixteen subjects had disobeyed the would-be authority figure. Of these, eleven allowed the self-appointed commander to take over the shock panel and complete the experiment. However, the other five subjects intervened physically to prevent the confederate from shocking the learner. One of these five people actually picked up the confederate, carried him away from the shock panel, and stood guard over him until the experimenter returned! Most of the eleven who allowed the confederate to continue the experiment tried to talk him out of shocking the learner. Nothing like this kind of behavior was ever directed to the actual experimenter who fit the stereotype of an authority figure in every way. The experimenter was always treated politely and regarded with respect. Woe betide him who attempts to command if he doesn't come from the "commander mold."

What happens when a person who does not have the quality of authority challenges the commands of someone who does? In another experiment (Milgram, 1974) care was taken so that the authority figure maintained his position of command but still ended up in the "electric chair." In this experiment, after the experimenter's introduction, the learner demurred. Being unable to reassure the learner, the experimenter struck a bargain. He would agree to play the role of the learner in order to demonstrate that the shocks could be tolerated, if the confederate who drew the learner lot would agree to accept shocks in a subsequent session. Of course, the person who was supposed to be the learner agreed to the experimenter's suggestion. The chosen learner was then given an ancillary role. The experimenter was strapped into the chair and the experiment began. At the first demand by the experimenter to discontinue the experiment every subject refused to deliver more shocks, even though the chosen learner had assumed the role of authority figure and insisted that the subject continue according to agreement. When the experimenter who had authority quality commanded the subject to stop shocking, the subject stopped, ignoring the commands of a person who lacked authority quality.

SOME DETERMINANTS OF OBEDIENCE NOT INVESTIGATED BY MILGRAM

Bound by the Chains of Command

In the Milgram experiments, orders went directly from the experimenter to the subject. However, in real life, orders are often filtered through a sometimes vast chain of command. For example, in Viet Nam, the men in Lt. William Calley's command were allegedly ordered to kill women and children by Calley, who, in turn, was allegedly ordered to "waste everybody" by his superior, Medina, who, in turn, may have been ordered by superiors to instruct his officers to "waste everybody." It is apparent that it is easier to give such orders than to carry them out. Thus a transmitter—or conduit in John Dean's Watergate terminology—would be more likely to carry out orders than an executant who must actually implement the orders.

To investigate this possibility, Wesley Kilham and Leon Mann (1974) conducted an experiment which was almost exactly like Milgram's prototype experiment. The major differences were that Kilham and Mann's learner was not attributed with a "heart condition," their learner screamed as well as pounded on the wall, there were two experimenter's confederates and female as well as male subjects participated. One confederate played the usual learner role, while the other played either the transmitter role, if the subject was assigned to the executant role, or the executant role, if the subject was assigned to the transmitter role. The transmitter monitored the learning task and conveyed orders to the executant concerning what level of shock to deliver to the learner in the event of a wrong answer on the word-pairs task. Under these circumstances, 54 percent of the subjects in the transmitter condition obeyed fully, while 28 percent of the subjects obeyed in the executant condition. The last link in the chain of command is likely to be the weakest.

Compellingness of Commands

The amount of pressure to obey that is applied to the subordinate by the authority figure should influence the degree of obedience. The greater the pressure the greater the likelihood of obedience. Compellingness of an authority's orders is determined by degree to which orders are strong and insistent and often repeated.

One of my students, Jack Cox (1971), investigated compellingness of commands, by varying the amount of pressure put on subjects to complete a nonsensical task. When Cox's subjects arrived at the lab, the experimenter escorted them individually to a cubicle and explained that he was working for a professor in the psychology department who needed some "graphs" for his research. The subject was then given a stack of fifty papers each of which had a line of boxes across the top and bottom. The subject was told to carefully draw diagonals in each box for each page, thus creating "X's" to fill all of the boxes. The subject was not informed that it was impossible to complete all fifty papers in the time limit imposed by the experimenter.

In the low-compellingness condition, the experimenter *asked* the subject to complete as many graphs as he could. However, the experimenter explained to the subject that he was not required to complete all of the graphs and that he could leave at any time. The experimenter than left the cubicle without mentioning a twenty-minute time limit.

In the moderate-compellingness condition, the experimenter *told* the subject that he was required to complete all of the papers within twenty minutes. As he exited, the experimenter commented that he would be back in twenty minutes to check the subject's performance. In the high-compellingness condition, the procedure was the same as in the moderate condition, except that the experimenter remained in the cubicle in order to monitor the subject's performance.

Results showed that the more compelling the experimenter's demand that the subject complete the boring and meaningless task, the more units—papers—of the task were completed by subjects. Furthermore, before the actual experiment began, the experimenter had told subjects that he was not quite ready for them and thus he would allow a colleague to administer a short questionnaire to the subject while he waited for the actual experiment. This ruse was to make the subject think that the questionnaire had nothing to do with the experiment. Actually the questionnaire measured "authoritarianism." Authoritarianism is a personality trait defined as the degree to which a person is respectful, courteous, and ingratiating in the presence of authority. Within each condition, subjects' authoritarianism scores were correlated with their index of obedience, the number of units of the task completed.

For the low-compellingness condition, the correlation was strong and positive as well as statistically significant. This result means that the more authoritarian subjects were, the more they obeyed the experimenter's orders to produce graphs. In the moderate-compellingness condition, correlation was positive, but weak and not statistically significant. Thus when moderate pressure to obey was applied by the experimenter, the authoritarianism trait had little influence on level of obedience displayed by subjects. Finally, in the high-compellingness condition, the correlation was near zero, indicating that the trait authoritarianism had no influence on level of obedience. That is, nonauthoritarians obeyed as fully as highly authoritarian individuals. These results suggest that if enough pressure is applied by an authority figure, there is a tendency for everyone to obey regardless of their particular personalities. Only when compellingness is low would the trait "authoritarianism" influence the level of obedience.

One must be cautious in generalizing from Cox's trivial-task to the profound and consequential task used by Milgram. But, with that word of caution in mind, it seems that the more compelling the command the more obedience would be obtained. Further, these results are consistent with those generated by Milgram and his colleagues when they attempted to relate level of obedience to authoritarianism and other personality traits. Compellingness of commands is but one of the situational constraints which act to produce obedience. Cox's experiment suggests that whenever situational constraints such as compellingness are strong, they will overwhelm personality traits such as authoritarianism and cause individuals to obey equally well. Milgram (1974; also see Elms and Milgram, 1966) and his colleagues found no strong relationship between obedience and various personality traits including authoritarianism, probably because compellingness was strong in Milgram's experiments as well as many other situational constraints (i.e., impressiveness of the equipment and prestige of the setting).

Because of the lack of correlation between personality test scores and the behavior of obedience, Milgram has reasoned that obedience stems from forces in the social environment rather than from within the individual. Therefore, don't blame the people for obeying, blame the situation in which the people are found. This "social forces are more important than personality traits" position of Milgram's is consistent with his repeatedly stated conception of his subjects. According to Milgram his subjects were not sadists or sycophants eager to obey any order regardless of who gave it, or under what circumstances, or what its consequences might be. Rather they were typical Americans who were overwhelmed by powerful social forces.

Another Battle of the Sexes: Who Obeys the Most

Of the some 1,000 subjects who participated in Milgram's experiments, only 40 were women. Because 65 percent of these women obeyed fully in the prototype experiment, Milgram has implied in his book (1974) and film (see references) and stated publicly on television that there is no evidence for sex differences in obedience. This is puzzling because an inspection of the reference list for his book reveals that he is aware of others' research which has shown sex differences in obedience to authority.

In one of these experiments done outside of Milgram's laboratory, Charles Sheridan and Richard King (1972) adopted a procedure very similar to that of the prototype experiment, with the major exception that a real victim was employed. The "learner" was a puppy who was being taught some new behaviors by the use of electric shock as punishment for incorrect responses. The puppy was judged to be cute and attractive according to some independent ratings. The shocks delivered to the puppy by the male or female teachers were strong enough to elicit squirming and yapping behavior, but not strong enough to harm the puppy. Results showed that 100 percent of the female subjects fully obeyed the experimenter's demands to shock the puppy, while the corresponding figure for males was 54 percent. Females did show upset while shocking the puppy. They winced, squirmed, and showed other signs of discomfort as much as males. Additionally, females attempted to "cheat" more than males, by depressing the shock switch for the shortest duration possible in order to minimize the shock's effects on the puppy. This was in spite of the fact that duration of switch depression had no effect on shock duration. However, sex differences on switch depression were not statistically significant. Thus although women may have suffered more due to their obedience, they obeyed more than males.

The Kilham and Mann (1974) experiment to investigate the executant and transmitter roles employed both male and female subjects. Sixty-eight percent of the males in the transmitter condition obeyed fully, while the corresponding figures for females was 40 percent. The analogous figures for the executant condition were 40 percent for males and 16 percent for females. Over both conditions, 54 percent of the males and 28 percent of the females obeyed fully.

Why did females obey less in this study? One obvious possibility was that females, because they receive different training than males, are less willing to harm another. It is masculine to aggress and to do harm "when it is justified," but such behavior is rarely considered to be consistent with the feminine role. However, here is an obvious answer for which there is contrary evidence. Women obeyed as much as men in Milgram's experiments, and more than men in Sheridan and King's research.

An alternative explanation considered by Kilham and Mann stems from a pecularity of their experimental design. Although subject, victim, and collaborator were always of the same sex, the experimenter was always male. Thus female subjects had to take part in shocking a member of their own sex at the behest of a member of the opposite sex, but such was not the case for male subjects. Perhaps in this era of female awareness, females reacted against a male's command that they harm one of their own. However, this argument is *post hoc,* and therefore is only one of many hindsight explanations which could be invoked.

So far the score is 1-1-1. In the Milgram experiment females showed exactly the same level of obedience as men. In the Sheridan and King experiment females showed more obedience than males, but in the Kilham and Mann experiment females showed less obedience than males. These experiments were similar, but they yielded different results. If the reader can see a pattern here, he or she is more perceptive than I.

Faced with these confused results, another of my students, Greg Smith (1973), felt the need to get back to fundamentals. As a first step to solving the riddle of sex difference in obedience, he thought it might be fruitful to investigate a variable which had not been considered in previous research: sex of the experimenter.

For ethical reasons, and also to make life as simple as possible in this first approximation, Smith chose a simple, plausible, and non-severe obedience situation. When subjects arrived at the experimental room, they found a note from the experimenter indicating that he or she would return in a while to administer a "pursuit rotor" task but in the meantime subjects were told (not asked) to staple some questionnaires together. The note was signed "Janet Weiss" or "George Weiss" depending on the condition in which the subject was to perform. A male or a female coat was conspicuously draped over a chair inside the room and each cover page of the questionnaire bore the name of the male or female experimenter. Upon the first "click" of the stapler, the experimenter who was just outside the room began timing a fifteen-minute period. The index of obedience was the number of questionnaires that the subject stapled in the constant amount of time.

Smith was hoping to discover some kind of interaction between sex of the experimenter and sex of the subject. For example, it may be that when there are no dire consequences of obeying, people obey authority figures of the same sex more than they obey figures of the opposite sex. However, no interaction was obtained. Regardless of the sex of the experimenter, females obeyed more.

It seems that the best conclusion to draw about sex difference in obedience is not to draw a conclusion at all. Results of experiments are simply too mixed to support a generalization about sex differences. This decision not to decide contradicts Milgram, who continues to state that there are apparently no sex differences in obedience. Maybe he is correct, but at present there are insufficient data to confirm his position.

AN EXCEPTION TO THE RULE

Earlier it was stated that social desirability prevents individuals from seeing themselves as willing to perform immoral acts at the behest of authority. Individuals will say that they would disobey an authority figure who commanded them to behave immorally. However, before going on to consider a general explanation of obedience, it is necessary to consider an exception to this statement.

There are situations for which obedience is so strongly institutionalized that people are able to see through the haze of social desirability and recognize that they would commit acts at the behest of authority which would normally be considered immoral. Everyone knows that in the armed forces you do what you are told regardless of the consequences. Obedience and membership in the armed forces go hand and hand. Thus one would expect that many people would be able to see themselves as obeying an army commander's order to kill civilians.

Herbert Kelman and Lee Lawrence (1972) have provided some data in support of the notion of "institutionalization of obedience." They asked a sample of rather typical Americans whether they would behave like Lt. Calley's troop: obey orders and shoot civilians. Contrary to predictions of Milgram's subjects who were asked to predict their obedience to an order to harm another, 51 percent indicated that they would "follow orders and shoot." Also, contrary to the predictions that Milgram obtained, 66 percent thought that "most people" would obey. Thus there are cases where people can see themselves as doing almost anything in the name of authority.

AN EXPLANATION OF OBEDIENCE

Why do people obey authority even when the consequences are tragic? It is not due to peculiarities of individuals, according to these researches. In some cases individual differences simply do not exist: almost everyone obeys. Furthermore, cultural explanations seem inadequate. Milgram's prototype experiment was replicated in Germany which is supposed to have an authoritarian culture (Milgram 1974). Although more obeyed in Germany (85 percent), the percentage is not out of line with results reported for American subjects. In Italy, also supposedly an authoritarian culture, the level of obedience was about the same as in Germany. The Kilham and Mann experiment was done in Australia. As we have seen, the overall obedience level was lower than in America, but not much lower.

It seems that obeying orders is a universal phenomenon characteristic of all human beings. Why this should be seems straightforward: it is functional. When people find themselves in a situation which they don't understand and in which they are uncertain how to behave effectively, they rely on an individual who appears to understand the circumstances and have command of them. It pays to obey the commander of the situation. Most usually one is rewarded with positive outcomes. In fact, it pays off so often, and has paid off for so long in our lives that we develop a habit of obedience. That it is appropriate to obey becomes a hidden assumption, one that we take for granted and thus never question. Because it has become such a thoughtless process, when ordered to do something immoral or inappropriate, we may do what we always do: obey.

In view of this powerful tendency to obey, how does one avoid being sucked into the vortex of powerful forces which surround, support, and are part and parcel of an authority figure? The answer is certainly not to stop obeying orders. No orderly society can exist without hierarchies of authority and authority figures. Neither is the answer to question every order. To do so would be completely disruptive. The answer is to make obedience a thoughtful process. Each of us should consider our life situation and in so doing recognize what constitutes reasonable, moral, and legitimate orders for our particular life situation. If we thus make obedience a thoughtful process, in advance of receiving orders, we may have a conception of what is a reasonable, moral, and legitimate order firmly in mind. This strategy will allow us to readily discriminate between a just and an unjust order without agonizing over every order we receive. Of course, this method of dealing with the tendency to obey presupposes that we admit we can be controlled from without, rather than always being the master of our own fate.

WAS LT. CALLEY A VICTIM OF AUTHORITY?

Now that the reader is armed with some information about obedience, it would seem beneficial to consider a real-life case of tragic consequences due to "blind obedience." Lt. William L. Calley's case appears to be one in which soldiers were given an order to slaughter civilians and thoughtlessly carried out the order.

Lt. Calley has frequently been depicted as inhuman; a killing machine turned loose in the jungles of Viet Nam. Because this view has been so widely accepted, it seems important to consider other possibilities. Perhaps Lt. Calley is really not much different from you and me. It may be that under the circumstances of Viet Nam, many of us would have behaved like Calley.

Consider the situation in which Calley found himself. He was fighting in a war different from any other in United States history. Probably most U.S. citizens, for one reason or another, disapproved of the war as it was being conducted. This atmosphere certainly raised the question in Calley and his fellow soldiers as to the value of what they were doing. Further, like no other war in memory, the enemy was not readily identifiable. The enemy might be in the uniform of North Viet Nam, or in the black "pajamas" of the Viet Cong, or very often in the amorphous dress adopted by the civilians of Viet Nam. Thus the enemy could lurk anywhere undetected, and could be anyone a soldier might encounter, including women and children. Finally, the most diabolical weapons in the history of warfare were employed. Hidden "anti-personnel" devices could be encountered at any time. Mines designed to blow a man's legs off rather than destroy a tank were scattered everywhere. The emphasis was on taking lives rather than taking territory.

All of these unique factors acted to confuse and frighten Calley and probably most other soldiers in Viet Nam. Under circumstances like those which prevailed in Viet Nam, people are reduced to a bare survival level. At this level of functioning, one does whatever is necessary to survive from moment to moment.

Who was the enemy and how was he to deal with the enemy? Calley, like many others, probably couldn't find an answer to his survival problem, and thus found himself in an extremely perplexing situation, nearly impossible for anyone to understand. It is little wonder that he turned to someone who appeared to have command of the situation, Capt. Medina. Medina allegedly told Calley that everyone was the enemy, and therefore the way to handle the situation was to "waste everyone." Calley obeyed and, in turn, many of his troops obeyed when he conveyed the order. Was this monstrous behavior, or an understandable, though tragic, reaction to the total circumstances of Viet Nam? If the latter, none of us can be sure that we wouldn't have submitted to authority as did Calley.

SOME ETHICAL CONSIDERATIONS

Reactions to Milgram's work were varied to say the least. Some laughed, while others were outraged. Those who laughed had not carefully examined the data and therefore could not believe that Milgram's subjects behaved as he claimed. Those who were outraged were not concerned with what Milgram's subjects did, but with what Milgram did to his subjects. The ethical question boiled down to this: were the results Milgram obtained worth the cost in possible psychological damage to his subjects?

Once a famous author was invited to speak on research ethics by an august group of psychologists. He wished to make the point that some kinds of research cannot be justified on humanitarian grounds, regardless of the potential importance of the outcome. He chose the following example. During World War II the Nazis did a series of experiments which potentially could save the lives of many of their fighting men. It was important to know the symptoms of drowning, in order to possibly save pilots downed in the water. Thus, they hooked up physiological measures to concentration-camp inmates, and monitored their responses while they were drowned.

This extreme example was chosen in order to drive home an important point. But what about the relatively mild experimental situation created by Milgram? He led subjects to believe that they were harming or possibly killing a fellow human being. Was it sufficient to tell the subjects that the learner was in fact not harmed? Or would all the elaborate dehoaxing in the world fail to alleviate the sense of guilt caused by knowledge that subjects had been *willing* to harm someone, even though no actual harm was done?

Milgram did have 40 of his approximately 1,000 subjects interviewed by a psychiatrist one year after their participation. There was no evidence that any of these people were harmed by the experience of being in the experiment. But based on this small sample who were interviewed for a short period of time, how can one be sure no harm was done to subjects? It seems impossible to be sure, and Milgram may have doubts himself.

In an interview with *Esquire* magazine (Meyer,1970), Milgram seemed to display some defensiveness by apparently assuring the interviewer that, had someone else invented the prototype experiment and he had served as a naive subject, he would have been among the few who disobeyed. In this same interview he appeared to have admitted to a feeling of uneasiness when he encountered ex-subjects on the street. Finally, the subject profiles that Milgram included in his book were interesting to me more for what is implicit in them than for what is explicit. Reading between the lines of Milgram's (1974) description of his subjects and their reactions revealed to me that he may harbor some negative feelings about them. For example, one female subject is described as a "worn-out housewife" (p. 79), a male subject as "very slow . . . and impassive" (p. 49), another male as "somewhat brutish" (p. 45), and a third male as " curt and officious" (p. 47). Rarely, it seemed to me, did he have anything positive to say about them, and, looking at each description as a whole, only one or two seem positive. In general, the subjects appeared to me to be described as self-serving, morally blunted, and low in intelligence. These subtly negative assessments of his subjects are in sharp contrast to overt statements he has used to characterize them. In his film he characterizes his entire sample of subjects as typical, normal people who would consider hurting others repugnant.

His possible defensiveness, his apparent uneasiness around ex-subjects, his alleged underlying negative feelings about the subjects argue that Milgram may have some residual guilt about possibly harming his subjects that he may have attempted to alleviate by blaming the subjects for their behavior rather than himself. If one assumes the subjects were dull and brutish one would not wonder that they were willing to shock another person and thus one could assume that they deserve any guilt feelings they might have about their behavior.

Milgram has been made aware of my comments concerning him and his research. In a personal conversation, he has thoughtfully and openly responded to these comments. Milgram is certain that he does not feel negatively about his subjects and that he does not harbor guilt feelings about his treatment of his subjects. Although he recognizes that a variety of unconscious feelings he *might* possess could be "read into" his descriptions of his subjects, he himself is unaware of any negative feelings or guilt feelings. He pointed out that in trying to be accurate in his portrayals of his subjects he has included some genuinely negative descriptions, but also some genuinely positive descriptions. For example (Milgram, 1974), the "worn-out housewife" is also described as possessing "a soft manner from which [others] benefit" (p. 79). In one of the descriptions that is positive overall, the subject is described as "mild-mannered and intelligent" (p. 51).

Milgram also indicated some doubts about the attributions made to him by Meyer (1970) in the *Esquire* article. He did not feel that he told Meyer "I would not do what many of my subjects did if I were in the experiment." Rather, he feels he communicated that he would *hope* he would not obey fully as many of his subjects did. In this context Milgram also expressed the feeling that he considers himself as not really different from his subjects. He seemed to have a feeling of identity with his subjects.

In addition, Milgram told me that the feeling of uneasiness that supposedly was characteristic of him when he encountered his former subjects on the street (Meyer, 1970 as interpreted by myself) was more a "funny feeling." The "funny feeling" took the form of wondering about the larger implications for society of what the subjects had done. Milgram reported that in general his face-to-face encounters with his subjects have been positive.

Milgram reminded me that others have responded to his work and to himself in a favorable manner. He has won a sociopsychological award from the American Association for the Advancement of Science, and his book (1974) has been among one of the very few social science books to win a prestigious literary award. These facts affirm for him his belief that he has no reason for feelings of guilt.

Milgram also discussed the recent TV movie about his work (*The Tenth Level,* CBS, 1976). He does not see the movie as a condemnation of himself or his research. The movie itself was not seen in a favorable light by Milgram. He sees the movie as more an exercise in theatrics than an accurate account of his experience and of his research. However, he does not see the blame for these faults to lie with the script writer.

When asked about the harassment that he has received, Milgram indicated that he has become resigned to some harsh treatment. He feels that a person who has come into the public eye by virtue of a controversial but esteemed scientific contribution is going to be subject to some negative feedback.

In relating Milgram's reactions, I am not reneging on the comments that stimulated his reactions. I believe that I have made a legitimate *possible* interpretation of how Milgram's work may have affected him. The reader is encouraged to peruse Milgram's absorbing book to make a judgment as to the correctness of my interpretation.

Also in Milgram's behalf, it may be said that there was no precedent to guide his behavior. At the time that Milgram began his research, social psychologists had not formally attempted to create guidelines for treatment of subjects. Furthermore, Milgram made exhaustive attempts to alleviate any anxiety in his subjects and to ascertain whether they were harmed by their experience as subjects. Subjects were apparently allowed to talk about their feelings just after the experiment until they appeared to have resolved any conflicts which resulted from participation. Not only were some subjects interviewed by an objective medical specialist to ascertain any possible harmful effects, but also each subject was sent an exhaustive questionnaire to assess possible harmful effects. Questionnaire results revealed no evidence of harmful effects and, in fact, pointed out many positive effects of participation. Several subjects indicated that they had learned something of personal importance about themselves. Of course, these results do not prove that subjects were unharmed, but few researchers since have been more thorough in attempting to alleviate anxiety in subjects and assess possible harmful effects of participation.

In sum, it is not possible to say whether Milgram was justified in doing his research, but it has been done and there can be no question about the importance of it. Milgram's work is the single most important contribution to understanding social behavior that anyone has ever made.

THE LESSONS OF MILGRAM'S EXPERIENCE
AND BLIND OBEDIENCE IN THE
WATERGATE EPISODE

The earlier statement that some people were outraged by Milgram's research was probably an understatement. Several articles and a play were written condemning Milgram and his work. In fact, Milgram was harassed so unreasonably that his feelings of guilt, if they exist, may be more due to the way he has been treated than to the way he treated his subjects.

In view of the uproar created by Milgram's treatment of his subjects, one would expect that steps would be taken to set guidelines for treatment of subjects. In fact, the American Psychological Association began to form such guidelines several years ago. However, has all this formal and informal discussion of ethics for treatment of subjects affected researchers so that now more caution is generally exercised than before Milgram's work became known? Unfortunately, a research example to be considered below indicates that these discussions of ethics have not had a great impact on current researchers.

And what about the lesson of Watergate? The wide exposure given the tragedies of blind obedience which beset the young men of the White House should have had an impact on the general public. Surely millions of television viewers were profoundly influenced by such incidences as the sight of young Gordon Strachan breaking into tears because he had wrecked his life through blind obedience. But were they? If people were influenced by the Watergate disclosures of blind obedience, they would be wary of "government officials" who would induce them to break the law.

Stephen West, Steven Gunn, and Paul Chernicky (1975) sought to investigate the impact of Watergate in an experiment which was conducted soon after the Senate Watergate hearings were televised. Their experiment involved an elaborate plot to convince a sample of college students that a local private investigator needed help to break into a nearby company in order to obtain some "records."

When first approached by the private investigator who was generally known to the subjects, each subject was asked to meet with the investigator at a local restaurant in order "to discuss a project which you might be interested in." At the meeting, the subject was presented with elaborate break-in plans including aerial photographs of the target office. The technique proved to be highly plausible and convincing. After the plans for the break-in were revealed to the subject, he was asked to participate as a look-out.

There were three basic conditions in the experiment. In one condition subjects were told that the company in question had broken the tax laws and that the IRS had commissioned the investigator to obtain records necessary for successful prosecution. In this condition subjects were assured that the government guaranteed immunity from prosecution if they were apprehended. A second condition was identical, except that no immunity was offered. In a third condition, the investigator was supposedly employed by a local advertising firm which had offered him $8,000 to obtain some "designs" from the target company. In this case the subject was offered $2,000 to participate. In all conditions refusals by subjects were met with strong pressure from the private investigator.

Results were alarming and indicated that the lesson of Watergate was not learned very well. In the condition where the authority figure had the official sanction of the government which offered immunity from prosecution, 45 percent of the subjects were willing to participate in an illegal break-in. In the no-immunity condition, only 5 percent agreed to participate, and in the reward condition, 20 percent agreed to participate. These percentages can be compared to the 10 percent of control subjects who agreed to participate as a look-outs in a break-in done just to see if the experimenter's plan would work, rather than to steal anything.

These results suggested that the habit of obedience is too deeply ingrained to be seriously affected even by a widely known event like Watergate with its serious implications. Knowledge that the young men of the White House had suffered tragedy because of blind obedience failed to deter many of these subjects. It seems that changing people's conceptions of obedience will be a long and difficult process. Perhaps the place to start is the way we train our children.

As for West and his colleagues, it must be said that they did carefully debrief their subjects and that their defense for what they had done was reasonable and thorough. Also, their results seem important. However, if the effect of Milgram's experience of being harassed for alleged mistreatment of subjects were not weakened by time and much lip service to ethical treatment of subjects, would West and his colleagues have induced experimental subjects to break the law?

3

Whatever happened to the

Good Samaritan?

According to popular reports, Kitty Genovese was assaulted for thirty-five minutes and finally killed while thirty-eight witnesses watched, but did nothing. A man was attacked on a metropolitan subway and left bleeding from stab wounds, but no one helped, not even after the assailant left the scene. An eighteen-year-old switchboard operator was sexually assaulted in her office, but escaped momentarily to run naked and bleeding to the street. Forty witnesses watched but failed to help as the assailant attempted to drag her back inside. For forty minutes a woman lay on the sidewalk of Fifth Avenue, stunned by the shock and pain of a broken leg. Hundreds went by before a cab driver stopped to help. Recently, in the dead of the Illinois winter, a motorist shot himself to death as he huddled in his car which was disabled beside a major thoroughfare. He left a note to indicate that the failure of anyone to come to his aid was more than he could bear.

EXIT HOMO SAPIEN, ENTER HOMO URBANI

Various "armchair psychologists" have attempted to explain these tragedies. "Alienation due to city crowding," said one commentator. Others attributed the incidents to apathy, indifference, or even sadism. Still another commentator suggested that man had evolved to Homo urbanus: the stress of city life had selected out those who could not be stoic in the face of human misery. Obviously an unflattering picture of mankind was being painted. It seems that many individuals felt that the underlying evil of mankind was sufficient to explain the tragedies chronicled above.

Fortunately, social psychologists Bibb Latané and John Darley chose science rather than morality as the means of understanding failure to intervene in a crisis.

THREE DECISIONS TO MAKE

Latané and Darley (1970) suggested that three decisions have to be made before a person will aid another in a crisis. First, one must "decide" that something unusual is occurring. One can decide not to notice certain kinds of events, and certain kinds of events may so resemble ordinary, everyday occurrences that they may not be deemed unusual. Thus if one refuses to be aware of people lying in the gutter in the rundown section of a city, one is hardly likely to offer aid.

Second, one must decide, given that unusual circumstances are judged to be occurring, whether the circumstances constitute an emergency. Finally, given that an emergency is occurring, one must decide whether or not to offer help. Three experiments by Darley, Latané, and their colleagues will be described in order to illustrate these three decisional levels or stages.

The first experiment might be called the "smoke study" (Latané and Darley, 1968). Male college students were asked to complete a questionnaire about urban living. In a "strangers condition" each subject completed the questionnaire while in a room with two other subjects. In a "confederate condition" subjects performed with two collaborators of the experimenters who were told to act indifferent no matter what happened. Other subjects completed the questionnaire while alone. As the subjects worked, the room began to fill with smoke.

Two basic questions were considered. First, who would notice the smoke more rapidly, persons who were alone or persons in groups? In order to answer this question, subjects were observed through a partly concealed one-way mirror. Observers recorded whether subjects noticed the smoke within five seconds after it was introduced into the room. The results indicated that noticing the smoke in the first five seconds was significantly more likely when subjects were alone than when they were in groups.

A second question was that of who was most likely to report the smoke to the experimenter, subjects in the group conditions or subjects who were alone? More reporting occurred in the alone condition than in the strangers condition, and the least reporting occurred in the confederate condition.

Obviously the presence of others inhibited reporting, especially if some of those present were particularly nonreactive and indifferent.

For the purposes of our discussion of the three decisional levels, the most important finding of the smoke study was that the presence of others inhibited noticing that "something unusual is occurring." When others were present, it took longer for subjects to conclude something unusual was happening. If one is not aware that something unusual is happening, the opportunity to assess the situation as an emergency and to decide to intervene will be precluded. In the smoke study eventually all of the subjects saw the smoke. However, sometimes people may not become aware that events which are unfolding around them are at all unusual. The presence of others may contribute to this lack of awareness. It may be that the motorist who shot himself wasn't even noticed by those who passed by. The occurrence of a car parked by a highway is so usual that motorists may not be aware of its presence anymore than they are aware of the telephone poles and the signboards that go zipping by.

A "lady in distress" study by Latané and Judith Rodin (1969) illustrates the second decisional stage: deciding whether or not some unusual circumstance constitutes an emergency. In this study, male college students reported to the Consumer Testing Bureau on their campus in order to participate in a "marketing study." When they entered the bureau testing room they encountered some games scattered about and were greeted by a female secretary. She handed them a questionnaire to complete and exclaimed that she would be in the adjoining room, should they have any questions. As she entered the room, she drew a curtain over the threshold and almost immediately began to make sounds indicating that she was climbing to reach an object which was above her grasp. Actually the sounds came from a tape recorder which she started upon entering the room. Soon a great "crash" was heard followed by a cry and the utterance "Oh my foot . . . my ankle." There were three two-person group conditions, aside from the usual alone condition. In a "friend" condition, subjects brought a friend with them. In the "stranger condition," subjects performed with a stranger who was a fellow subject. In the "confederate" condition subjects performed with a collaborator of the experimenter who was instructed to be indifferent. The amount of helping was the same for the alone and friends conditions, but more helping occurred in these conditions than in the strangers condition. The least amount of helping occurred in the confederate condition. Incidentally, as in other such studies, the time lapse between crisis onset and the emergence of help followed the same course as amount of helping: the more people present, and the more nonreactive those people were, the longer it took for help to arrive.

At first glance it may appear that there was no inhibition in the friends condition. However, it may have already occurred to the reader that there were more people available to help in the friends condition. Obviously, just by chance, you would expect more helping in the friends condition than in the lone condition. Therefore, the fact that the amount of helping was the same in the two conditions indicates that even friends inhibit one another. Friends did inhibit one another, but not as much as strangers inhibited one another. This result indicates that "inhibition due to the presence of others" (the bystander effect) refers to not just the number of people present, but also the way the people who are present behave. Friends as compared to strangers are more likely to communicate openly and less likely to display indifference and nonreaction. The greatest inhibition and thus the least amount of helping occurred in the confederate condition. This was because confederates were instructed to be nonreactive and to act especially indifferent when the crisis occurred.

In the lady-in-distress study it was obvious that "something unusual" was occurring, but was it an emergency? Apparently as a function of whether another person was present and how those others reacted, subjects tended not to assess the unusual circumstances as an emergency. Thus the presence of others may cause individuals to fail to assess a situation as an emergency, even if objectively it is an emergency.

The lady who fell on Fifth Avenue must certainly have been noticed by many and most of those who were at all aware of her presence on the sidewalk must have regarded that presence as unusual. But was she in an emergency state? Perhaps she was drunk or drugged or "crazy." At any rate, many of those who passed the woman must have decided that she had not suffered a calamity of emergency proportions.

Finally, given that it is obvious that an emergency is occurring, what will determine failure to help? Darley and Latané's "seizure" study (1968b) will illustrate the final decisional stage: deciding whether or not to intervene in an emergency. Female college students were told, upon arrival at the laboratory, that they were to participate in a discussion about "personal problems associated with college life." Each was placed in an isolation booth without meeting the other discussants and told that for the sake of anonymity and candor they would talk to others over a microphone and listen to others via a speaker. Some subjects were alone with the eventual victim. In a "one other" condition, the subject was led to believe that another person as well as the victim was present. Finally, in a "four other condition," the subject was led to believe that four other persons were present in addition to the victim. Subjects were told that each person present would initially talk for two minutes, and as each talked, the others' mikes would be off. Actually all "others" were tape recordings so that speeches would be the same across conditions. The victim always talked first, and the real subject talked last. During the first round, all speeches revealed typical college student problems. However, with some chagrin, the victim indicated that he was prone to seizures particularly when under stress. Almost immediately upon beginning the second round, the victim began to stutter and stammer as he exclaimed that he was having a seizure. After about two minutes, the victim's mike automatically cut off. A help response was recorded when subjects left their booth and reported the seizure to the experimenter's assistant before six minutes lapsed. More helping occurred in the alone condition than in the one-other condition, and more helping occurred in the one-other than in the four-other condition. The conditions were ranked the same in terms of scores for speed of helping. Again, the more people present, from the subject's point of view, the less help given. Thus, the more people present in a crisis, the greater is the inhibition of helping behavior.

Perhaps the most important finding of this study was that there were no signs of apathy. Of course, helpers were not apathetic, but neither were nonhelpers. When the experimenter opened the booths of nonhelpers, he was almost universally greeted with an inquiry to the effect, "Is he O.K.?" Some nonhelpers were found to be trembling with anxiety, others showed general nervousness and symptoms such as sweating palms. Before the booths were entered, exclamations such as the following were heard over the intercom: "My God, he's having a fit," "Oh God, what shall I do," "Hey, I think number one is very sick." These and other findings make it clear that popular notions of apathy and indifference do not provide an adequate explanation of failure to intervene in an emergency. The answer apparently is to be found in the observation that the presence of others inhibits witnesses of emergencies.

The subjects in the seizure study were in a situation somewhat like that of at least a few witnesses of the Kitty Genovese murder. As we'll see at the end of this chapter some of those who were watching Kitty knew that others were also watching, but were not sure what those others were doing. Thus the presence of "others" may have inhibited some of the people who were present when Kitty was killed.

PLAY IT COOL AND LET THE OTHER GUY DO IT

But why does the presence of others inhibit noticing, defining a situation as an emergency, and helping in an emergency? What explains the bystander effect? So far we've only considered the decisional stages and the observation that the presence of others has an inhibitory effect, but not the explanation of that inhibitory effect. Darley and Latané (1968a) pose two social processes to explain the bystander effect. One of these, social influence, is seen as operating primarily in the early decisional stages and only when individuals are face to face, or can observe each other in some way. In our society, and in other societies as well, it is impolite to stare at others or pry into others' business. Also, one must maintain one's "cool" in public. Misassessing a situation while in the presence of others, especially strangers, is to "blow one's cool." This is why we sometimes walk the streets in large cities as if we had blinders on. This is why the public transit rider learns to carefully fold his newspaper so as to virtually cover his head, while being careful not to touch anyone in the process. Residents of large cities are bombarded with stimuli. If they didn't learn to filter out some of this stimulation, they would fold under the stress.

Imagine the anxiety that a person would suffer from if that person were a resident of a large city and were set to notice every case of someone shouting at someone else, every case of someone sprawled in a tenement doorway or slumped over the seat of an automobile. Imagine the embarrassment such a person might suffer if he or she rousted the motorist to find him merely taking a nap. He might be told to "butt out" and he might be laughed at by others passing by. Thus one must "screen out" many "unusual events" and when one does notice an unusual occurrence, one must often conclude "it's not an emergency."

The "smoke" study (Latané and Darley, 1968) provides some good examples of the process of social influence. In this study, subjects were observed through a one-way mirror. Alone subjects tended to look about the room freely, which appears to account for their quick observation of the smoke. However, subjects in the other two conditions, where three were present, tended to bury their heads in the questionnaire. Social influence ("don't stare at strangers") caused these latter subjects to be slow in noticing. Further, social influence causes persons not to assess the situation as an emergency, when they do notice. Something akin to "pluralistic ignorance" occurs. This is when each person falsely believes that everyone else believes something or other. By the time a given individual in the three-person condition looked up, everyone else was "playing it cool." Thus each person appeared to the others as if he or she believed nothing serious was occurring. The extremes to which subjects went in order to "play it cool" (not misassess the situation) were truly amazing. Some began to cough, but did nothing. One exclaimed that he had probably been smoking too much and another got up to open a window instead of reporting to the experimenter. Obviously this kind of denial required rationalizations. Some said the smoke was probably steam, air-conditioning vapors, or possibly smog (the study was done in New York City). Two subjects independently indicated that the smoke was "truth gas," introduced into the room in order to elicit truthful answers to questionnaire items! In this experiment and in others, subjects steadfastly claimed not to have been influenced by other persons who were present.

The second process for explaining inhibition is "diffusion of responsibility." This process operates after the first two stages are passed and it is clear that an emergency is occurring. A typical person will feel some responsibility for helping a distressed person in an emergency. If other persons are also witnessing the emergency, each will feel that they share the responsibility with the others who are present. Thus each will "diffuse" some of the responsibility for helping to others and the more people present the less the responsibility accepted by each individual who witnesses the emergency. A diluted sense of responsibility, therefore, may account for failure to help, given that an emergency is obviously occurring.

Diffusion of responsibility was employed by Darley and Latané (1968b) to explain the results of their "seizure" study. Because subjects in this study knew that others were present, except of course for the alone condition, but were isolated from those others, they could not have been affected by "social influence." Their failure to intervene as a function of the number of others thought to be present must have been due to diffusion of responsibility. In the Kitty Genovese case, some witnesses may have strongly suspected that Kitty was being killed, but diffused responsibility to others who they knew were also aware of her plight.

The tension and anxiety shown by nonhelpers which were evident when the experimenter opened their booths indicated that it wasn't that these people had decided not to help, but rather that they were assuming that someone else *might be helping* and they were themselves in the process of deciding what to do. Given that the onlooker can't see whether others have acted, diffusion of responsibility probably delays a nonhelper's decision to help until he concludes that someone else has probably helped. Such was the case in the seizure-study and probably was also true of some of the witnesses of the Genovese murder. Alternatively, the decision to help may be delayed until the observed inaction of others convinces the nonhelper that there is some good reason why no one has helped (e.g., it might be dangerous to help).

As the reader has probably noticed, there is no reason why social influence and diffusion of responsibility should be regarded as rival explanations of inhibition. Both may operate in the same situation. The lady-in-distress study (Latané and Rodin, 1969) is a good case in point. In this study some nonhelpers indicated that they thought the fall was not serious (social influence), while others indicated that they thought someone else would help (diffusion of responsibility). The former probably decided that it wasn't an emergency, while the latter probably accepted that there might be an emergency, but diffused the responsibility to help.

In the case of the young telephone operator who was attacked in front of forty witnesses, both social influence and diffusion of responsibility may have operated within a single witness. Not only were many witnesses present, but each could observe the behavior of the others. Thus a given witness may both have diffused responsibility to others and have been strongly influenced by the inaction of others.

SOMETIMES THE BYSTANDER EFFECT DOESN'T OCCUR

These studies indicate that a simple social phenomenon, the bystander effect, accounts for failures to help someone in need. Further, social influence and diffusion of responsibility seem adequate to explain the bystander effect. However, research subsequent to Darley and Latané's has revealed that the bystander effect doesn't always occur. Sometimes the presence of others does not inhibit and thus social influence and diffusion of responsibility do not operate. Therefore, it becomes important to know when the bystander effect occurs and when it doesn't. That it doesn't always occur is evidenced by Shalom Schwartz's and Geraldine Clausen's (1970) study. Their study was patterned after the "seizure" study and differed from the latter in only a few important details. As before, subjects were in isolation booths and someone had a "seizure." However, in the Schwartz and Clausen experiment males as well as females were subjects. Also, since the experimenter left the scene, which was not the case in the original study, subjects could help either by searching for the experimenter or reporting to other "subjects" (indirect help) or by trying the victim's door (direct help). In contrast to the original study, the bystander effect occurred only for females and only in the case of indirect help.

DOES HE REALLY NEED HELP?

It seems that the most important determinant of the bystander effect is the degree of ambiguity of the crisis situation. It may be that laboratory studies are inherently ambiguous and that the bystander effect occurs only in ambiguous circumstances. Subjects come to a laboratory expecting to be in an experiment, not to witness an emergency. Thus the occurrence of an emergency may be perplexing to them. In the seizure study, subjects couldn't actually see what was happening; in the smoke study there were no flames to suggest a fire; and in the lady-in-distress study the tape recorded crisis vaguely indicated an injured leg. However, in several studies in natural settings, it was abundantly clear that an emergency was occurring. For example, Jane and Irvin Piliavin did two studies of emergencies aboard metropolitan subway cars. In the first study (Piliavin, Rodin, and Piliavin, 1969) a man walked aboard, to the middle of the car, and then fell. In one condition he carried a cane and in another condition he carried the proverbial brown bag distributed by liquor stores and he smelled of liquor. Fewer people helped the "drunk" than helped the disabled person, but the bystander effect was not observed: whether there were many people aboard the car when the man fell or only a few had no effect on helping. In a second study (Piliavin and Piliavin, 1972), also aboard a subway, the victim who carried a cane either fell and bled from the mouth, or fell but did not bleed. More helping occurred when the victim did not bleed than when he did bleed, but again, the number of people aboard when the fall occurred made no difference.

Incidentally, the Piliavins explained the results of these two studies by asserting that the cost of helping was great when the victim was drunk or bleeding as compared to the cost of helping when the victim was disabled or not bleeding. Drunks are repugnant compared to ordinary people, and not only is blood repugnant, it suggests that the victim may have some serious medical problem. This cost factor may, *in part,* explain why no one helped in the case of the man who was stabbed and left bleeding on a subway. Another possible explanation of the actual case will soon become apparent to the reader.

To investigate whether the bystander effect is more likely to occur under ambiguous circumstances, Russell Clark and Larry Word (1972) varied the ambiguity of an emergency. Male subjects volunteered to participate in a study of "sexual attitudes." Specifically they were told that after they completed a standard survey questionnaire on sexual attitudes they would attempt to convince a female to liberalize her point of view. Undoubtedly this cover story distracted the subjects from thinking about the purpose of the study. After the experimenter had departed, leaving the subjects to their questionnaires, a uniformed maintenance man entered the room where subjects were working. After he carried some venetian blinds and a ladder past the subjects into an adjoining room, the maintenance man closed the door behind him and began to make sounds as if he were working. Shortly thereafter a crash was heard. The crash was either followed by the maintenance man's cry, "Oh my back, I can't move" and other sounds indicating that he was injured (unambiguous condition) or only the crash was heard (ambiguous condition). Subjects were either alone, or formed into two- or five-person groups. For the ambiguous condition, the more people present, the less the helping, but for the unambiguous condition the presence of others made no difference. In the unambiguous condition the maintenance man always received help, regardless of how many people were present. Thus the bystander effect appears to occur in ambiguous emergencies, but not in unambiguous emergencies.

According to popular accounts of the Kitty Genovese case, such as those found in introductory social psychology texts, it was abundantly clear to all thirty-eight witnesses that Kitty was being murdered. As the reader will see, such was not the case at all. But you may wonder, how could a witness mistake a murder for anything else? I might find it hard to believe myself if it were not for an incident which occurred to me. One winter, a few days before Christmas, I heard some horrible, incoherent cries coming from behind a drive-in grocery store that I was approaching. Behind the store in an alley, I found a young woman, nude from the waist down, and covered with blood. She was convulsing violently and appeared unaware of my presence. As I tried to comprehend what had occurred, a hunting scene from my childhood intruded on my consciousness. Her convulsions looked like those of a mortally wounded animal just before it dies. I covered her with my sweater and went to call an ambulance. Upon returning to the alley, I fully expected that I would find her lifeless. However, she was still convulsing when the ambulance took her away. I was sure that she would never make it to the hospital alive.

Needless to say, Christmas was bleak that year. I still hadn't been able to get the incident out of my mind two weeks after it occurred, when a neighbor told me that he knew the girl. I had assumed that she had been raped and beaten so severely that she probably had expired before arriving at the hospital. Actually, her boy friend had beaten her, but she was not seriously injured and was out of the hospital by the day after the attack. Apparently her hysterical behavior had been more a result of being rejected than a result of the beating she had sustained. I had been completely wrong in my interpretation of the incident. I had assumed a murder had been committed, when, in fact, the victim was only roughed up. As we shall see, some of the witnesses to Kitty Genovese's murder assumed the opposite of what I had assumed. They assumed that nothing serious was happening to Kitty, when, in fact, she was being murdered.

SHORT-CIRCUITED

Recently, Darley and his colleagues, Allan Teger and Lawrence Lewis (1973), were able to show that the bystander effect does not occur if "bystanders" are looking at each other when the emergency begins. Their study was much like the lady-in-distress study except that subjects were led to believe that they were to participate in an experiment concerning "artistic ability" and the "victim" was a maintenance man working in a room adjoining the experimental room. Some subjects made a sketch of a model horse while alone, but other subjects sketched in the presence of a fellow subject. In a face-to-face condition, subjects sat across from one another with a model in between. In a back-to-back condition, each subject had his own model and sat facing away from the others. Results showed that the bystander effect occurred for the back-to-back condition, but not for the face-to-face condition. That is, there was less helping in the back-to-back condition than in the alone condition but the help rate was about the same for the face-to-face and alone conditions. Also, the amount of helping in the face-to-face condition was about what would be expected by chance when two people are available.

Apparently when subjects were face-to-face they saw the startle response of one another at the onset of the emergency. Thus the social-influence process was short-circuited and each saw the situation as a definite emergency. After one has revealed one's own concern by showing a startle response and has seen others' concern by observing their startle response, no one is motivated to "play it cool and be careful to correctly assess the situation."

A CHILD IN DISTRESS

Because social influence and diffusion of responsibility are social processes involving social norms such as "don't stare" and "in an emergency, everyone shares the responsibility," they would be learned during the socialization process. If so, young children who have not fully learned all the rules of social behavior should not be subject to the two processes, and thus should not show the bystander effect. However, older children, who are more fully socialized, should know the "rules" better and should show signs of adult behavior. Therefore, older children should show at least a trend in the direction of the bystander effect.

Ervin Staub (1970) staged a lady-in-distress-like scenario for kindergarteners, first graders, second graders, fourth graders, and sixth graders. An experimenter led the children, either singly or in pairs, to a room where they were to color some pictures. Soon after their arrival, the experimenter "discovered" that she had forgotten the crayons. Before she left to get the crayons, she mentioned "I'd better check on the girl in the next room. . . . I hope that she doesn't stand on the chair again." The experimenter then went to an adjoining room to observe the subjects through a one-way mirror. After a brief time lapse, a timed tape played the sounds of a crash and a child in distress. Results showed that kindergarteners generally failed to respond and showed about the same amount of helping when in pairs as when alone. First and second graders showed a clear trend to more helping in *pairs* than when alone. Fourth graders showed a trend in the direction of more help when *alone*. Although weak, sixth graders also showed the adult trend. Thus the bystander effect doesn't occur for young children who have not yet learned to play the helping game according to the social influence and diffusion of responsibility rules.

KNOCK, KNOCK, "WHO'S THERE?"

So far only emergencies have been considered, which gives rise to the question of whether the bystander effect occurs in situations which are not emergencies. Emergencies are situations in which a person is injured or ill or about to be injured or become ill. A nonemergency, then, is a situation in which some person needs help, but is not in any immediate danger of injury or illness. Two studies suggest that the bystander effect occurs in nonemergencies. Peter Levy, Diane Lundgren, Marc Ansel, David Fell, Betty Fink and J. E. McGrath (1972) created some simple "demand without threat" situations. Subjects showed up in the laboratory expecting to participate in a routine experiment. They were told that they would be timed in completing some math problems. Subjects were alone or with one or two confederates. While they were completing the problems, one of the following simple-help requests was made: several taps on the experimental-room door were made at regular intervals; several verbal requests to be let in were made at regular intervals; someone called the experimenter's name over an intercom speaker in the experimental room. Results showed that for all three types of simple-help requests, the bystander effect was observed. That is, the more people present, the less the helping.

A nonemergency experiment by Dennis Hurley and myself (Hurley and Allen, 1974) was done in a natural setting rather than a university laboratory. The number of people present was varied by creating a flat-tire scenario either on a highly trafficked roadway or a country road with low traffic density. On the highway there were many people present at any given time, but on the country road, few if any were present at any given time.

A woman and an inflated spare tire were situated beside a car with an obvious flat tire. The implicit help request was "change my tire or take me to a filling station." A greater proportion of people helped on the country road than on the highway. Thus the bystander effect also occurred for a "real-life" nonemergency.

FALLEN BY THE WAYSIDE

To this point it's been shown that the bystander effect holds for ambiguous emergencies. It also holds for unambiguous nonemergencies (cases where the request for help is clear, but the victim is not in any danger). However, it does not occur for young children or in a case where bystanders are looking at one another when the crisis begins. Although these generalizations are robust, it might be interesting to examine an apparent exception before going on to other matters. Dave Mason and I (Mason and Allen, 1976) did four experiments which were suggested by the roadside study. Again a highly trafficked highway and a little-traveled country road were used, but this time the emergency character of the help-needed situation was manipulated as well as the degree to which the help-needed situations were ambiguous. Each of the following situations was created on both road settings: 1) ambiguous nonemergency-auto parked at the side of the road with the driver seated, upright behind the wheel; 2) unambiguous nonemergency—the flat-tire set-up as in the previous roadside study; 3) ambiguous emergency—auto parked at a 45° angle to the road, suggesting a skid, and the driver slumped over the wheel; 4) unambiguous emergency—auto at 45° angle, passenger side door open with the driver slumped out of the car, emergency flashers on.

A bystander effect was observed if a greater proportion of motorists stopped to render aid on the country road than on the highway for each of the four situations. Results indicated that neither ambiguous situation had any appreciable effect on motorists. There was very little helping in either situation and no difference between the two road settings in amount of helping. Significant bystander effects were found for the two unambiguous situations. The finding of a bystander effect (more helping on the country road) in the unambiguous non-emergency confirms the results of the previous roadside study (Hurley and Allen, 1974). However, the finding of a bystander effect for an unambiguous emergency is practically unprecedented. Couple this latter finding with our observation of *no* bystander effect in the ambiguous emergency, and our results can be regarded as the opposite of those reported by most other researchers. It could be that those other researchers have been incorrect in concluding that the bystander effect doesn't hold for unambiguous emergencies, but, frankly, I believe that our ambiguity manipulation failed. Instead of creating ambiguous and unambiguous emergencies, we may have created *obscure and moderately ambiguous* emergencies, respectively. In isolation, a person slumped out of a car which is angled off the road would likely be assessed as an emergency. However, we failed to take into account the larger context. Motorists were zipping by at about 60 MPH or more (even then people were ignoring the 55 MPH speed limit). Under these circumstances motorists are bombarded with stimulation. They are seeing signs, and cars, and houses, and a multitude of other stimuli flash by. In order to concentrate on the road ahead, much of this stimulation must be filtered out. Thus our subjects (motorists) may have gotten only partial information about the "emergencies." For our "ambiguous emergency" motorists probably received too little information to conclude "emergency," or perhaps they never noticed the car at all. But for our "unambiguous emergency," they were probably not sure. That is, the situation was actually ambiguous at least to a moderate degree. Thus, on the highway motorists who passed our "unambiguous emergency" may have diffused responsibility to other passersby who were always in view. However, on the country road many who saw the "unambiguous emergency" stopped to help, because often there was no one else in view.

Some evidence for this interpretation comes from reports phoned to the local police. We had the cooperation of local as well as state police who were informed of the scene we were creating.

Some motorists reported that the victim had been thrown from the car, pinned under the car, was lying in the ditch and other less extreme, but equally inaccurate accounts. In fact, the phoned reports were so bizarre that the local police dispatcher, who was also informed in advance, concluded that either a real accident had occurred near the mock accident or the experimenters had met with misfortune. As a result, a police car and an ambulance were sent to the mock accident and the experimenters were politely told to discontinue the experiment. In sum, when the overload of stimuli is great, as it is while driving, an objectively clear-cut "emergency" may become ambiguous and when many others are present, responsibility may be diffused.

These roadside studies may help to further clarify why the motorist who received no help shot himself. On the crowded superhighway, the parked car may not have been noticed at all by some passersby. Others may have seen the car but got so little information that they concluded, "it's a farmer checking his fields," or "a motorist taking a breather," or "it's just an abandoned car."

There were some interesting incidental observations made in the course of the highway-country road studies. Whenever a motorist stopped to help, he was thanked, congratulated on his altruism, and told that there was no problem after all. Almost all of the helpers seemed very pleased with themselves for having been good Samaritans. This should remind us of something which has not been emphasized in this narrative so far: valuable social rewards often accompany helping someone in need.

Also, in complex real-life situations such as those existing in the highway studies, altruism may not be the only reason for stopping to help. On a couple of occasions in the nonemergency situations, a carload of men stopped to help the woman. However, when the experimenter arose from the back seat of the woman's car in order to give the men an explanation, they quickly drove away. Perhaps these men had something other than altruism on their mind.

BEYOND THE BYSTANDER EFFECT

Beyond the bystander effect there are a couple of other considerations which are relevant to rendering help to others. It may have occurred to the reader that sometimes people may not help simply because, if they do, they may endanger themselves. For example, if one attempts to stop the attack of an assailant, one may find himself or herself subject to the assailant's attack. Surprisingly, however, there has been little experimental attention to this obvious possibility. One exception seems to be a study by Gerald Borofsky, Gary Stollak, and Lawrence Messe (1971).

In this experiment, male and female subjects were told that they were to participate in a "psychodrama." They were confronted with several confederates who were introduced as other subjects. Some of the collaborators were students like the actual subjects, but two of them were drama students. First the experimenter asked the confederates who were not actors to run through a scene while everyone watched. After the nonactors completed their turn, the experimenter complimented them, suggested some improvements, called the actors to take a turn, and left the room to get some papers from his office. The actors, who were to act out a family quarrel, began routinely, but soon became engrossed in their roles to the point that finally one slapped the other. The slapee then proceeded to beat up the slapper. The subject-behavior of interest was intervention to help the victim or break up the fight. Some subjects saw a male beat up a female, while others saw a female beat up a male, a male beat up a male, or a female beat up a female. The lowest frequency of intervention was for a male beating up a female. Subjects apparently believed that a real fight was occurring, with one possible exception: a female beating up a male evoked laughter. It seems plausible to suggest that intervention was low for the male beating up a female because the situation connotes a lovers' fight. As any policeman will indicate, one of the most dangerous situations he faces is intervention in a fight between spouses or lovers. In one case that I know of, when a policeman attempted to break up a husband-and-wife fight, both victim and assailant turned on the policeman. A fight between intimates is often considered as "nobody's business" and tends to be highly irrational and emotional. For this reason somebody who "butts in" could be injured or killed by the assailant. Thus people who fail to intervene when a man is attacking a woman may fear for their own safety. As we will see, this factor probably played an important role in the Kitty Genovese case.

In the Borofsky (1971) study, a single female was the only person who intervened when the male was beating up the female. This result brings to mind an actual event. A Chicago man was attacking his wife, while several onlookers stood frozen in a state of inaction. Finally, a smallish and rather grandmotherly woman came upon the scene and scolded the attacker until he stopped thrashing his wife. Perhaps some kinds of people have more license to "butt in" than others.

The other consideration beyond the bystander effect has to do with an entirely plausible hypothesis which has received little support. Several studies have shown that a bystander is more likely to intervene if he has skills which are relevant to the calamity of the distressed person than if he lacks such skills. Thus if a person witnesses a case of injury or illness and that person has medical training he is more likely to intervene than if he lacks it. But shouldn't the other side of the coin hold also? If a person lacks crisis-relevant skills, but there is another person present who has these skills, shouldn't the presence of the latter inhibit the intervention of the former? It seems a reasonable hypothesis, but Darley and Latané (1968b), Schwartz and Clausen (1970), and the Piliavins (1972) and their colleagues have all failed to produce clear support for an inhibitory effect due to the presence of an individual with crisis-relevant skills. In order to determine the source of these failures, a student of mine, Mike Alender (1972), contrived an experiment to control for possible interfering factors which may have prevented the demonstration of the inhibitory effect in previous studies. His basic procedure was much like that of Clark and Word's (1972) study in which a maintenance man fell off a ladder. When subjects showed for the experiment they were ushered to a cubicle and introduced to another "subject" who was acting under instructions to be indifferent no matter what happened. The confederate was either described as just another student or a pre-medical student who worked part-time for the emergency unit of the local hospital. As the experimenter gave "subjects" bogus instructions for a dummy task, a maintenance man interrupted to ask "where is the light that needs changing?" The experimenter pointed to the end of the corridor, finished his instructions, and left the "subjects" with their task. Simultaneously, the maintenance man proceeded with his ladder to the end of the corridor.

Before the experimenter left, he created different circumstances than in previous studies by indicating that he was leaving the entire area and would not be back for several minutes. Thus, when the maintenance man "fell off his ladder" and cried for help, the subject could not cop out and report to the experimenter or anyone else, as

the corridor and all adjoining cubicles were empty of potential helpers. If the subject opened the door in order to help, he would be confronted with the possibly seriously injured person and bear the whole
responsibility for helping unless, of course, he chose to diffuse the
responsibility to the "other subject."

There was significantly less helping when the "other subject"
was described as a medic than when he was described as just another
subject. This result is probably best understood in terms borrowed
from the Piliavins and their colleague, Judith Rodin (1969, 1975).
These researchers characterize a potential helper as weighing the cost
of intervention against the cost of nonintervention. Costs of intervention include disruption of whatever one is doing, loss of the time required to render aid, risk of legal liability and so on. Costs of nonintervention include loss of self-esteem and social approval as a
result of not helping a fellow human being who has suffered a calamity. When both costs are high, as they were in Alender's study, one
will attempt to reduce the cost of nonintervention. This can be done
by assuming "there is someone present who is better qualified to help
than I." In such a case, the job of helping is left to the better qualified
person. Thus subjects in the medic condition reduced the cost of
nonintervention by letting the medic do it.

The Piliavins have very recently supported their "cost" theory
by still another subway study with Rodin (1975). They manipulated
cost of intervention by either stigmatizing the victim by giving him a
"port wine stain" birthmark on the face, or leaving the victim's appearance normal. Again, the victim fell on the subway. Here the cost
of nonintervention was constant and high, but the cost of intervention
was highest when subjects had to help a disfigured victim. When the
victim was disfigured, less help was given if a uniformed medic was
standing near by than if the medic was absent. The medic made no
difference if the victim was not stigmatized. Thus, given high cost of
nonintervention and also high cost of intervention, the presence of a
person with crisis-relevant competence will inhibit helping.

THE KITTY GENOVESE CASE

After examining the intricacies of helping behavior it would seem interesting to detail an actual emergency case in order to analyze it in

terms of the research results that have been considered. Popular accounts of the Genovese case, which include a recent TV movie, are generally inaccurate and do not do justice to the complexity of the situation surrounding the murder. Thus I will outline an account given in *Chief,* co-authored by Albert Seedman and Peter Hellman (1974). Seedman was chief of New York City detectives and in charge of the Genovese murder investigation.

Kitty Genovese was an attractive barmaid who worked in the borough of Queens in New York City. According to all available information, Kitty was a nice person who had many friends and was generally well-liked. On the night of her murder she and a date had gone to his brother's house for dinner. After dinner, she and the date retired to a bar for a drink. Declining an invitation to go to his place, Kitty said goodnight and drove to Ev's bar, her place of employment. Some pleasant chitchat with customers detained her until 2:00 A.M. On the way home she may have noticed a white compact car following her, because, once out of her car, she headed for the well-lighted boulevard in front of her apartment complex, rather than chancing the back entrance. She barely made it onto the boulevard when the attack began. A small man in an overcoat slashed her with a knife. Kitty wailed for help, screaming that she had been stabbed. Activity across the street began immediately. A man named Hatch leaned out the window of his apartment and shouted "Let that girl alone." Had he just heard screams or had he heard Kitty's anguished cry that she had been stabbed? At any rate Hatch did nothing further, and the attacker fled to his car.

By now many people were looking down on Kitty as she lay on the sidewalk. One onlooker complained that she could not see well enough. Her husband suggested that she turn off the apartment lights. Now she could see well enough to warrant pulling a chair up to the window. This person must have had a clear view of Kitty as she slowly arose from the pavement. If so, she must have been uncertain as to what had happened to Kitty, because Kitty *did not stagger* as she walked toward the rear entrance of her apartment. Perhaps her boy friend had just knocked her down, or maybe they had just shouted at each other and he had left in anger. For the people on the boulevard the situation was probably ambiguous.

However, as Kitty turned the corner off the boulevard another set of witnesses could hear and possibly see her. Some of these people must have known that something was terribly wrong. Just as she turned the corner she was spotted by Emil Power. He reported seeing her stagger. Finally she entered an apartment building a few doors down from her own and fell on her back in the stairwell. Probably Harold Kline, Kitty's friend who lived upstairs, did not hear her call his name, but others did hear.

Meanwhile, the people on the boulevard were still watching as the assailant returned to finish Kitty. He showed the same psychopathic, casual air which characterized him even under interrogation. As he checked the doors along the boulevard he appeared as if he were on a Sunday stroll. It was almost as if he "knew" that no one would interfere—and no one did.

After the assailant checked the nearby train station, Emil Power saw him head for the set of apartments where Kitty lived. Power picked up the phone to call the police. "Don't," said his wife, *"thirty people have probably called by now."* For Power and his wife the situation must have been less ambiguous than it was for the people on the boulevard, but not nearly as clear-cut as it must have been for the people who lived in Kitty's apartment complex. Kitty's neighbors must have known that she was being slaughtered virtually on their doorsteps.

Now Power held his breath as the assailant tried the doors in Kitty's apartment complex. Finally he found his prey. She moaned loudly enough for a few neighbors to hear as her killer renewed his attack. He alternately stabbed her and attacked her sexually.

Upstairs Harold Kline paced the floor. He was at the point of deciding whether to help. He called a friend who advised him to call the police. But if he used his own phone, the assailant might overhear and turn on him or find out later and seek revenge. He called some of Kitty's neighbors; they couldn't advise him. Finally, he must have decided that it would be safe to call if he did it somewhere else. Thus he let himself out the window and scaled a steep roof to a neighbor's apartment where he called the police. Thirty-five minutes had lapsed since the attack had begun. More time lapsed before the ambulance arrived, but Kitty was still alive when they took her away. However, on the way to the hospital, she suffocated from an accumulation of blood in her chest which collapsed her lungs. It is possible that if someone had called earlier, Kitty would have made it to the hospital alive, and perhaps emergency room personnel could have saved her.

Harold Kline may have been cowardly, but he was not indifferent to Kitty's fate. By the time the police arrived he was drunk, guilt-ridden, and distraught. A policeman named Sang took an immediate dislike for Kline. Sang couldn't understand why Kline had not helped Kitty, but he tried to hold his temper. Sang ordered Kline to leave the scene of an interview with a neighbor. He did leave, but once downstairs Kline was heard cursing and venting his frustration on a door panel. That did it for Sang. Kline was arrested for disorderly conduct.

Popular accounts of the Genovese murder imply that no one even thought of helping Kitty. This, of course, is not so. Not only did Power start to call the police, but a young woman named Georgette Share actually contacted the local desk sergeant by phone. However, she hung up before saying a word. Was she afraid of "becoming involved," or was she afraid that the assailant would find out and make her his next victim?

At first, accounts of the case were buried on the back pages of the New York papers. But then Abe Rosenthal, *Times* Metropolitan Editor, got wind of the fact that fully thirty-eight bystanders had witnessed some aspect of the attack and had "done nothing." Now the case became infamous around the world. It was reported in Moscow (*Izvestia* called it a case of "stone jungle morals"). A play and song were written about it, Mike Wallace did a CBS special on it entitled "The Apathetic American," and Abe Rosenthal wrote a book about it, in which he asked himself if he would have behaved differently from the witnesses. As a result of all this publicity, the people in the section where Kitty lived were subjected to considerable harassment. It was as if they had murdered Kitty. People who had not lived through the incident could no more understand the behavior of these people than they could understand why Nazi concentration camp inmates waited for their fellows to die so that they could steal their food and strip their corpses of useful clothing. It is easy for one to condemn the behavior of others in a given situation if one has not experienced the situation himself.

Explaining a Complex Real-Life Emergency

As is already apparent, neither "apathy" nor "the bystander effect" can fully account for the behaviors of persons who were present when Kitty was killed. Probably the people on the boulevard, at least some of them, were unsure as to the seriousness of Kitty's plight. Some of them may have decided that she was not in a state of emergency,

while others, being unsure, diffused the responsibility to the faceless figures behind the illuminated apartment windows. However, Emil Power must have been leaning in the direction of "it's an emergency," but there must have been some doubt in his mind. If so, his behavior, and that of his wife, was an extraordinary reflection of diffusion of responsibility.

As for Kitty's immediate neighbors, there can be no doubt. They knew that she was being attacked. Probably just plain fear caused them not to intervene. But should these people be condemned? The problem is that we just cannot project ourselves into their circumstances. But let's try to make an approximation. If you suddenly came upon a man attacking a woman with some weapon or other, wouldn't you assume that, if you interfered, the assailant would turn on you? Would you be willing to risk your life for a stranger? As for the other onlookers, they were probably like most of us, sure that they could not be influenced by others (the inaction of others in this case). Those who are unaware that they can be overwhelmed by powerful social pressures are likely to fall victims to such pressures.

It is only when we are aware that we can be controlled from without that we are able to resist such control. An incident described to me by a young woman indicates this tendency not to recognize that one can fall under the spell of a social situation. This person witnessed a shouting match between a teenage girl and a middle-aged woman. The two women shrieked obscenities and threats at one another for an appreciable period of time, but did not actually harm one another. The witness was disturbed by her own behavior. She watched the entire exchange between the antagonists as if she were paralyzed; she felt the need to escape the scene, but was unable to do anything. While the witness watched, she never considered what she might do. It was only later that she realized the implications of her inaction. With nobody to intercede, the two cursing women might have made good their threats to do bodily harm to one another. Even after thinking about it for some time, the young woman never seemed to realize that she had fallen under the control of the scene she was watching.

The Apprehension of Kitty's Murderer

The person who murdered Kitty was caught quite by accident. It seems that he was also a petty thief. Some time after he murdered

Kitty, he was approached while carrying a TV out of someone's apartment. When asked what he was doing, he replied, "Oh, I'm just helping these people move." Fortunately, the neighbor who observed the theft knew enough about the owners of the TV to doubt that they were moving. As a result he consulted a friend who lived nearby and they both agreed that the owners of the TV were merely not home. Thus as the killer-turned-thief inexplicably returned to the scene of the theft to retrieve his screwdriver, one of the neighbors called the police while the other ripped the distributor from his car. Why were the TV owners' neighbors so bold whereas Kitty's neighbors had been so meek? The TV owners' neighbors didn't know that the thief was also a vicious killer, and petty thieves are not nearly as frightening as killers.

The killer returned to find that his car wouldn't start. Unruffled, he simply locked the car and walked away. However, by now the police had arrived in a squad car. Having available two men who could identify the thief, they easily located him, called him to their car and placed him under arrest. It was as simple and undramatic as that.

Of course, the police did not at first know that they had so easily apprehended the man who killed Kitty Genovese. Fortunately, the killer was first interrogated by a bright, young detective named John Tartaglia. Tartaglia had an uneasy feeling about the slight but audacious thief. He knew the details of the Genovese case and thus immediately recognized the significance of the fact that the young thief was driving a white compact car the trunk of which contained some pornographic materials. Abandoning questions about TV thefts for the moment, Tartaglia pressed the young man about two attempted assaults. To his surprise, the thief confessed to both assaults. Emboldened by this success Tartaglia, now surrounded by other detectives, asked the man if he had murdered Kitty. Only slight pressure was needed to get the confession. It seemed too good to be true, but a check with other officers revealed that the young man's recollections of details jibed with the facts of the case. They had their man.

The intensive interrogation which followed revealed a number of interesting facts. The killer, Winston Mosely, was a skilled technician who was obviously intelligent. He was married and had children and several dogs. Mosely expressed genuine affection for his family. He also treated his dogs humanely. However, this orientation was contradicted by his feelings and behaviors with regard to women. In fact, Mosely's behaviors were often contradictory.

He hated women. To him they were not human. His wife was the exception, since she was "like women were supposed to be." His hatred stemmed from the fact that his mother had left him and his father, and his first wife had been an adulteress. Thus he could slaughter Kitty, and another woman as was later discovered during interrogation, but act indignant when asked whether he was concerned for his children's safety and whether he stole TV's indiscriminately. He was sure his children would be OK when he left them alone on the night of Kitty's murder. His dogs would protect them and besides who would hurt children? Yes, he stole TV's, but not just from anybody! He never stole from customers of his father's TV repair shop, even though he had ample opportunity to do so. "I'm not that kind of creep," he said. He could talk calmly about repeatedly stabbing Kitty and repeatedly shooting the other woman, but on the way home from murdering Kitty, he stopped to warn a man who was asleep in his idling car that he was in danger of carbon monoxide poisoning. On trial, Mosely faced an assistant district attorney so terrorizing that he caused a psychiatrist to defecate in his pants on the witness stand. Yet the D.A. could not rattle Mosely. He simply didn't see anything wrong in what he had done.

Why Kitty? It was all happenstance. Mosely was out driving around one evening, when he happened to notice an attractive woman getting into her car. The woman turned out to be Kitty. He kept her in his rear view mirror until she turned, then he U-turned and pursued her. After she stopped he was out of his car before she was. When she saw him, she elected to run rather than attempt to get back into her locked car. He ran after her, fumbling for his hunting knife as he went. She was running fast so he didn't bother to order her to stop. He leaped on her back and stabbed her several times. Now he tried to drag her away, but her screaming awakened several people on the boulevard. Mosely saw their lights come on. Someone shouted at him. *Mosely could not make out what the man said.* Thus it is likely that most of the onlookers *could not make out Kitty's cry* that she had been stabbed. Why did he run? Incredibly he was afraid of being identified, so he left to move his car and to put on another hat. Before he returned, he waited and listened. No doors were slamming. No one was coming out to help Kitty, so he returned.

One of the interrogating detectives asked, "Weren't you afraid that someone would call the police?" Mosely's face reflected a faint smile. "Oh," he said, "I knew they wouldn't do anything. People never do." The detective continued this line of questioning. The situation was different at Kitty's apartment complex. Surely he was aware that the neighbors were watching and saw everything except, perhaps, what he was doing when he hovered over Kitty in the stairwell? Yes, he was aware. Moreover, someone had seen him as he was sexually assaulting Kitty who lay virtually lifeless at the bottom of the stair. Mosely said that he was lying between Kitty's legs when, out of the corner of his eye, he saw someone open the door at the top of the stairs and peer out. It was the "guy upstairs," but Mosely wasn't worried. He knew that Kline wasn't any more likely to help than the others.

4

Beauty and the Beast

A few years ago, ugly-baby jokes were popular. Remember the one about the man seated on a bus who was approached by a woman carrying a baby? Immediately he leaped up from his seat and said, "Here lady, take my seat, and have a banana for your monkey." Pretty funny, huh? It seems that physically unattractive people begin to be a source of amusement very early in their lives.

Of course, adult "ugly" people provide much amusement also. Not too long ago, a peculiar public protest had national television newscasters chuckling. A group of unattractive women were protesting an airline company's refusal to hire them because of their appearance. Isn't it funny that a group of "ugly" people would consider themselves discriminated against to the point that they felt the need to organize a protest? If you think that is funny, what do you think of Uglies Unlimited, an actual national association of men and women who say they are victims of discrimination (*U.S. News and World Report,* Aug. 23, 1976)?

At a well-known all-male university in the Southwest, there was an award given at every post-football game party. The lucky recipient was the young man judged to have the ugliest date. The greater part of the fun was giggling and pointing behind the back of the award winner and his date. People who associate with "ugly" people are "funny" too.

During college fraternity and sorority rush, members are always looking for "sharp" people to pledge their organization. A little careful observation indicates that "sharp" means physically attractive. But that's not all. "Sharp" also means intelligent and socially adept. Pretty people are covertly assumed to have other valued attributes.

An administrator of a famous ballet school was interviewed on a national TV show. He was asked, "With all the fabulously talented dancers that you must audition for a position at your school, how do you decide which to choose for the few places available?" His reply was "You're right. We do have many talented applicants. It's difficult to decide among them in terms of talent. From among the obviously talented, we choose those who are comely of face and figure."

And then there was the popular song:

> To those of us who know the pain
> Of valentines that never came,
> And those whose names were never called
> When choosing sides for basketball.

It was long ago and far away.
The world was younger than today
And dreams were all they gave for free
To ugly duckling girls like me.

—"At Seventeen," by Janis Ian
Mime Music, Ltd., and April Music, Inc.,
1974-75

WHAT DO PEOPLE SAY ABOUT THE IMPORTANCE OF PHYSICAL ATTRACTIVENESS?

A couple of years ago, I gave a guided tour of the psychology department to a group of visiting high school students. At the end of the tour, I "treated" them to a lecture on social psychology. During the lecture I took advantage of the fact that they were a captive audience and asked them some questions. One of the questions was, "What characteristics do you consider to be most important for deciding whom you would like to date?" Their answers were tallied on a blackboard. Such attributes as "good conversationalist," "same interests as mine," "good dancer," "shows me respect," "intelligent," "humble," and of course, "beautiful" or "handsome" were frequently cited. The single most frequently mentioned attribute was "good personality." However, one "old boy" in the back of the room displayed uncommon candor and insight. He said, "I don't kear nutten about nutten, 'cept how they look."

In a formal assessment of what people say about physical attractiveness, Rebecca Vreeland (1972) asked a group of Harvard college boys to list the traits that they *thought* were most important for selecting and liking a date. As you might expect of Harvard boys, such attributes as highly intelligent, intellectually sophisticated, and well-dressed were considered to be important. Physical attractiveness was considered to be more important than all of these attributes, but considerably less important than "being a good conversationalist."

John Hudson and Luva Henze (1969) were interested in determining how various criteria for selecting a spouse varied in order of importance over a twenty-eight-year period. They found that in 1967 "good looks" was ranked eleventh out of eighteen characteristics by

males (a rank of one was most important), and next-to-last by females. These rank orderings differed only a little from those obtained
in 1939 and 1956.

These various surveys which involve asking people what they
think about the importance of attractiveness clearly reveal that although people believe that physical attractiveness is important, other
characteristics are seen as more important than attractiveness. Thus
when asked, people play down the importance of being "pretty" or
"handsome." However, if the actual behavior of people and their reactions to others are systematically observed, quite a different picture
develops. There is a discrepancy between the admitted importance
of physical attractiveness, and its actual importance in determining
the everyday behavior of people.

BEAUTIFUL = DATABLE

It should be obvious that physical attractiveness is important for date
selections. After all, "date" implies a short-term relationship, and
"superficial" characteristics like physical attractiveness are expected
to be important for short-term relationships. Thus Elaine Walster and
her colleagues Vera Aronson, Darcy Abrahams, and Leon Rottmann
(1966) assumed the importance of physical attractiveness for selecting and liking dates, and investigated the "matching hypothesis." This
hypothesis can be stated as follows: people will prefer dates whose
physical attractiveness is close to their own. The matching hypothesis
seems reasonable, because when people go to the "dating market,"
what they can "buy" is determined in part by what they can "sell" in
return.

To test this hypothesis, Walster and her colleagues set up an
elaborate experiment in computer dates. Incoming freshmen at the
University of Minnesota received an advertisement for a dance along
with all the other materials freshmen receive upon their first regis-
tration. The advertisement indicated that for the dance, the "computer" would match each student with someone with similar interests.
Even though subjects had to pay for their tickets, the response was
overwhelming. After the first 376 males and 376 females had attempted to purchase tickets, sales were terminated.

When the subjects came to buy their tickets, they were required to complete some questionnaires. Some of the questionnaire items were routine, such as requests for age, sex, height, and religious affiliation, but some were important for the present purposes. Among the latter were a measure of self-esteem (liking of self) and a measure which might be called indices of "social skills." A rough measure of intelligence was also obtained by looking up high school academic rank and college entrance scores. Also, ratings of the physical attractiveness of subjects were surreptitiously made at this time by the student helpers who administered the questionnaires.

Actually, dates were assigned to each other at random. This insured that all possible pairings of attractiveness, intelligence and so on existed. The night of the dance, subjects were supposed to meet at the dance site, but a few enterprising males arranged to pick up their dates at their place of residence. The first two-and-a-half hours of the dance were taken up by conversation and dancing. After this period, there was a pause during which males and females were separated so that they could anonymously respond to the questions "How much do you like your date?" and "How much would you like to date her (him) again?" A few months after the dance, males were contacted to determine whether or not they had asked their dates out again.

Results were surprising. The subject's own physical attractiveness level made no difference. Whether or not a subject was attractive or unattractive he or she preferred an attractive date both in terms of liking and desire to date the person again. Further, males subsequently asked attractive girls for more dates than unattractive girls, regardless of whether they were "handsome" or "ugly" themselves. Thus the matching hypothesis received no support. "Beautiful" and "ugly" people preferred beautiful dates.

In fact, attractiveness was so powerful, that nothing else mattered. Both male and female subjects preferred attractive to unattractive dates, regardless of whether the dates were intelligent or stupid, socially skilled or socially inept, liked themselves or didn't like themselves. Physical attractiveness was the sole important determinant of liking dates and selecting dates on subsequent occasions. Other research has shown that there is some tendency for unattractive people to demand less attractiveness in their dates than do attractive people.

However, this tendency is weak and may be thought of as superimposed on the stronger tendency for everyone to prefer attractive dates (Berscheid and Walster, 1972).

Walster and her colleagues were as surprised as the man in the street. They had accepted people's statements that attractiveness is important, but less important than other factors. One researcher put it this way: we have neglected to investigate physical attractiveness until this late date (mid-60s) for fear of finding out how important it really is.

Why do people cling so tenaciously to their beliefs about social behavior and its determinants? In the case of "beauty," it is probably because we like to think that it's what's inside a person that counts. A person's humanity, innate good sense, and congeniality are what *ought* to matter. To think that people give much weight to superficial characteristics like physical attractiveness would be repugnant to most of us.

But What About the Long Run?

The dating study of Walster and her colleagues has been replicated many times. Later there will be occasion to mention some of these replications. The results are amazingly consistent across studies. For almost every replication, attractiveness proved to be far more important than any other determinant of liking dates and of dating choices. But there is something else common to these several dating studies. Like the Walster study, only one or two dates were involved. Perhaps physical attractiveness is more important than other attributes only for short-term relationships. More "internal" factors like "personality" may increase in importance as relationships increase in duration, whereas superficial characteristics like attractiveness may decrease in importance with increase in duration of relationships. This point of view seems entirely logical. When you first meet someone, the only information by which you can judge them is superficial in nature. It takes time to determine what kind of personality they have, but you can tell whether they are "pretty" or not in an instant.

The notion that attractiveness may decrease in importance while other more internal factors increase in importance as relationships extend into time may be particularly true of dating relationships. Any high school student knows that on initial dates one tries to look his or her nicest and be on his or her best behavior. Thus, on first dates people tend to erect a "proper social behavior" barrier to their "true selves." It may take several dates before people are willing to let down their defenses and disclose their real, personal characteristics.

"Getting to Know You . . ."

Eugene Mathes (1975) adopted the above logic in an experiment involving long-term dating. When his college-student subjects showed up for the initial session of the experiment, they were surreptitiously rated on physical attractiveness and were required to complete a questionnaire measure of the personality attribute anxiety. At the same time they signed a contract to complete five dates during the course of the experiment. Male and female subjects were randomly assigned to each other, with the restriction that all possible combinations of attractive-unattractive and high and low anxiety were created. At a subsequent session, the experimenter introduced the participants to one another and instructed them to set up the actual dates at their own convenience. This procedure was to make the encounters more like real-life dates. Subjects were also told to privately rate each other on "likeability" after each date.

Mathes reasoned that on the first date and possibly the second, attractiveness would determine liking of dates, because subjects would not have had the opportunity to know each other. Therefore, attractiveness would be the only available criterion for liking. However, on later dates after subjects had gotten to know each other they would be relatively inattentive to physical attractiveness and show greater liking for low- as opposed to high-anxious persons.

Alas and alack, it didn't turn out that way. Instead of attractiveness becoming less important as a determinant of liking across the five dates, attractiveness *increased* in importance from the first date to subsequent dates. Further, high-anxious subjects were liked more than low-anxious subjects, and this effect did not change over the five dates. This latter failure in prediction may have been due to a misinterpretation of the anxiousness measure. Highly anxious people may perform some annoying behaviors, but they are more compliant to the wishes of others, and many persons like someone who will give them their own way.

However, the attractiveness-vs.-anxiousness finding is more dif-

ficult to explain, and again it is necessary to depend on hindsight.
Perhaps the personality variable investigated was weak and unimportant thus causing subjects to continue to rely on attractiveness for
making likeability ratings. It has often been noted that the failure of
personality factors to rival attractiveness in importance may be because factors that don't particularly matter have been investigated.
Later, I will return to the contention that, in future experiments,
stronger personal factors than anxiety must be compared with
attractiveness.

Mathes' surprising finding might have been due to the nature of
his procedure. Contrary to what happens in real life, subjects had to
complete the series of dates. In real life, if people don't like each
other, they stop dating. People who stay together initially in a real-
life dating series may do so because they regard each other as physically attractive, but whether they continue to like each other and
continue to date may depend upon such personality traits as loyalty,
personal stability, and selflessness. What's needed to test this *post hoc*
explanation is a study in which attractiveness is pitted against other
attributes for couples who are asked to complete a series of dates, but
are allowed to stop dating whenever they like.

It could also be that the rationale for the long-term dating study
is faulty. So-called "superficial" characteristics may be more than
temporary substitutes for the criteria that "really count" in evaluating
others, such as stability, loyalty, and humanity. Charles Potkay
(1971) reports that clinical psychologists sometimes do as well in
judging their clients when judgements are based on superficial criteria
as when judgements are based on well-respected formal tests (e.g.,
the inkblot test). Future research may reveal that the "superficial"
characteristic attractiveness continues even in the long run to be more
important than "what's inside" for the determination of maintenance
of a relationship and liking of a relationship. A hint that this possibility is genuine comes from Ellen Berscheid and Elaine Walster in
their (1972) discussion of a study which found that women who
were judged to be pretty while in college were dissatisfied with their
marriage twenty-five years later. These researchers speculated that
as their subjects' looks faded so did the positive regard that they had
come to expect from their husbands, and dissatisfaction with the relationship was the result.

Although this study did not replicate (Murstein & Christy,

1976), there is evidence that middle-aged women are concerned about "fading beauty" (Nowak, 1976). Also, there is evidence that middle-aged husbands who see their wives as attractive and whose wives see them as attractive are happy with their marriages (Murstein & Christy, 1976). Perhaps attractiveness is important for determining perceptions that are related to marriage satisfaction, even for the middle-aged who may have been married for a number of years.

But enough of the clear vision of hindsight. Based on the data which is available at this time, it must be concluded that the overwhelming importance of attractiveness relative to other possible determinants of dating preferences is not necessarily confined to short-term dating.

Princesses Don't Marry Frogs

It's apparent that physical attractiveness is very important for the realm of dating. However, even long-term dating is a transitory state. People may date for a year or two, but they get married for a lifetime.

Thus a more important consideration than how attractiveness influences dating relationships is the importance of attractiveness for determining the selection of marital partners. Norman Cavior and Patrick Boblett (1972) addressed themselves to this consideration in straightforward fashion. They simply recruited a sample of married couples, took their pictures individually and had the pictures rated on physical attractiveness. The attractiveness ratings of husbands and wives were then correlated. The resultant correlation coefficient of .73 indicated that there was a strong tendency for handsome men to marry beautiful women and unattractive men to marry unattractive women (a coefficient of 1.00 would have indicated perfect correspondence between the attractiveness ratings of husbands and wives). This same result also has been found by other researchers. Thus the matching hypothesis of Walster and her colleagues (1966) is strongly confirmed for marital selections. The high correspondence between the attractiveness of husbands and wives implies that people seek out someone to marry who is at their own level of attractiveness.

Cavior and Boblett did the analogous correlation for dating couples. In this case the correlation coefficient was positive but small (.19) indicating only a small tendency for people to date individuals whose physical attractiveness is similar to their own. This outcome fits very well with results reported above. A low correlation is predicted by the observation that an individual, regardless of his or her own attractiveness, seeks and likes an attractive date. But the slight correlation is consistent with the observation that there is a small tendency for attractive people to demand more attractiveness in their dates than do unattractive people.

Thus attractiveness is important in marriage as it is in dating, but in a different sense. Attractiveness is important for dating not only in the sense that everyone seeks and likes attractive dates, regardless of their own attractiveness, but also in the sense that other possible criteria for selecting and liking dates appear unimportant in comparison to attractiveness. However, attractiveness is important for marriage in the sense that a person's attractiveness determines to a significant degree whom he or she may consider as a potential spouse. Attractiveness appears to be a limiting factor in marital selection. An unattractive person cannot consider as a possible spouse someone whose attractiveness far exceeds his or her own. Such a person can reasonably consider only persons who are toward the unattractive end of the attractiveness continuum. It is improbable that they would be acceptable to an attractive person. Conversely, "it wouldn't do" for very attractive persons to consider as potential spouses individuals whose attractiveness level was much less than their own. As will be supported below, attractive people are expected to do well in life, and being married to an attractive person is part of what constitutes "doing well." An attractiveness credibility gap is acceptable, in fact even desirable, in the realm of dating, but when it comes to choosing someone to marry, an attractiveness credibility gap can take on the proportions of the Grand Canyon.

There is another way to say the same thing about the importance of attractiveness for mate selection. Intelligence has long been recognized as an important factor in mate selection. It may be that a person seeks someone as a spouse whose intelligence level is similar to his or her own. Evidence for this contention comes from the fact that the correlation between indices of intelligence for husbands and wives is positive and strong (coefficient range in the .60's). This means that the intelligence correlation coefficients for spouses are in the same order of magnitude as the corresponding coefficients for attractiveness of spouses. Thus a person's attractiveness level may be as important in determining whom he or she will marry as his or her intelligence level.

HOW SOON THEY LEARN

At this point it can be conceded that physical attractiveness is an extremely important criterion for determining social choices. Other traits or characteristics which have proven to be important determinants of social behavior have been shown to be effective very early in life. In fact, one of the tests of the power of a characteristic for determining social behavior is how early in life it begins to influence children and how early its influence is recognized by children. For example, it is now widely accepted that male and female children are treated differently almost from the day they leave the maternity ward. Children learn their sex and that of their siblings and parents very early, as well as the general deportment appropriate for their sex.

Likewise, children learn at a very young age to discriminate by race and that black persons are regarded as "bad" while white persons are regarded as "good."

That race and sex are powerful determinants of social behavior should be evident. Evidence in support of the power of these variables will be considered elsewhere in this book. But does physical attractiveness belong in the same class as race and sex? The evidence considered above leads to the prediction that it does. If it does, the effects of attractiveness should be evident in the behavior of young children and in the reactions of people to young children. Let's see.

Karen Dion (1973) attempted to find out whether young children have developed the concept "attractiveness" well enough to correctly identify attractive and unattractive persons. Further, if children can identify "pretty" and "ugly" people, she wanted to know whether they attributed different characteristics and behaviors to the two kinds of people.

Dion's subjects were thirty-four boys and thirty-one girls whose ages ranged from three years to six-and-a-half years. These subjects were shown twelve photographs of some children who were strangers to them. The photos depicted three attractive boys, three attractive girls, three unattractive boys, and three unattractive girls. The classification of the twelve photos was based on th aettractiveness ratings of eight adults. First, the subjects were shown the photos of six children of one sex and asked which two would they like as friends and which two would they not like as friends. The procedure was repeated for the photos depicting children of the other sex.

Next, subjects were shown all twelve photos and asked to "Find someone you think" displays a certain social behavior. The question was asked of each subject for several social behaviors including the following: "Hits without a good reason," "Scares you," "Might hurt you," "Very friendly to other children," "Doesn't like fighting or shouting," and "Doesn't hit even if someone else hits first."

Finally, the twelve photos were arranged in pairs such that each pair contained a picture of an attractive child and a picture of an unattractive child. The members of each pair of photos were of the same sex. Each subject was shown each pair of photos and for each pair was asked, "which child is prettier?" for female photos and "which child is cuter?" for male photos.

Results for this last task indicated that the child subjects were very accurate in identifying the photos that adults had judged to be attractive. Furthermore, younger and older children were compared as to accuracy and no significant difference was found. Thus young children show attractiveness discrimination similar to adults, even those as young as age three. Race discrimination is also found in three-year-olds (Renninger and Williams, 1966). If people learn that "pretty" and "ugly" people are different very early in life, they would be expected to attach a great deal of meaning to the difference by the time they reach adulthood, just as they do in the case of black persons vs. white persons.

But do "pretty" and "ugly" become rich in meaning only at adulthood? Dion's child subjects showed a significant tendency to prefer the attractive children as friends. Also, all the positive or socially approved social behaviors listed above were more likely to be attributed to attractive than to unattractive target children. Conversely, all the negative or socially disapproved social behaviors listed above were more likely to be attributed to unattractive than to attractive target children. This is the first hint that "pretty" or "beautiful" is "good" and "ugly" is "bad." As we shall see, these connotations of "beautiful" and "ugly" become greatly elaborated in adulthood.

Dion's study was somewhat hypothetical in that subjects reacted to strangers presented in photographic form. Would her results hold if subjects reacted to their actual peers instead of strangers? She and Ellen Berscheid (1974) did a study which was very similar to the one described just above and which is relevant to this question. The major difference was that each child subject was shown a board containing photos of his entire elementary school class. Classmates had been rated on physical attractiveness by adults before the experiment began. From the entire class each subject was asked to pick out three children he or she especially liked and three that he or she especially disliked. As in the previous study, subjects were asked to "find someone who" performs certain social behaviors, or displays certain traits.

Younger (4-5 years) and older (5.5-6 years) males and older females who were attractive were more popular with the subjects than were their unattractive counterparts. However, younger unattractive females were more popular than their attractive counterparts. It took an additional year or two to learn that attractive is better than unattractive when applied to females.

Results for the attribution of social behaviors and traits were similar to those found when subjects reacted to strangers rather than actual peers. For example, unattractive males were seen as engaging in more antisocial aggressive acts than attractive males, and a similar trend was found for the attribution of nonconforming behaviors. Attractive children, regardless of sex, were seen as more independent than unattractive children. Finally, unattractive females were seen as more fearful than attractive females, and unattractive children, regardless of sex, were seen as more "scary" than attractive children. Thus when actual peers are the target of attributions, it was still true that attractive was "good" and unattractive was "bad."

Self-Fulfilling Prophecy

Sometimes we kick people around and when they react with aggression or other undesirable behavior, we say, "See, I told you they were mean." Of course, the expression "they're mean" amounts to an expectation that they will behave like "meanies" in the future, and it tends to make them all the meaner. This is the logic of the self-fulfilling prophecy and it seems to apply to the case of attractive and unattractive people. If "unattractive" is "bad," people may treat unattractive individuals badly and expect them to behave badly. As a result, unattractive individuals behave badly which reinforces the notion that "unattractive is bad." On the other side of the coin, if attractive is good, people may treat attractive individuals well and expect well of them which could predispose them to behave desirably.

In a study of attractive and unattractive children which is relevant to the self-fulfilling prophecy, Karen Dion (1972) presented some coeds with photos of children who varied in physical attractiveness according to ratings previously made by nine graduate students. Along with the photo, subjects received an attached description of an antisocial act supposedly committed by the child depicted in the photo. In effect, they were told, "We would like to know how a detached observer would judge this act, if she is given the same basic information as the person who was at the scene of the act." It was implied that detached observers would have an "extra dimension to their judgments" in contrast to direct observers.

Other variables investigated besides attractiveness included sex of the child in the photo and severity of the act. Each subject received a photo depicting a boy or a girl who was attractive or unattractive, and who had committed a mild or severe antisocial act. An example of a mild act was the throwing of a snowball at a child resulting in a "sting." A severe act was the throwing of a snowball with a piece of ice in it resulting in a deep cut which bled.

After viewing the photos and reading the descriptions, subjects were asked a number of questions. Among these were the following: How likely was the child to have committed such an act in the past? How likely was he to commit such an act in the future? How does the child usually behave on a typical day? How undesirable was the act? In addition, subjects were asked to rate the child in their photo on a number of personality traits.

Results showed that for the severe transgression, female subjects judged that such acts were more typical of an unattractive than an attractive child. That is, more chronic antisocial behavior was attributed to unattractive children than to the attractive children. Further, unattractive children were judged to be more likely to commit antisocial acts in the future than attractive children. These results clearly indicate that the subjects, many of whom would become mothers and teachers, assumed that unattractive children misbehave relative to attractive children and expected that they will continue to do so.

On the personality traits, attractive children were seen as more honest and more pleasant than unattractive children who had committed the same antisocial acts. Does the former finding imply that unattractive children are expected to be liars? If so, an unattractive child would be at a distinct disadvantage when pitted against an attractive child in a contest of "who's to blame" for some undesirable outcome.

Finally, regardless of severity of the act, a given act was judged to be less undesirable if committed by an attractive child. It may be that people see less misbehavior in attractive children, because whatever they do is judged less severely.

But how do attractive and unattractive children fair in terms of punishment for transgressions? Karen Dion (1974) has done yet another study which addresses this question. She had men and women mete out punishments to boys and girls for mistakes on a picture-matching task. Women were more lenient to attractive boys than to

unattractive boys. For men, sex and attractiveness made no difference. Thus women, who have the most exposure to young children,
allow "pretty boys to get by with murder."

Teacher's Pet

Robert Rosenthal (1966) gave an intelligence test to some elementary school children, but told their teachers that the test measured
"academic growth potential." The teachers were then led to believe
that the test results indicated that certain of their pupils would show
"unusually great academic development during the coming school
year." Actually, the children to whom unusual growth potential had
been attributed were randomly chosen and didn't differ from their
classmates. Thus the teachers were given the expectation that some
of their pupils would show great intellectual progress during the next
year. One year later the children were retested with the same intelligence test used initially. First and second graders showed a significant
increase in measured intelligence. Apparently the teachers communicated their positive expectations to the students which spurred them
to greater intellectual heights. Also, the teachers may have helped
their expectations come true by devoting more time and attention to
those they thought were "intellectual bloomers." At any rate, positive
expectations were associated with positive intellectual outcomes.

The practical importance of differential expectations about attractive and unattractive children is not clearly indicated by the
studies cited above. If, however, these differential expectations could
be shown to be held by persons who directly influence the real outcomes of children, their practical importance would be apparent.
Rosenthal's experiment suggested that it is important to determine
whether schoolteachers have different expectations about the academic potential of attractive and unattractive children.

To investigate teachers' expectations about the academic potential of attractive and unattractive children, Margaret Clifford and
Elaine Walster (1973) sent permanent record "report files" and attached photos to elementary school principles who, in turn, distributed them to their fifth grade teachers. The report files actually all
contained the same information. The only thing that varied was the
sex and the prerated level of attractiveness of the child depicted in the
photo. A cover letter addressed to each teacher indicated that the

researchers were interested in evaluating various kinds of report file forms in order to identify the forms which would best fit the needs of educators. The teachers were asked to help in the evaluation process by examining a file and responding to several questions about the information included in the file. Since attaching of photos to report files was routine in the state in which the teachers worked, no rationale for including the photo was presented. The teachers were asked the following questions about the child whose file they examined: What do you estimate the child's I.Q. to be? What do you estimate the child's social status with peers to be? How interested are the child's parents in school? What level of education do you think the child will be able to attain?

First, all answers except the one to the question on social status were transformed into a single index of Perceived Educational Potential. On this overall measure, attractive children received higher scores indicating that they were seen as having greater educational potential. When the overall measure was broken down into its component parts, it was revealed that attractive children were expected to have high I.Q.'s, more interested parents, and go farther in school than unattractive children. Finally, attractive children were expected to have far better relations with their peers than unattractive children.

Thus teachers may have different expectations about attractive and unattractive pupils. If so, they may communicate these expectations to their attractive and unattractive pupils and "make their prophecies come true" by investing different amounts of time and attention to the two sets of pupils. As a result, the academic development of unattractive children could be impaired.

BEAUTIFUL IS GOOD!

Beautiful Is Success in Life

Already it is apparent that for both children and adults, attractive children are expected to have better outcomes and display better behavior than unattractive children. However, it remains to be seen how these attributions are expanded and elaborated as both the attributor and the target of attributions mature into adulthood. A series of experiments was addressed to one aspect of the expectation that beauty in adults is associated with "good" behaviors and "good" outcomes: attractive people are expected to have more success in life in terms of both social and professional success. One of these experiments which supports "beautiful is success in life" is detailed below. Others will be considered in another context within this chapter.

Karen Dion, Ellen Bersheid, and Elaine Walster (1972) sought to determine whether adult attractive target persons are assumed to possess more socially desirable personality traits and are expected to lead better lives than unattractive target persons. To this end, thirty males and thirty females were asked to be in an "impression formation" experiment. Subjects were told that persons can form detailed impressions based on minimal information about others, but that the dynamics behind this process were not known. To shed some light on the process of "impression formation," subjects were told that the impressions of untrained college students were to be compared with those of trained professionals for a set of target persons previously observed by professionals. Finally, the experimenters suggested that possibly one of the factors important for impression formation may simply be God-given ability: some people may have the ability to form accurate impressions while others don't. Thus subjects were led to believe that when their impressions of target persons were compared with those of professionals, some of them would show the same level of accuracy as trained professionals, while others would not. Presumably, "accuracy" of impressions was to be established with reference to some personality data on each target which was made available because all targets were participants in a continuing longitudinal study of personality.

Each subject was shown photos of three target persons who varied over three levels of attractiveness. That the targets were classified as attractive, average, or unattractive according to preratings was not disclosed to subjects. Half the subjects received photos of male college students and half received photos of female college students. First the subjects rated the targets on general personality traits such as "exciting" as opposed to "dull" and "sincere" as opposed to 'insincere." Next, subjects were asked to pick the photo of the person who they thought had the most, least, and intermediate degrees of several other personality traits (e.g., friendliness and social poise). The more targets were seen to possess one of these traits, the more favorable was their rating for that trait. Some of the traits involved in these two rating tasks had been previously formed into an index of social desirability. A "socially desirable" trait is one that is desirable for persons to have or one that is socially approved. A subject's overall social-desirability rating of a given target person was the sum of the ratings given to that target on each of the several traits constituting the social desirability index.

In an additional rating, subjects were to select one target who was most, one who was least, and one who was intermediate in likelihood of having each of several life experiences. The life experiences were divided into four categories: 1) marital happiness, 2) parental happiness, 3) social and professional happiness, and 4) total happiness (the sum of the first three categories). Sample questions asked of subjects from category (3) were, "Which stimulus person (target) is most likely to experience deep personal fulfillment?" "Which is least likely?" "Which is intermediate?"

Finally, subjects were to assign each target one of three occupational levels for each of ten occupational categories. For each occupational category the three levels corresponded to three degrees of status. For example, one category was "military," and the three levels were "sergeant" (low status), "captain" (average status), and "colonel" (high status). Subjects were to assign "sergeant" to the target most likely to be limited to the lowest level, and "colonel" to the target most likely to attain the highest level.

Results showed that "beautiful is good" regardless of whether the reference is marital happiness, occupational status, or social desirability. Attractive as compared to unattractive targets were seen as having more socially desirable personalities, were expected to have more prestigious occupations, were expected to have less trouble finding an acceptable marital partner and have happier marriages, and were expected to have happier social and professional lives. Based on this data Dion and colleagues suggested that people have developed a stereotype of attractive persons such that the possession of the valued attribute "attractiveness" implies the possession of a host of other highly valued attributes. Beautiful people are assumed to be good in every way.

Beautiful is Talented

Beautiful means not only success in life, but talent as well. Beautiful people are expected to be intelligent and skilled in numerous ways. To demonstrate this point David Landy and Harold Sigall (1974) presented some male students with essays which were either well-written or poorly written. The essays had supposedly been done for an English class and turned into the instructor with accompanying background information about the authors so that they could be entered in a contest. Actually the "contest story" was to justify attaching cards which contained mundane information about the authors of the essays. All subjects received essays with the same card attached, but for some subjects the card contained a photo of an attractive female college student while for others, the card contained the photo of an unattractive female student. Still other subjects received a card without an accompanying photo.

In sum, each subject received a well-written or poorly written essay and an accompanying information card which contained a photo of an attractive or of an unattractive female, or no photo at all. The experimenter explained that he had acquired the essays for a social-judgment experiment in which subjects would read the essays and accompanying information and then make judgments about the essays and their authors.

The essays were to be judged on an essay-evaluation measure and a general quality measure. The evaluation measure involved having subjects indicate whether the ideas in the essay were dull or interesting, whether the essay reflected a high or low level of creativity and whether the style of the essay was poor or good. The quality measure involved simply a good/poor rating of the essay as a whole. The authors themselves were rated on whether they were high or low in overall ability and on whether they were high or low in intelligence, sensitivity, and talent (called the writer-impression measure).

The essays of attractive authors were rated higher than those of unattractive authors on both the general quality measure and on the essay-evaluation measure. However, closer examination of the data revealed that on both measures the difference between the ratings was significant only for the poor essay condition. A similar finding was reported for the ratings of the authors themselves. Both on the writer-impression measure and on the overall ability measure, attractive authors were rated more favorably than unattractive authors, but the difference was significant only for the poor essay condition.

Thus when people produce good work, their level of attractiveness makes little difference in the evaluation that they receive. However, beauty compensates for poor work, in that poor writers who are beautiful receive more favorable evaluations than poor writers who are ugly. It seems that attractive people can get by on their looks, while unattractive people must be skillful to succeed.

The Midas Touch

All of the above data indicating that beautiful is good suggest that beautiful people should attract like a magnet, because others would want to associate with them in the hope that some of the "goodness" would rub off.

Sigall and Landy (1973) did another two experiments to determine the effects of association with beauty. In the first of these an average looking male target was associated or merely present with an attractive female who was either dressed to enhance her beauty or to make her appear unattractive. Both people were confederates of the experimenter. The two confederates were seated side by side in chairs facing the one to be occupied by the subject. After the subject arrived and took his or her seat, the experimenter entered and asked if all present were there for an experiment. When only the subject and the male target answered in the affirmative, the experimenter asked the female confederate if she would help him. In the associated condition she took the target's hand and said, "No, I'm just waiting for my boy friend." In the unassociated condition, she said, "No, I'm waiting for Dr. Jones."

The experimenter then left only to return shortly in order to escort the subject and the target to separate cubicles. The experimenter first approached the subject in his private cubicle and informed him that he was to participate in a person-perception experiment in which various information was to be exchanged between subjects, presumably to provide a basis for forming impressions. "But first," said the experimenter, "I would like to get your first impression of the other subject" (actually the target). The experimenter then supplied the subject with a questionnaire and left, ostensibly to instruct the target. Among the items on the questionnaire was "My over-all impression of the other subject is _____" (some degree of positive or negative), "I think that I would _____ the other subject" (some degree of like or dislike), and various other items for measuring other dimensions such as confidence, friendliness, and likability.

On the overall-impression measure, subjects gave the target the most favorable ratings in the attractive-associated condition and the least favorable ratings in the unattractive-associated condition. The unassociated conditions were intermediate in favorability of ratings. Thus if an individual is associated with beauty, evaluations given him by others are enhanced. Further, ratings were more favorable in the unattractive-unassociated condition than in the unattractive-associated condition. This means that association with "ugliness" may cause a person to receive lower evaluations than he would normally receive. Similar results were obtained on the liking measure: the target was liked more when associated with the attractive confederate than when unassociated with her, but the "association with ugliness effect" was not observed. The target was seen as more friendly, confident, and likable in the attractive-associated condition than in the unattractive-unassociated condition.

Not only does "goodness" rub off on those associated with beauty, but "badness" may rub off on those associated with ugliness. However, only if people are aware of the rub-off effect at some level of consciousness would beautiful people "attract like a magnet." One index of awareness is the degree to which people expect to be positively evaluated when associated with beauty and negatively evaluated when associated with ugliness.

In their second experiment Sigall and Landy (1973) concocted a situation in which male subjects were led to believe that they would be associated in the eyes of others with an attractive female, associated with an unattractive female, or would merely be present with an attractive or unattractive female while others formed impressions of them. Shortly after the subject showed up for the experiment, an attractive female who was actually an accomplice of the experimenter arrived. Again, she was either dressed to enhance her beauty or to make her appear unattractive. The experimenter ushered both persons into a room and informed them that they were to be targets in an impression-formation experiment designed to discover how impressions develop. In preparation for the evaluators who had not yet arrived, the targets were asked to copy some information onto a questionnaire form. Ostensibly this procedure was to provide the evaluators with information upon which to base their impressions. Actually it was to convince the subject that he was to be a target in an impression-formation study. The experimenter went on to say either that the two targets would be presented to evaluators as boy friend and girl friend or as strangers. Apparently the subject was expected to accept this information as more grain for the impression-formation gristmill, but actually it was to create an associated condition (boy friend-girl friend) or an unassociated condition (strangers).

Finally, the experimenter asked the targets to attempt to anticipate the evaluations that they would receive by responding to some questionnaire items similar to those used in the previous experiment (e.g., intelligent–unintelligent, likable–not likable, talented–untalented). Thus the subject indicated how he thought he would be evaluated.

Results showed that when the target thought the evaluators would see him as being associated with an attractive female, he anticipated the most favorable evaluations, and when he thought the evaluators would see him as being associated with an unattractive female, he anticipated the least favorable evaluations. Expected evaluations were intermediate in favorability when the target thought he would be seen as unassociated with the female. Thus subjects expected to be downgraded when associated with ugliness and upgraded when associated with beauty.

These results suggest that individuals may associate with beautiful people because they expect that some of the "goodness" (i.e., positive attributes) connoted by beauty will rub off on them resulting in positive evaluations. The notion of "rub-off" implies that the associates of beautiful people are assumed to obtain their "goodness" through osmosis. This possibility is akin to the "guilt by association" belief: if you associate with someone enough you will soak up his or her characteristics. Thus people may assume that merely associating with "goodness" makes one "good."

However, there are other possible explanations of why individuals give positive evaluations to the associates of beautiful people. Some of these fall under the heading of "assumptions implicit in winning the favor of a beauty." For example, a boy who wins the attentions of a beautiful girl must "have something on the ball"; i.e., he must be outstanding in many ways. It takes ability to win a beauty. Also, individuals may assume that a beautiful person can have his or her choice of associates, and thus whoever he or she chooses must be outstanding.

These hypotheses imply that the assumption of "goodness" that is made about the associates of beautiful people is not necessarily accurate. A boy who wins a beautiful girl may in fact be the "out-standing" person he's assumed to be or he may be a dull, socially inept stumblebum who was lucky. In the latter case the assumption "outstanding" which was based on association with beauty would be inaccurate. Thus, the assumption that "the associates of beautiful people are good in many ways" is not necessarily fact. It can be regarded as a fact only as a result of assessing the intelligence, likability and so on of the associates of beautiful people. But just as the process of the self-fulfilling prophecy can help an attractive child do better in school, the positive feedback received by the associates of beautiful people may help them to actually do better in life.

The Influence of Being Beautiful or Ugly on Self-Esteem

Self-esteem refers to the degree to which individuals see themselves in a favorable light. It is widely believed to be dependent on the favorability of the regard that individuals receive from important people in their lives. Doesn't it seem reasonable to expect that all the positive regard that attractive people receive and all of the negative regard that unattractive people receive should influence their self-esteem? Some research by myself and Steve Wroble (1975) suggests an affirmative answer to the question.

For these purposes the experiment that we performed can be described simply. Male subjects were given a questionnaire containing many items designed to assess beliefs about general issues. Buried among the items was one which asked subjects to describe themselves by generating five descriptive adjectives (see the discussion on Adjective Generation Technique in the Racism chapter). This was the measure of self-esteem. While subjects were completing the questionnaire, four raters rated their physical attractiveness from behind a one-way mirror. Attractive subjects described themselves significantly more favorably than unattractive subjects. The correlation between attractiveness and self-esteem was .60. Recently, I was able to replicate these results. Other researchers have reported essentially the same results for female subjects (Berscheid, Dion, Walster, & Walster, 1971; Mathes & Kahn, 1975). Beautiful may also mean higher self-esteem.

Incidentally, self-esteem is apparently not the only way that attractive and unattractive people differ in actual characteristics and behaviors due to being treated differently. Although some researchers have reported that attractive people actually score higher on intelligence tests than unattractive people, other researchers have failed to find any difference (Tinken, 1976). However, there is some evidence that attractive female college students do better academically than unattractive female students (Singer, 1964). Also, attractive females are more popular as dates than unattractive females (Berscheid et al., 1971; Krebs and Adinolfi, 1975). Finally, attractive people are more socially active (e.g., invited to more parties and other social gatherings and belong to more organizations) than unattractive people (Berscheid et al., 1971; Tinken, 1976).

SEARCHING FOR LIMITS OF THE IMPORTANCE OF ATTRACTIVENESS

After appreciating the research described above, it doesn't seem reasonable to quarrel with the conclusion that the importance of physical attractiveness is much greater than most of us had been willing to admit. However, this research goes beyond the indication that attractiveness is more important than most people had thought. Attractiveness appears to be more important than almost any other factor for a large number of attributions and social choices. In fact, one might conclude from the research cited above that "attractiveness rules all."

Such a conclusion makes one uncomfortable. It has always been true that whenever someone claims that a single factor is sufficient to account for an entire social domain, he turns out to be incorrect. As is considered elsewhere in this book, Milton Rokeach's claim that congruence of belief is sufficient to account for prejudice so that other factors like race are of little importance proved to be in error. It is difficult to imagine that when there is sufficient data available, beautiful people will have been found to almost always finish first in social-choice derbies regardless of what other factors are in the race.

For these reasons, several researchers have been concerned in recent years with determining the limits of the importance of attractiveness. A consideration of the strategies they employed and what they found will constitute the remainder of this chapter.

Beauty vs. Other Powerful Factors

A strategy adopted by myself and my students involved the assumption that attractiveness seemed to be more powerful than other factors merely because it had not been compared with very powerful factors. It was expected that if attractiveness were compared to factors of more central importance to social interactions than factors which were investigated in previous research, attractiveness might be beaten.

To this end, Mike Meredith (1972) compared the importance of independence and honesty to attractiveness as criteria for dating choices. Male subjects were asked to look at yearbook pictures of college females and read the personality summaries accompanying each picture. Each female was to be rated on desirability as a date based on the picture and personality description. Each picture was of an attractive or unattractive female (based on preratings), who was described as honest or neutral with regard to honesty, and who was described as dependent on others or independent. Bogus information was included with each personality description. Honesty and dependency were indicated in slightly different ways across the personality descriptions in order to disguise the purpose of the experiment. There were two pictures for each of the eight conditions generated by combining levels of attractiveness, honesty and independence. Thus each subject was presented with sixteen pictures. The pictures were in a different random order for each subject. This latter procedure was to minimize order effects and further disguise the purpose of the experiment.

The results were disappointing. Although the honesty and physical attractiveness effects both were significant, attractiveness was by far the most important in determining dating choices. The independence effect was not significant. Thus attractiveness was "almost the whole bag."

We went searching for a new factor. Some research had indicated that the amount of "basic trust" intimates have for one another is important for maintenance and satisfaction in romantic relationships. Further, basic trust seemed to increase with time in the relationship, indicating that it may be of critical importance in the long run. Because basic trust is the confidence one has in the affection and loyalty of a partner, it makes sense that it would be important for long-term relationships. Therefore, it was reasoned that although physical attractiveness may get people together, it is basic trust that keeps them together. Attractiveness, then, may be replaced in importance over time by trust.

To test this hypothesis, Mark Shepard (1973) replicated Meredith's experiment, but substituted information on trustworthiness for information on honesty and independence of college females who varied in attractiveness. Also, Shepard used two groups of male subjects. One group was instructed in the same way as Meredith's subjects, while the other group was told to "indicate your desire to date each of these girls steadily."

At first glance, the results seemed encouraging. Both the attractiveness and trustworthiness effects were highly significant and about equally important in determining desirability ratings. However, examination of the joint effects of attractiveness and trustworthiness and the effects of length of the assumed relationship put a halt to the celebration. First, trustworthiness did not increase in importance when subjects assumed "going steady" as opposed to dating once, and attractiveness did not decrease in importance with length of the relationship. Second, trustworthiness didn't make much difference for attractive targets. They received high ratings whether they were described as trustworthy or not. However, unattractive targets received high ratings only if they were described as trustworthy. Thus trustworthiness was important mainly for unattractive targets. Beautiful girls are desirable as dates even if they are untrustworthy, but ugly girls have to be relatively trustworthy to be desirable.

Next, I began to look for a different kind of factor to rival attractiveness. As is discussed in detail in another part of this book, race, like attractiveness, seems to dominate certain kinds of social relationships. Race is the uncrowned "king" in its social domain just as attractiveness is for its domain. Thus race might be potent enough to challenge attractiveness. But there is another important characteristic of race which made me think that it might rival attractiveness. It is highly visible, and equally as apparent on the first glance as is attractiveness. Maybe the reason that attractiveness had not met its match is because it had not been compared with a factor that is as visible.

Thus I did still another dating study (Allen, 1976). "Dating" was chosen as the social relationship to investigate, because attractiveness is known to be important for dating and because race *should be* important for dating. The latter is the case because the dating relationship is akin to the type of relationship for which race has proven to be of primary importance. Dating involves intimacy and race has been shown to be important for intimate relationships.

In a first experiment, white male and female subjects viewed full-body color slides of members of the opposite sex. The critical slides were of members of the opposite sex who had been rated as attractive or unattractive and who were white or black. The black and white targets had been carefully matched on attractiveness ratings. Also, there were a number of filler slides along with the critical slides. This was to make plausible a promise expressed to subjects just before the slides were seen. The promise was that each subject would be able to actually date one of the targets that they had *rated as a highly desirable date*. This promise required the apparent availability of large number of potential dates.

Subjects were told that they were to make "desirability as a date" ratings based on the slide and accompanying "interest information" which was read to them with each slide presentation. Actually the interest information was contrived to distract the subjects from the purpose of comparing race and attractiveness. Subjects were told to indicate their willingness to participate in the actual date portion of the study by writing their telephone number on their "date rating" form. The reason for the "actual date" instruction was to cause subjects to make their ratings under the assumption that they were making a real dating choice rather than a hypothetical one. The "real date assumption" was strengthened by the fact that the experiment had been advertised as a dating study, and excluded people who were going steady, engaged, or married. Also, several actual date studies had recently been conducted at the subjects' university. On the same day that choices had been made, my assistant began calling the people who had furnished their phone numbers. All subjects were asked to meet with me at a mutually convenient time to "set up the date." I considered a subject fully committed to the actual date if he or she showed up for the meeting. At the meeting it was explained to subjects that there was no actual date and also why the deception was necessary.

The data for male and female subjects were analyzed separately because they had been run in separate groups and had been exposed to different targets. The results for females indicated highly significant effects for both race and attractiveness. White females strongly preferred an attractive male and a person of their own race. The joint effects of race and attractiveness were significant. The white, attractive male target was rated much higher than all of the other targets. That is, the attractive, black male was lumped together with the unattractive targets as date rejects. Also, a special analysis was done to determine how much weight females gave race and attractiveness in making their desirability as a date ratings. This analysis revealed that females gave race more weight than attractiveness. Thus for females race was more important than attractiveness. At last attractiveness has a rival.

The "commitment to the date" data were disappointing. Only six of the seventeen females committed themselves to the date by providing their telephone number and only four of the six showed for the date-arrangement session. Further, race discrimination and attractiveness discrimination for the desirability ratings were the same for subjects who committed to the date as for subjects who did not commit.

The results for males were similar. Again, both the race and attractiveness effects were highly significant. White males also preferred attractive members of the opposite sex and members of their own race. The joint effects of race and attractiveness were of the same form as those for females: the attractive white female was rated well above the other targets in desirability as a date. But there was a difference in the relative weight given race and attractiveness by males as compared to females. For males attractiveness was more important than race.

The commitment data were also disappointing for males. Only five of twenty-six males committed and showed for the date arrangement session. Also, commitment failed to relate to desirability ratings. The probable reason for these failures was that subjects were not encouraged to participate in the actual date portion of the study, and contrary to instructions, some subjects entered their telephone numbers after seeing the slides.

Since it is obvious that whether subjects were committing themselves to a blind date or not could make a difference in ratings, a second experiment was done. In this experiment, everything was the same as in the first experiment, except that subjects were strongly encouraged to participate in the actual date portion and some subjects were in a "blind date" condition, while others were in an "informed" condition. Those in the blind-date condition were required to commit themselves before they saw the slides of potential dates. Subjects in the informed condition were not asked to commit themselves until after they had seen the slides.

Overall the results for females were similar to those obtained in the first experiment. Again, both the race and attractiveness effects were highly significant, the white attractive male was rated above the other targets, and race was given more weight than attractiveness. But this time, commitment as indicated by showing up to the date arrangement session did make a difference in desirability ratings. The male is the controller of the dating situation. If he doesn't like a girl on the first date, he can take her home early and never call again. For him, blind dates are no great risk. But for females, blind dates can be big trouble. If she doesn't like a guy on the first date she may be faced with fighting him off all night and with concocting excuses not to date him again. Females have good reason to be more cautious about blind dates, and cautious they were in the present case. No female subjects entered their phone numbers in the blind-date condition. However, six of the eleven subjects in the informed condition entered their phone numbers and showed for the date arrangement session. Further, blind-date subjects, all of whom were uncommitted, showed a different pattern of desirability ratings than informed subjects. These females acted as if "beauty is only skin deep." For white targets, female subjects discounted attractiveness by giving similar ratings to attractive and unattractive targets. Subjects in the blind-date condition had decided that they were not going on the actual date before making the ratings and thus they could afford to indicate by their ratings that "good looks don't matter so much." But their counterparts in the informed condition were in a sense still deciding as they were looking at the slides of targets. For them attractiveness discrimination was strong.

The results for males were the same as in the first experiment. Further, the majority of these subjects committed themselves to the date and showed for the date-arrangement session. The number of subjects committing themselves in the blind-date condition did not differ significantly from the number committing themselves in the informed condition. Finally, commitment didn't relate to desirability ratings for males. Males apparently employed the same criteria in the same way for deciding on a blind date as they did for deciding on dates with persons about whom they had information. And why not? For them there is little risk involved. These results suggest that race is a genuine rival to attractiveness for determining social choices. Also, results suggest that people (females at least) may choose as if "beauty is skin deep" only if their choices are such that they won't have to relate to or be identified with those chosen. When it comes down to the nitty-gritty of making consequential choices, "beauty pervades the whole body."

Extrapolating from these and other results, it seems possible that women give appreciable weight to several criteria, including attractiveness, in making their dating choices, while males emphasize attractiveness above other criteria. This means that a male might still be seen as a desirable date even if he is unattractive, so long as he has other positive qualities, but an unattractive female is less likely to fare well on the dating market, even if she has compensating qualities. As one researcher put it, if it's one's fate to be ugly, it is better to be male.

The race results are consistent with the notion of racism as discussed elsewhere in this book. White persons did not find blacks desirable as dates even when the latter were attractive. Further, whereas females in the blind-date condition of the second experiment discounted attractiveness, they did not discount race. Thus, even in the case of nonconsequential choices made by whites, if the target's skin is nonwhite, "beauty is skin deep" does not hold.

When Beauty is Irrelevant

My students and I adopted still another strategy for finding the limits of the power of attractiveness. We reasoned that attractiveness is bound to be irrelevant for some kinds of behaviors having social ramifications. As a first try for supporting this hypothesis, we focused on the possible influence of an experimenter's attractiveness on a subject's responses to an experimental task. An experimental task may be ego-involving or nonego-involving. An ego-involving task is one which appears to the subject to provide an opportunity to perform "well" or "poorly" and thus to appear skilled or unskilled. Such a task would entail scores implying desirable or undesirable performance. A nonego-involving task would not appear to the subject to provide the opportunity to appear skilled or unskilled. Scores on a nonego-involving task would have no meaning with regard to desirable or undesirable performance. Such a task would be one on which subjects could not do "well" or "poorly."

We reasoned that if a task is ego-involving, subjects might try to "look skilled," if they had a reason to do so. The presence of an attractive experimenter might be sufficient reason for subjects to want to appear in a favorable light. However, the presence of an unattractive experimenter would not be sufficient reason for subjects to want to appear in a favorable light. Thus it was predicted that, if an experiment task is ego-involving, subjects would perform at a higher level for an attractive than for an unattractive experimenter. However, if an experimental task is not ego-involving and therefore does not provide an opportunity to "look skilled," the attractiveness of the experimenter should make no difference in performance. Subjects confronted with an attractive experimenter and a nonego-involving task would make no special effort to enhance their performance, because it would be a waste of time. A strong performance on such a task would not be expected to result in a favorable impression on the attractive experimenter.

To test these predictions, Brian Donley and I (1977) conducted an experiment which employed a "verbal learning" task much like the one used by Stanley Milgram (see the Obedience chapter). In this experiment all subjects were male and the experimenter was female. For some subjects, the verbal learning task was described as "a measure of I.Q." This instruction was assumed to impart "ego-involvement" to the task, because most people assume that they will be seen in a favorable light if they perform well on an I.Q. test. For other subjects, the task was described so that subjects would assume that their individual performance would have no particular meaning. About half of the subjects in each of these two conditions were confronted with an experimenter who was attractive. The remaining subjects in each condition were confronted with the same experimenter who was made up to be unattractive. As in the Milgram experiments, the experimenter presented the subjects with word pairs and asked them to memorize the pairs. Later she presented the subjects with "stimulus" words for each pair and asked them to recall corresponding "response" words. A subject's "score" on the task was the number of response words that he correctly recalled. A high score, then, would indicate that many response words were correctly recalled.

Results were not as we expected. There was no difference in average scores for subjects confronted with an attractive experimenter-ego-involving task, unattractive experimenter-ego-involving task, and unattractive experimenter-nonego-involving task. However, average scores were higher under these three circumstances than they were when the experimenter was attractive and the task was nonego-involving. An attractive experimenter in the nonego-involving condition *lowered* scores relative to the other conditions. Apparently, when the task was nonego-involving, male subjects confronted with an attractive experimenter ignored the task and attended to the experimenter. The attractive experimenter was a source of distraction, rather than a stimulus for enhanced performance. Thus attractiveness of an experimenter may be irrelevant, if the experimental task is ego-involving. In the ego-involving condition, performance level did not vary with the experimenter's attractiveness level. However, an experimenter's attractiveness level may be relevant if the experimental task is nonego-involving. In the nonego-involving condition, the presence of an attractive experimenter lowered performance level.

We accept these results even though they were not predicted, because they have been replicated. John Hartnett and his colleagues (1976) found that an attractive female experimenter distracted both male and female subjects in the case of three tasks which were similar to our nonego-involving task.

When Beautiful Is Bad

Marshall Dermer and Darrel Thiel (1975) also quarreled with the notion that beautiful is always good. They suggested that beautiful may not be so good for those who are not beautiful themselves. That is, unattractive people may not endorse the stereotype of beautiful people as being good. To examine this possibility, they replicated the Dion, Berscheid, and Walster (1972) study described above. Dermer's and Thiel's study was essentially the same as that of Dion and colleagues with the following important exceptions: 1) only female targets and subjects were used, 2) very attractive as well as very unattractive targets were used along with targets of intermediate attractiveness, 3) the subjects themselves were rated on physical attractiveness and categorized into three levels of attractiveness, 4) items included in Dion's and colleagues' Social Desirability measure and other measures were weeded out and analyzed separately if they were found not to fit with most of the items constituting the measures, and 5) additional measures were included upon which unattractive subjects might find attractive people wanting (e.g., since attractive people marry well, they might be seen as having bourgeois orientation including status consciousness and greed).

Results showed that on the Social Desirability index used by Dion and colleagues, which was divested of the modest-vain and altruistic-egotistic items, attractive targets were rated more favorably than unattractive targets, with intermediate targets being intermediate in favorability of ratings. However, unattractive subjects did not share this overall effect with other subjects. They did not rate attractive targets as more socially desirable than unattractive targets. Further, all subjects saw attractive targets as being more vain and egotistical than unattractive targets or intermediate targets. These results provide some evidence of a jealousy effect. On the other hand, these attributions may be accurate assessments of attractive persons' actual characteristics.

On the marital happiness measure of Dion and colleagues, attractive targets were rated most favorably on the part relating to being an understanding spouse and a responsive sexual partner, but attractive targets also were expected to be more likely to have a divorce and extramarital affairs. On the parental competence measure of Dion and colleagues, unattractive subjects so downgraded attractive targets that an overall effect was generated indicating that attractive targets were expected to be poor parents. On the "occupational status of target and spouse" measure and the "social professional happiness of target" measures which were analogous to measures used by Dion and colleagues, attractive target persons' spouses were expected to have prestigious occupations relative to the spouses of other targets, and were expected to have more social and professional happiness than other targets. However, on Dermer's and Thiel's Bourgeois Orientation measure, attractive targets were seen as believing most that money leads to happiness, were expected to be status-seeking snobs, and expected to be unsympathetic about the condition of oppressed people. The general trend of these results was replicated in a second experiment in which male and female subjects were used.

Although Dermer and Thiel confirmed the notion that beautiful is good, they also showed that beautiful is not always good. Beautiful people were seen as being more socially desirable and were expected to be happier in life. However, they were also seen as vain, egotistical, adulterous, greedy, status-seeking, and unlikely to sympathize with oppressed people. In a word, the orientation of attractive persons was seen to be one of selfishness: get all the goodies in life for myself and the hell with everyone else. All that glitters is not "good," apparently.

Another study by Dennis Krebs and Allen Adinolfi (1975) produced results consistent with "beautiful is sometimes bad." Sixty male and sixty female students were selected for their study on the basis of the acceptance ratings they had received from their same-sexed dorm mates. On the basis of these ratings, thirty subjects (fifteen male and fifteen female as was the case for other categories) were classified as highly accepted, thirty as average in the acceptance accorded by their dorm mates, thirty as rejected by dorm mates, and thirty as isolated (infrequently mentioned as desirable or undesirable dorm mates). These persons were rated on physical attractiveness by strangers and were given a series of personality tests. Results showed that the highly accepted group was rated as being more physically attractive than the average acceptance group, which, in turn, was rated as more attractive than the isolated group. However, unexpectedly, the rejected group was rated as being the most physically attractive. Was jealousy operating in this case? The personality tests revealed a more probable reason why the most attractive persons were rejected by their dorm mates. This group of males and females were higher on the personality factor "Independent-Ambitiousness" than the other groups and lower than other groups on the factor "Affectionate Sociability." Thus attractive individuals in this study actually were more selfish than others in the sense of displaying the characteristic of ambitiousness and other characteristics, implying little need to rely on and to relate affectionately to others.

PUTTING BEAUTY IN ITS PLACE

These recent results which indicate that beauty is sometimes a liability do not refute "beautiful is good," but rather qualify it. All the data considered, it is still the case that attractiveness is more important than either researcher or layman has been willing to believe. Nevertheless beautiful people do not always finish first. For social choices and social relations which require a high degree of selflessness, co-operation, and empathy, beautiful people may be seen as wanting and, in fact, may actually lack the required characteristics. For example, a beautiful woman may have a distinct advantage over other candidates for a job as restaurant receptionist, because such a position requires "social charm" and "good looks." However, the same woman may have difficulty acquiring a job as a social worker, because she is stereotyped as self-centered and unresponsive to the needs of others. Undoubtedly other liabilities of being attractive will be uncovered in the future, but they will not likely outweigh the advantage of being beautiful.

Thus, we are left with a difficult question. It is, how can the discrepancy be eliminated between the rather minor importance that people ascribe to attractiveness when they are queried about its importance and the actual major importance of attractiveness in determining behavior? A foolproof prescription cannot be provided as an answer, but I have some suggestions. It would be silly to state that, henceforth, individuals should ignore attractiveness as a criterion for evaluating, reacting to, and relating to others. We couldn't, even if we were so inclined. But it's possible to adopt the following strategy. Different people have different assets in the form of physical and psychological characteristics. One should be applauded for his or her strong points and encouraged to exploit them. However, attractiveness is but one positive characteristic that a person might possess. Let those who are attractive receive their just and proportional rewards, but let's not automatically assume that the possessor of good looks also has most of the other assets that we value. Since intelligent persons are not automatically assumed to have great social skills, why then assume that an attractive person is intelligent and has other valued characteristics? The place to begin to break the tie between attractiveness and other assets is by monitoring our reactions to one another and to children.

It is little wonder that children learn to confuse beauty with goodness if in order to show them affection or to reward their efforts we call them "pretty" or "handsome," and if they frequently overhear us praising people for their beauty or condemning people for their ugliness. Children also get the message about beauty when they observe their parents primping in order to gain the favor of other adults or primping them for school every morning so that they may gain the favor of their peers. If we can teach our children not to confound beauty with other characteristics that we value, some day beauty may become no more important than we currently believe it ought to be.

Racism in America?

5

There are many definitions of racism. A common factor in these definitions is that antiblack sentiment pervades American culture. Of the sources of evidence that have been used to support this charge, historical evidence has probably been most frequently cited: European society, which produced most of the early American settlers, was itself engrained with racism. Thus antiblack sentiment was imported to America by the first settlers and became part and parcel of the fledgling American culture. Because antiblack sentiment was present at the settling of America, it was blacks who were enslaved when slavery became accepted in America. An account of the historical evidence concerning racism is presented below.

The literature of sixteenth-century Europe was replete with references to black as "bad" and white as "good." Black was linked with "dirty" and words or phrases such as "black magic," "Black Prince," and "blackguard" all connoted evil. On the other hand the whiteness of angels symbolized goodness, the white gown of the bride symbolized purity, and white *per se* symbolized cleanliness. Modern research has confirmed that the connotations of the "colors" white and black are closely related to the connotations of "white people" and "black people" (Williams and Edwards, 1969). The literature of the sixteenth century reflected the close relationship between the assumption that the "black is evil" and the assumption that black people are evil. For example, George Best (1577) (Schwartz and Disch, 1970) reinterpreted the Bible so that the wages of sin became the "curse" of black skin. According to Best, upon entering the Ark, Noah admonished his sons to abstain from carnal relations with their wives for the duration of their voyage. But Ham, wishing his progeny to dominate the earth, disobeyed his father. God witnessed this sin and commanded that the child of the crime of disobedience, Chus, and all of his children were to be "black and loathsome." Further, Ham and Chus were banished to Africa when the waters subsided, which supposedly accounted for the color of Africa's inhabitants. Fictions such as Best's apparently were widely accepted in Europe, particularly Anglo-Europe, which produced the great bulk of early American settlers.

The first significant number of blacks to arrive *en masse* in America disembarked at Jamestown in 1619 (*Report of the National Advisory Committee on Civil Rights*—Kerner Report, 1968). However, these early black Americans were not slaves. Slavery did not exist as an institution at the time. The Jamestown blacks were indentured servants who had been transported to America along with whites of the same status. As indentured servants, these people were obligated to work for their masters for a specific number of years. The obligation rose from the fact that their masters had financed their transportation to America. After repaying their debt, former indentured servants were as free as other Americans. At first, black indentured servants were treated in the same way as white indentured servants. At the end of their servitude they became landowning, taxpaying citizens, which partially accounts for the fact that there were a number of free blacks present in America at the time of the revolution (*Life*, 1968). However, in the period between 1619 and 1700, America lapsed into slavery. When this occurred, it was blacks who became slaves.

The process by which slavery evolved can be invoked to explain how it was that blacks, rather than others, were enslaved. Laws and legal precedents came into existence which set the stage for the enslavement of blacks (Schwartz and Disch, 1970). Laws were passed which made sexual contact between black and white indentured servants illegal. Wills were accepted in court which specified that white indentured servants were only obligated to their contracted term of service, while black indentured servants were to serve their master's family after his death for the remainder of their lives. Tax laws were written which considered blacks and whites separately for the purposes of taxation, and, in some cases, dictated that blacks be regarded as property. Other laws provided that a black indentured servant could not serve as a supervisor to white indentured servants. There was also a case in which a black indentured servant was punished for attempted escape by being bound to service for the rest of his life, while the white servants who fled with him were given punishments which didn't entail the permanent deprivation of their freedom (*Life*, 1968). With these subtle precedents as background, the following 1663 Maryland law made the tie between black skin and slavery explicit.

> All Negroes or other slaves within the province, and all Negroes and other slaves to be hereafter imported into the province, shall serve *durante vita*; and all children born of any Negro or other slave shall be slaves as their fathers were for the term of their lives (Tannenbaum, 1947, p. 67).

By around 1700 most of the other colonies had followed suit.

Thus black and white servants began with the same nonslave status in America, but when slavery became a fact of American life, it was the black servant who became the slave. There is, of course, no necessary reason for enslaving persons merely because they are of a different race from that of the majority members of a society in cases where slavery has been accepted. For example, during the time of the Roman Empire, any type of person could be a slave and any type of person could be a citizen. There were black Roman citizens and white Roman slaves. That it was blacks who were enslaved in America leads to the conclusion that antiblack sentiment preexisted slavery. The evolution of slavery in America, then, provides a strong argument that antiblack sentiment was present at the settling of America and at the beginnings of its culture.

But what does "pervasive antiblack sentiment" imply about the social behaviors of white Americans? Statements by prominent black revolutionaries and other notable social commentators of the 1960s seem to assert that hatred and rejection are universally reflected in the behavior of white people *vis-à-vis* black people.

Stokely Carmichael proclaimed that "For racism to die a totally different America must be born" (Schwartz & Disch, 1970, p. 512). Malcolm X declared " 'Conservatism' . . . means 'Let's keep the niggers in their place.' And 'liberalism' means 'let's keep the knee-grows in their place—but tell them we'll treat them a little better; let's fool them more, with more promises.' " (Malcolm X, 1964, p. 373). Even the rather conservative members of the Kerner Commission summarized their findings with regard to the 1967 riots by stating, "What white Americans have never fully understood—but what the Negro can never forget—is that white society is deeply implicated in the ghetto. White institutions created it, white institutions maintain it, and white society condones it." (*Report of National Advisory Committee on Civil Rights*, 1968, p. 2).

This latter declaration first appeared during the presidential campaign of 1968. Candidates for the highest office such as Richard Nixon and other politicians completely denounced the charge that antiblack sentiment characterized all whites and thus was the cause of the black American's plight. Indeed, the charge that all whites harbor antiblack sentiment is extreme. The common observation of at least some positive relations between blacks and whites seems to refute the claim that racism is evident in all relations involving whites

and blacks. Thus in spite of the compelling evidence which may be gleaned from history and the inflammatory statements which have been so persuasive, the racism charge seems hollow in the absence of concrete behavioral evidence. What then is the evidence, if any, that racism is reflected in the social behaviors of white Americans?

BELIEF vs. RACE

Milton Rokeach certainly would not accept the possibility that white Americans have uniformly inculcated antiblack sentiment in the process of adopting their culture. In fact, Rokeach (1960) has argued that people have no internalized disposition to discriminate by race at all. According to Rokeach, there is only one natural basis for making discriminations among individuals and this basis is *belief*. Individuals accept other persons who believe like themselves and reject those who believe differently regardless of the race of those others. This is the so-called "belief congruence theory." Of course, one of the first questions that is addressed to Rokeach when he presents these notions is "Why do we commonly observe racial discrimination?"

Rokeach's reply has been that what we observe is not real racial discrimination due to internal dispositions of individuals. Rather it is *apparent* racial discrimination due to the absence of belief information or due to the presence of external social pressure to discriminate by race. If white persons attempt to evaluate a black person but have no information about his beliefs, they assume that because he is of a different race he has different beliefs. Whites then would reject him on the basis of their assumptions about his beliefs. However, if these same white people had information about the black person's beliefs, race would become irrelevant and whether the black person was accepted or not would depend entirely on whether he or she believed as the whites did.

The other possible case of *apparent* racial discrimination would be when individuals must evaluate others under conditions where external social pressure to discriminate by race is present. In parts of our country, particularly the South, the pressure to show racial discrimination is strong enough so that white people are actually censured if they fail to show it. Under these conditions people may appear to discriminate by race in order to avoid sanctions that might be brought against them. Thus in some parts of the country a white person might actually have positive feelings about a black person who believes as he does, but would appear to reject the black person in response to social pressure. Rokeach (1961) has argued that if this pressure were somehow eliminated, thus leaving all people free to act according to their natural internal dispositions, white people as well as others would discriminate according to belief no matter what part of the country they were from. Racial discrimination is either discrimination on the basis of belief or a superficial response to social pressure.

Choosing Friends Among Black and White Believers and Nonbelievers

In order to support the theory Rokeach and his colleagues, Patricia Smith and Richard I. Evans (1960), conducted a study which employed white subjects from both the North and the South. First, subjects were asked to indicate their beliefs about several issues including socialized medicine, communism, labor unions, God, and racial integration. These issues were used to determine belief discrimination in the second phase of the study. Next, subjects were presented with pairs of target persons and asked to evaluate each member of each pair by indicating how easily they could see themselves as being friends with each pair member. Three kinds of pairs were presented to subjects. One kind, called "race pairs," involved varying race within the pair, but holding belief constant, an actual example being "A white person who believes in God" and "A Negro who believes in God." Only racial discrimination could account for any differences between the friendship ratings of members of such pairs, because only race was varied. A second pair type was called "belief pairs." For this type, beliefs of the pair members were varied and race held constant. An example was "A white person who believes in God" and "A white person who is an atheist." In this case, differences in friendship rating of pair members could only be due to belief discrimination. The third pair type was called "race-belief pairs," because both the race and the beliefs of pair members were varied. An example was "A white person who believes in God" and "A Negro who is an atheist." Here discrimination could be according to race or belief or both. Whether or not a subject believed like a given target person was established by reference to the belief expressions previously made by the subjects on the belief issues listed above.

Several sources of support for Rokeach's theory were inferred from the data produced by subjects. The "race-belief" pairs only were used in the first analysis. For each subject the total friendship rating given to black pair members who agreed with the subject was computed. Also for each subject the total friendship rating given to white pair members who disagreed with the subject was computed. These two total ratings were compared statistically and it was revealed that subjects favored a black person who agreed with them compared with a white person who disagreed with them. Thus white subjects expressed more friendship to a person of a different race who agreed with them than to a person of the same race who disagreed with them.

In a second analysis, four different total ratings were computed for each subject. First, using the "race pairs" only, each subject's total friendship rating of black pair members was computed. Next each subject's total friendship rating of white pair members was computed. In a third calculation involving the "belief pairs" only, each subject's total friendship rating of pair members who agreed with them was computed. Finally, using only the "belief pairs," each subject's total friendship rating of pair members who disagreed with them was computed. The total friendship ratings of black pair members were compared statistically with the total friendship ratings of white pair members and the total friendship ratings of pair members who agreed with subjects was compared statistically with the total friendship rating of pair members who disagreed with subjects. Subjects favored white pair members over black pair members and pair members who agreed over pair members who disagreed. However, the difference in friendship ratings of "agreers" and "disagreers" was greater than the difference between friendship ratings of white pair members and black pair members. Subjects discriminated more strongly in terms of belief than in terms of race. As Rokeach's theory would predict, belief was a more important criterion for discrimination than race.

In an additional analysis, the total difference between the friendship ratings given members of the "race pairs" was computed for each subject. This score was called the "race difference score." It was an index of racial discrimination. Also, the total difference between the friendship ratings of members of the "belief pairs" was computed for each subject. These "belief differences scores" were an index of belief discrimination. Finally, a "race-belief difference score" was determined for each subject by computing the total difference in friendship ratings of "race-belief pair" members. According to Rokeach's theory, people would rely more heavily on belief information than on race information when they are given both kinds of information. Of course, both kinds of information were included in the "race-belief pairs." Therefore, if the theory is correct, "race-belief difference scores" should be more closely related to the "belief difference scores" than to the "race difference scores." Results supported this prediction from Rokeach's theory. When given both race and belief information about targets, subjects discriminated primarily by belief.

Rokeach and his colleagues not only supported belief congruence theory in impressive fashion, but also produced data which seemed to indicate that race is not very important as a determinant of social relations. Since their subjects were white, their findings certainly didn't fit the notion that "racism affects most whites." However, there was one who was not so hasty to reject race in favor of belief.

Friends and Lovers

The unchallenged reign of belief as the sole determinant of discrimination was short lived. About a year after the publication of Rokeach, Smith and Evans (1960), Harry Triandis (1961) published a study which attempted to refute the theory. Triandis had two major objections to the claims implied by Rokeach's theory. First, he accepted the claim that belief might be more important than race for determining friendship choices as indicated on paper-and-pencil questionnaires. However, he could not accept the generalization of the greater potency of belief for all social relations, including those which entail much more intimacy than "friendship" as measured by Rokeach and his colleagues. According to Triandis, the hypothetical acquaintanceship of "friendship choice" represented a single, low degree of intimacy. Triandis asserted that if individuals must choose targets for social relations which entail more degrees of intimacy, race would be much more important than belief for determining acceptance. More specifically, Triandis predicted that race would be more important for the "social distance" continuum of social relations. This continuum entails degrees of intimacy ranging from acceptance as a marital partner or as "best friend" through refusal to allow targets to attend public school or refusal to tolerate their presence "in the country."

Second, Triandis objected to the loaded belief issues employed by Rokeach and his colleagues. Perhaps belief *is* important for determining acceptance in social relations if the belief information available concerns issues like God and communism. Most everybody has strong beliefs about God and communism. Thus they are likely to react strongly to targets who are attributed with extreme beliefs about these issues. But what would their reaction be to targets who are attributed with beliefs about less heated issues? Perhaps belief is a powerful determinant of acceptance in social relations only when information about beliefs on "heated issues" is available. Whether or not someone agrees with a person on more neutral issues such as jogging, stamp collecting, or health foods, may make no difference in his acceptance in various social relations.

Triandis (1961) did a study to support his arguments. To "cool down" the belief factor, Triandis had his subjects read Morris's thirteen "Ways of Life" and choose one way of life which was commensurate with their "philosophy," and a second way of life which was different from their "philosophy." The first choice was to represent "beliefs like subject's own beliefs" and the second choice was to represent "beliefs different from subject's own beliefs."

Subjects were then presented with a number of the same kind of "word target persons" that Rokeach and his colleagues had used. The word targets were constructed of all possible combinations of the following traits or characteristics: race (black or white), occupation (high status or low status), religion (same as subject's or different from subject's), and "philosophy" (same as subject's or different from subject's). Some example target persons were as follows: black, bank manager, same religion, different philosophy; white, coal miner, different religion, different philosophy; black, bank manager, same religion, same philosophy. When subjects saw "same philosophy" in the descriptions of targets they were to think back to the "philosophy" that they had previously picked as commensurate with their own. They were to "think back" in analogous fashion when they saw "different philosophy." For each target person, each subject was to indicate, using the social distance continuum, the most intimate social relation which they would be willing to enter into with the target person.

Results can be summarized easily. Although all four traits or characteristics investigated were of significant importance for determining acceptance in social relations, race was by far the most important determinant. "Philosophy," the stand-in for belief, paled in importance by comparison to race. Thus, Triandis argued that when choices involve greater degrees of intimacy than implied by "friendship choice" and involve beliefs on less heated issues, race of a target is a much more important determinant of acceptance of the target than the target's beliefs.

Rokeach Strikes Back

It took Milton Rokeach even less time to rebut Triandis than it took Triandis to react to Rokeach's theory. On the next page of the same journal in which Triandis presented his refutation, Rokeach (1961) answered Triandis. In essence, Rokeach claimed that Triandis had missed the point. According to Rokeach, Triandis had made a great deal out of what kinds of social relations one ought to investigate in comparing the importance of race and belief, while he ignored the most important consideration, the strength of the race and belief information. Rokeach believed that Triandis's belief factor was weak. First, were the vague and abstract "ways of life" or "philosophies" the same thing as specific beliefs on familiar issues? Rokeach didn't think so, and he seemed to have a good point. One can evaluate another person's specific beliefs, but his "philosophies" may never even be apparent. Second, the belief factor was further weakened by the difficulty of the task that subjects had to perform in order to appreciate "belief." Subjects had to remember the long and complicated paragraph description of the "philosophy" that they previously had chosen as like their own whenever they were confronted with the description of a target person having the "same philosophy." Their task was, of course, just as difficult whenever they encountered "different philosophy."

As for Triandis's charge that Rokeach had used loaded belief issues, Rokeach replied that his results held for all kinds of issues. Not only was belief more important than race for the issues of God and communism, but belief also was more important than race for less loaded issues like "labor unions" and "socialized medicine." This point by Rokeach is less telling. Perhaps he should have consulted with the presidents of General Motors and the American Medical Association before deciding that the latter two issues were relatively cool. At any rate, as we shall see, Rokeach ignored Triandis's criticisms and continued to *believe* that belief discrimination is the only kind of discrimination.

Coffee, Tea, or Guess Who's Coming to Work

Rokeach apparently completely rejected Triandis's criticisms. In his subsequent research, Rokeach made no effort to correct the "faults" which Triandis had claimed were evident in the 1960 study by Rokeach, Smith, and Evans. Instead, Rokeach became his own best critic. According to Rokeach, the following were the only serious difficulties with the 1960 study: 1) "Choices" were made by marking a questionnaire with a pencil. Sometimes paper-and-pencil choices do not correspond to real-life choices, and this is partly because they usually have no real-life consequences for the future. A subject completes his questionnaire and turns it into the experimenter and that's it. Would race or belief be most important in a real-life situation in which a person chooses someone for some relationship and they expected actually to interact with him or her in that relationship? 2) Word target persons were used. Word targets are simplex. They only have a few characteristics. Real people are more complicated. Further, when a subject encounters a word person, he knows that the person is hypothetical, i.e., the target could exist, but doesn't really exist. Would race or belief be more important if subjects had to choose from real, living, breathing human beings? 3) The 1960 study was a laboratory study (done in specially designed university facilities). Laboratory studies involve "controls"; i.e., many of the factors which would exist and possibly influence behavior in real life are eliminated (controlled) in the laboratory. This is why researchers must replicate their laboratory finding in the real world. It always is possible that what is found in a laboratory study will not be duplicated in the real world. Would the 1960 study results be replicated in the real world? In order to correct the self-styled faults of the 1960 study, Rokeach and a colleague, Louis Mezei (1966), did two laboratory experiments and one natural-setting or real world experiment. In all three experiments real people were targets, and choices having future consequences were made. All laboratory subjects and half of the real world subjects were white.

The laboratory studies were almost identical, and will be described together. Preliminary to the actual studies, all subjects completed a standard prejudice questionnaire. "Prejudice" will be discussed below, but for present purposes it is sufficient to say that subjects were classified as "high" or "low" in prejudice based on their questionnaire responses. When subjects later showed up for the actual study, they encountered an experimenter, as well as two black and two white persons who were posing as fellow subjects. The experimenter first had all "subjects" examine some belief issues. This procedure was justified by telling those present that the experiment was about discussion processes. Next, each "subject" introduced himself, following which the real subject was "elected" chairman. The chairman then was allowed to choose the issue to be discussed. This procedure insured that subjects chose an issue which was important to them. A fifteen-minute discussion then ensued. During the discussion, one black and one white collaborator agreed with the subject, and one black and one white collaborator disagreed with the subject. After the fifteen-minute period, the experimenter called the real subject aside under the guise of "checking his notes." After the "note checking" was completed, the experimenter exclaimed that he wanted to interview each "subject" individually. As these interviews would take some time, the real subject was asked to choose two members of the discussion group to accompany him on a coffee break while the other two members were being interviewed. Choices were made under two different conditions. About half of the subjects were told to choose two persons to go across campus to the student union for coffee. The other half were told to choose two persons to go nearby to a private room for coffee. These "public" and "private" conditions were instituted in order to determine whether social pressure in the public condition would increase the importance of race as a determinant of choices.

Subjects who participated in the real-world study were applicants for maintenance jobs at a mental hospital. When they arrived for their job interviews they were ushered into a "waiting room." Besides the experimenter posing as a hospital employee, guess who else subjects encountered in the waiting room? You've got it—two blacks and two whites posing as job applicants. The experimenter then suggested that all applicants participate in a discussion of some problems that they might have to deal with should they be hired. Each "problem" amounted to a belief issue. Of course, one black and one white agreed with the real subject and one black and one white disagreed with the subject during the course of the discussion. After the discussion, subjects were asked to record anonymously the names of the two persons that they would prefer as fellow workers.

Because two factors in the studies (the previously recorded personal prejudices and the public or private nature of the coffee breaks) made no difference in choices, and neither did race of the job applicants, the results of all three studies will be discussed together. The possible choices available to each subject were as follows: 1) one person of each race, both of whom agreed with the subject; 2) one person of each race, both of whom disagreed with the subject; 3) two persons of the subject's own race, one of whom agreed and one of whom disagreed; 4) two persons, neither one being of the subject's own race, one of whom agreed and one of whom disagreed; 5) a person of the same race who agreed with the subject and a person of the other race who disagreed; and 6) a person of the same race who disagreed and a person of the other race who agreed with the subject. If belief was most important, the preponderance of choices should have been the two persons who agreed, regardless of race (choice 1). However, if race was most important, the preponderance of choices should have been the two persons of the same race, regardless of belief (choice 3). Across all three studies involving a total of one hundred-eighteen subjects, forty-seven subjects chose two persons who believed as they did (choice 1), but only seven subjects chose two persons of their own race (choice 3).

The results seemed to support Rokeach's theory strongly. However, closer examination of Rokeach's and Mezei's data revealed that mixed race, mixed belief choices (5 and 6) were prevalent. In fact, in the laboratory studies, both choices 5 and 6 were actually made more frequently than the choice of two people who held the same beliefs as subject (1). Post-experiment comments solicited from subjects in one of the two laboratory studies revealed that some of the subjects who chose the mixed race–mixed belief combinations were motivated by a desire to have a stimulating continuation of the discussion over coffee while others who chose this combination were motivated to appear fair-minded. Choosing one person who agreed and one who disagreed was ideal for discussion, because it insured that the subject had an ally against one lone adversary. Discussions are more fun when there are two against one. Choosing one person of each race was ideal for appearing fair-minded, because it insured that both members of a given race were not left behind. Selecting choice 1 may also have involved the motivations "to continue the discussion" and "to appear fair-minded." In selecting choice 1, subjects were choosing one person of each race and providing an opportunity for continued discussion without dissent. It seems that in the laboratory studies the motivations to "continue the discussion" and "to appear fair-minded" were at least as powerful determinants of choices as the need to select persons who agreed with oneself.

Obviously, the overall greater frequency of choices of two persons who agree (choice 1) was generated by real-world study results. In this study, many more subjects chose two people who agree regardless of race than chose any of the other five choice categories, including the mixed race, mixed belief categories (choices 5 and 6). However, we are only left to assume that the need to select persons who believe as oneself motivated subjects who chose two persons who agreed, because post-experiment comments were not solicited in the real-world study. It is conceivable that subjects who chose two persons who agreed (one of each race) did so in order to have completely harmonious discussions on the job should they be hired. Also they may have chosen one person of each race (both of whom agreed) in order to appear fair-minded to the hospital administration, represented by the experimenter.

The probable reason why prejudice-level and public-private conditions had no effect in the laboratory studies is because choosing someone to go get a cup of coffee might be considered trivial by subjects. Even a prejudiced white person might be willing to go get a cup of coffee with a black person, even if he had to do it in public. Choosing someone as a coffee companion certainly doesn't entail intimacy. As a matter of fact, neither does indicating acceptance of someone as a work partner. It has long been known that white persons are willing to work with black persons, even though they wouldn't accept blacks in more intimate relations (Harding *et al.*, 1954).

In spite of the difficulties with Rokeach's research, his theory has held up remarkably well over a decade and a half of research. When nonintimate social relations are considered, a large number of studies has shown that belief is more important than any other criterion for social choices, including race. Before Rokeach presented his theory, it did not occur to very many of us that we are capable of strong discrimination against those who do not agree with us.

When Neither Race Nor Belief Is Most Important

The experiments with Louis Mezei (1966) represented Milton Rokeach's last direct contribution to the race vs. belief controversy. Likewise, in 1966 Harry Triandis published his last direct contribution to the controversy. His co-researchers for this last study were Wallace Loh and Leslie Ann Levin.

Target persons for the Triandis, Loh, and Levin (1966) experiment might best be described as "picture persons." The targets were color slides of a young black man or a young white man accompanied by tape recordings supposedly of their voices. The young men were either dressed neatly in a business suit or in laborer's overalls. Their recorded voices either espoused pro- or anti-integration beliefs. Finally, they talked either in excellent English or in poor English. Thus the targets presented to subjects were composed of all possible combinations of the following characteristics or criteria for choices: 1) race (black or white), 2) belief (same as or different from what the given subject had expressed on a questionnaire), 3) dress (high social status or low social status) and 4) quality of spoken English (excellent or poor). Example targets were a white man dressed as a laborer, who spoke excellent English and espoused a belief different from a given subject, and a black man who was dressed in a business suit, who expressed the same belief as the given subject in poor English.

White college students served as subjects. Subjects responded to each target person on four different measures. Responses on two of these measures amounted to "making choices for social relations." One of these two was the now familiar friendship measure. The other was the social distance measure. This latter measure was derived from the social distance continuum described above (Triandis, 1961). It consisted of "accept as a neighbor" and "accept as kin through marriage" submeasures; i.e., subjects were asked to indicate the degree to which each target was acceptable as a neighbor and as kin through marriage. Responses on the other two measures were more "social reactions" than "choices for social relations." One of these latter two measures entailed expressing admiration for the targets, while the other entailed evaluating the targets. The evaluation measure was an index of general feelings about the targets. Since the process of making "social reactions" to targets and the process of choosing targets for "social relations" appear equivalent, the phrase "social relations" will be used to refer to both types of measures.

The results will be considered in terms of the relative importance of each trait or criterion for determining each social relation. For *friendship* choice, quality of spoken English was by far the most important criterion. Subjects were much more accepting of targets who spoke well than of targets who spoke poorly. Race was the second most important criterion, followed by dress and then belief. Belief was not only last in importance, it was the only criterion that failed to generate statistically significant results. The results for evaluation and admiration were, for practical purposes, identical: again, quality of spoken English was clearly the most important criterion. However, for admiration and evaluation the effect of belief was also strong and highly statistically significant. Targets whose beliefs were congruent with those of subjects were evaluated more favorably and were more admired than targets whose beliefs were incongruent with those of subjects. Race and dress were tied for last place in importance and neither showed significant effects. The results for *social distance* revealed that race was much more important than the other criteria. White subjects were much more accepting of white targets than of black targets. Quality of spoken English was second in importance. Belief and dress effects were nonsignificant and tied for last in importance.

The results of this particular study are especially illuminating. In a way, Triandis, Loh, and Levin resolved the race vs. belief controversy. The resolution can be stated simply: whether race or belief is most important depends on the social relation. Neither race nor belief is generally more important than the other. Race was most important for the intimate social distance, social relation. For the other three social relations which did not entail intimacy with the target, race was more important than belief for friendship choice, but belief was more important than race for both evaluation and admiration.

However, neither one was as important as quality of spoken English. Admittedly, the great importance of quality of spoken English may be because it implied many characteristics or criteria. "Speaking the King's English" *implies* high education level, high social status, high intelligence and probably much more.

There is another reason why the study by Triandis and colleagues is important. It suggests that one might expect race to be of great importance for determining social relations only for relations which entail intimacy with target persons. Race effects were not consistently important for the nonintimate social relations investigated by Triandis and his colleagues. In fact for all three nonintimate social relations, race was less important than quality of spoken English. However, for the intimate social distance relations, race beat all the other criteria, even the criterion of quality of spoken English. The results of many other studies have confirmed these observations. Whenever *intimate* social relations are investigated, race invariably is of great importance for determining acceptance in the relations, but when *nonintimate* relations are investigated, race is rarely of much importance.

Further, other work by Triandis and his colleagues (see Goldstein & Davis, 1972) has shown that some individuals tend to discriminate by belief but not by race for all kinds of social relations. Other individuals tend to discriminate by race but not by belief for all kinds of social relations. For some individuals, belief is almost always important and for other individuals, race is almost always important.

Incidentally, it is fortunate that the Triandis, Loh, and Levin (1966) results have been replicated by several other researchers as indicated below. It appears that their procedure was such that subjects might have had difficulty imagining that the targets possessed the characteristics attributed to them. Apparently, only one black man and one white man were photographed to make the slides. Thus sometimes the black man was dressed in a business suit and sometime he was dressed in overalls; sometimes he spoke well and sometimes he spoke poorly and each time subjects were to assume that he was a different person! Of course the same was true of the white model for the slides. To compound the problem, the same actor was the "voice" of all sixteen target persons. The fact that their results

have held up under replication, in spite of their questionable procedures, indicates that the effects that they reported must be robust.

WHEN RACE ACCOUNTS FOR NOTHING AND WHEN IT ACCOUNTS FOR MOST EVERYTHING

The Triandis, Loh, and Levin (1966) experiment was Triandis's last
direct participation in the race vs. belief controversy. Thus both of
the major protagonists dropped out of the controversy, each probably
thinking that he had resolved it. Their withdrawal apparently caused
a decline in interest in the controversy, because there was a paucity
of published research on the subject from 1966 until the early 1970s.

Involving and Noninvolving Social Relations

During the lull in interest in race vs. belief I became interested in the
controversy, along with a lot of other people. After examining the
earlier published reports, I became convinced that intimacy was not
sufficient to characterize the kind of social relation for which race
was critical. The studies which had shown race to be important as a
determinant of social relations had focused on social relations which
not only implied intimacy, but also permanency and public commitment to target persons. For example, not only does accepting a person in a marital relation entail intimacy, it also entails legally en-
forced permanency and a high level of public commitment. A person
really becomes highly involved with another person when he or she
marries that other person. For these reasons I use the expression "involving social relations" for those social relations which entail permanency, intimacy, and commitment. Social relations which do *not*
entail permanency, intimacy, and commitment to an appreciable degree, I call "noninvolving" (Allen, 1971a; 1971b; 1975).

If an involving-noninvolving social-relation continuum is assumed, it is possible to think of most social relations as tending to fit
the definition of one of the extremes of the continuum better than the
other. For example, the social relations investigated by Triandis and
colleagues (1966) seemed to be distributed neatly at one end of the

continuum or the other. Friendship, Admiration, and Evaluation are noninvolving and Social Distance ("accept as a neighbor" and "accept as kin through marriage" scales) is involving. In some preliminary work (unpublished) in which various social relations have been rated as to how involving they were perceived to be, the following relations were among those rated as highly involving: become engaged to a target, telling one's innermost thoughts to a target, accepting a target of the opposite sex as a roommate, adopting a target as one's child, and accepting a target as a spouse in marriage. Social relations which were found to be noninvolving included the following: working with a target, giving an (automobile) ride to a target, accepting a target as an acquaintance, and accepting a target in a student-teacher relationship.

The advantage of the involving-noninvolving continuum is that it allows for more accurate predictions of when race is going to be an important determinant of choices for social relations than was allowed by attending only to the degree of intimacy entailed by social relations. If a social relation entails not only a high degree of intimacy, but also high degrees of permanency and commitment, race is highly likely to be important for determining choices for the relation. On the other hand, if a given social relation rather completely lacks the qualities of permanency, intimacy, and commitment, race probably will be unimportant in determining choices for the relation. For these reasons social relations will be evaluated with reference to the involving-noninvolving continuum throughout the remainder of this chapter.

When Race Doesn't Matter at All

After the 1960 study with Smith and Evans, Rokeach was prepared to say that racial discrimination may be appreciable in some cases, particularly when external social pressure is present or when belief information is absent. He had to say this, because he and his colleagues had found significant racial discrimination in the 1960 study. However, by 1965 Rokeach was implying (Rokeach and Rothman, 1965) that given no appreciable external pressure and *an especially high level of congruence between the beliefs of subjects and targets,* racial discrimination would be absent altogether.

To test this 1965 extension of Rokeach's 1960 theoretical statement, it was necessary first to locate an issue on which potential subjects held a very strong position (Allen, 1970; 1971a). Potential subjects were white students at Western Illinois University. This position then could be attributed to target persons, thereby establishing a high level of congruence between the belief of subjects and targets on the issue.

First, student publications were examined to discover currently "hot" issues around campus and how students stood on these issues. Seventeen issues were located upon which students apparently held strong positions. For example, students felt strongly that eighteen-year-olds should have the right to vote (the study was done before eighteen-year-olds could vote), students' sexual behavior was *not* the business of university officials, students should have the right to wear whatever style of clothing they please to class, and students arrested by local police should *not* also be subject to university disciplinary action (anti-double jeopardy position).

Seventeen statements then were written to support these positions on the issues. I assumed that students as a group agreed with all seventeen statements. What I wanted to know was with which statements did students agree the most? To answer this question, the statements were given to 119 subjects who were asked to rank them. These subjects were told to give a rank of one to the statement with which they agreed the most and a rank of seventeen to the statement with which they agreed the least. The "anti-double jeopardy" statement was ranked number one. Subjects clearly agreed with this statement more than any of the others.

Next a communication was written which strongly condemned double jeopardy; it indicated that subjecting a person to "prosecution" twice for the same offense was illegal, immoral, illogical, and downright unfair. All available evidence indicated that almost all students would agree strongly with this communication. Its basic theme was being advocated by student organizations representing all points along the ideological continuum.

A second communication was written. This communication was "about the weather" and was intended to contain no belief information. As it turned out, student-subjects apparently disliked this communication and may have assumed that anyone who would communicate such a message would *not* have beliefs congruent with their own.

In the actual experiment, 410 white students were told that they were to participate "in the preliminary stages of the development of a new reading test" (Allen, 1970). This special new test was supposedly designed to measure impressions gained from written materials as contrasted to the usual reading test which measures comprehension of content. Subjects were told that they would read a communication which had originally appeared as an article in a midwestern university newspaper (the subjects' university was located in the midwest). About half of the students were given the anti-double jeopardy communication to read while the other half read the weather communication. For about half the subjects in each communication condition, the communication was attributed to an eighteen-year-old white freshman (the subjects mostly were freshman), while for the other half, the communication was attributed to a black freshman. The racial identification information was mixed in with some irrelevant information about the communicators. The information about the communicators prefaced the communication.

After reading a communication, subjects were asked to give their impressions of each of five aspects of the communication. To disguise the purpose of the experiment, only one of these "aspects" was the communicator himself. "Impressions" of the communicator, of course, was the only rating relevant to testing Rokeach's hypothesis that racial discrimination is absent when there is a high level of correspondence between the beliefs of subjects and beliefs of targets. The specific prediction was that subjects would have equally highly favorable impressions of black and white communicators of the anti-double jeopardy communication. That is, subjects would show no racial discrimination when targets varying in race agreed with them to a high degree. Had there actually been no belief information in the weather communication, Rokeach would have predicted that subjects would favor the white communicator under the assumption that the black communicator disagreed with their beliefs. However, since subjects may have assumed that both black and white communicators of the weather communication did not believe as they did, it would be consistent with Rokeach's theory if subjects displayed equally un-favorable impressions of the two communicators. Someone who clearly disagrees with one's beliefs is rejected regardless of his race. Each subject gave his impression of the communicator by writing down five descriptive adjectives. The method by which the adjectives generated by subjects to describe the communicators were treated in order to derive an "impression score" needn't be covered here. Suffice it to say that a numerical score was derived for each subject to represent the favorability of their impression of their communicator (see Allen, 1970 and Allen and Potkay, 1973, 1977a, 1977b). However, the technique of asking subjects to generate adjectives to describe target persons deserves some attention. The technique, which is called the Adjective Generation Technique or AGT, has some advantages over standard rating methods like those referred to in the introductory chapter. Standard rating scales have anchors like "good and bad," "like and dislike," and "attractive and unattractive." For such scales it is obvious which is the "good" end and which is the "bad" end. Thus, if subjects want to be lenient in rating others or make themselves look good through self-ratings, it is easy to do.

The anchors also may provide cues as to the possible purpose of the study. If a subject knows the purpose of an experiment, or thinks he does, he may bias his responses in order to serve the presumed purpose, or even bias his responses in order to undermine that presumed purpose. For example, if "attractive-unattractive" scales are used to rate targets, subjects might suspect that the experimenter is predicting differences in attractiveness of targets associated with different experimental conditions. The subject might use the transparent attractiveness scale in order to give the experimenter what he thinks the experimenter wants.

However, with the AGT the experimenter provides the subject with no biasing anchors or other cues associated with the rating measure *per se*. It is not clear to subjects whether "like-dislike," "good-bad," or other rating dimension is relevant to the adjectives that they are generating. Thus, use of the AGT lowers the likelihood that subjects will be able to be lenient in rating targets. Also the AGT makes it less likely that subjects will discern the purpose of the experiment based on assumptions about the rating method and then react to that presumed purpose.

A second advantage of the AGT is that the subject, rather than responding to the external stimulus represented by anchors, produces the rating from within himself. Since the subject can use any adjective within his repertoire, rather than being limited to the rating dimensions provided by the experimenter, the subject's AGT ratings may be a richer and more accurate indication of impressions than ratings obtained with the use of standard rating methods.

Results of the analysis of AGT "impression scores" were as predicted. Racial discrimination was entirely absent. Subjects who read the "anti-double jeopardy" communication had very favorable impressions of the communicators to which it was attributed regardless of their race. Averages of the impression ratings of the black and white communicators of the anti-double jeopardy communication were almost identical in numerical value. Further, the black and white communicators of the "weather" communication had equally unfavorable impression ratings. Subjects apparently were "color blind" in forming their impressions of targets. Rokeach was correct. When subjects perceived a high level of agreement with targets on important belief issues, they did not show racial discrimination at all. They also showed no racial discrimination when they apparently assumed disagreement with targets.

A Little Change Makes a Big Difference

Although the hypothesis from Rokeach's belief congruence theory received impressive support in the experiment just considered, it should be obvious to the reader that the support was obtained with the investigation of a noninvolving social relation. Indicating impressions of other persons is noninvolving. It is comparable to indicating with paper and pencil whether another person might be an acceptable friend. Thus it is possible that the hypothesis, "if an especially high level of correspondence between the beliefs of subjects and targets is established, racial discrimination will be absent," would not be confirmed for an involving social relation. To examine this possibility, the above study was replicated with just one significant change (Allen, 1971b). As in the original study, the "anti-double jeopardy" and "weather" communications were attributed to black and white communicators. The procedure was virtually identical to that used in the original study. White students from the same university served as subjects. The only difference was that the social distance measure used by Triandis and colleagues (1966) was substituted for the AGT measure of impressions. In other words, an involving social relation was substituted for a noninvolving social relation. Instead of giving impressions of targets, subjects in the replication indicated how acceptable targets would be as "a neighbor" and as a "kin through marriage." Results of this experiment were essentially the reverse of the previous experiment. Although subjects did show weak belief discrimination, the results of the replication can be summed up as follows: subjects accepted white communicators much more than black communicators regardless of what they communicated. Racial discrimination might have been expected on the basis of past research, but this almost complete reversal was a surprise.

In both the original experiment and its replication the cards were stacked in favor of belief discrimination and against race discrimination because of the establishment of strong correspondence between the beliefs of subjects and the beliefs of targets. Impressions were investigated in the original experiment and this advantage for belief resulted in strong belief discrimination and zero race discrimination. However, in the replication, the involving social distance relation was investigated and racial discrimination was very strong but belief discrimination very weak. The contrasting results of the "impression" and "social distance" experiments confirmed the previous observation that race is important in determining choices for involving but not for noninvolving relations of white people. But the results of these studies suggested something further. Race must be more than simply important for determining choices for involving social relations. Race must be an overwhelmingly powerful determinant of choices for the involving relations of white people. This must be true because, although the cards were stacked in favor of belief discrimination, race discrimination replaced belief discrimination when an involving social relation replaced a noninvolving social relation.

UNPREJUDICED WHITE PEOPLE AND RACISM

The "impressions" and "social distance" experiments suggested that race may be a more important determinant of involving social relations than was previously assumed. But just how important is race for determining choices for involving relations of white people? Is it so powerful that it affects the choices of most white people, even those who claim not to discriminate by race? This is the question to be considered next. However, before considering the experiments which addressed the question, the unique target persons that were used in the experiments will be described.

O. J. Simpson vs. Johnny Unitas

The target persons used in previous research were artificial in some way or other. Word persons such as those used by Rokeach and colleagues (1960) and Triandis (1961) were wholly artificial in that subjects probably assumed that they were not reading the characteristics of actual persons. These criticisms may also apply to the communicator descriptions used by Allen (1970). The picture persons such as those used by Triandis and colleagues (1966) were artificial because (1) the persons were not actually present, (2) they were attributed with only a few characteristics, (3) subjects were not actually acquainted with them (subjects had no prior information about the targets), and (4) subjects probably sensed that the target persons had been contrived. Even the real and present persons who were used by Rokeach and Mezei (1966) were somewhat artificial since subjects were not actually acquainted with them and their characteristics (e.g., beliefs) were "staged."

For these reasons, public figures were used as target persons in the experiments described below. A public figure was defined as anyone who is known to most Americans. Public figures are not artificial, because subjects have knowledge of them before participating in an experiment, know that public figures really exist, and can regard them as real people. The latter is true because public figures have a multitude of characteristics instead of the few characteristics attributed to contrived targets. The public figures actually used in the experiments were selected from a pool of two-hundred persons whose names were gleaned from popular publications such as *Newsweek* and *Reader's Digest*. The only criterion for inclusion in the pool was that the given public figure was likely to be known to college students.

The names of all two-hundred public figures were printed on questionnaire pages so that they could be rated on the evaluative measure. The evaluative measure was developed by Charles Osgood and his colleagues (1957) as a general measure of feelings about target persons. If a person expresses very positive feelings about a target on the evaluative measure, it means that he probably likes most of the target's characteristics including beliefs. If a person expresses very negative feelings about a target, it means that he probably doesn't like most of the target's characteristics. A large number of subjects rated the two-hundred public figures on the evaluative measure, and an average rating was computed for each public figure. Next, pairs of public figures were selected, with one member of each pair being black and the other member being white. For this pairing process, only those public figures who had been recognized by subjects and about whom subjects had agreed in making evaluative ratings were considered. A black and a white public figure were paired if their average evaluative ratings were almost exactly the same and if they were of the same sex and sphere of fame or notoriety. As to the pairing criterion, sports figures were paired with sports figures, political activists with political activists, and entertainers with entertainers. The pairing process resulted in the selection of ten pairs of public figures. Example pairs were O. J. Simpson and Johnny Unitas, Flip Wilson and Bob Hope, Ella Fitzgerald and Barbra Streisand. Because of this pairing procedure, it was possible to assume that the target persons differed only in race.

Do Unprejudiced White Persons Show Racial Discrimination?

As mentioned previously, the first experiments to be considered were concerned with whether even white persons who claim that they do not discriminate by race actually choose whites over blacks for involving social relations. The first step in this consideration was to locate some people who would claim not to discriminate by race. A "prejudice test" was used for this purpose. Prejudice tests measure the degree to which people see themselves as discriminating by race. If a person's responses on a prejudice test indicate that he claims to discriminate by race, he is labeled "prejudiced." On the other hand, if a person's responses on a prejudice test indicate that he claims that he does not discriminate by race, he is labeled "unprejudiced." People whose responses are mixed so that it is not clear what they claim for themselves are labeled "ambivalent." Such people do not clearly make a claim as to whether they see themselves as discriminating by race.

To determine whether unprejudiced white people actually do show racial discrimination in choices for involving relations, a large group of white male and female college students were given a prejudice test (Allen, 1975). On the basis of their responses to the test, some members of this group were classified as "unprejudiced" while others were classified as "prejudiced" or "ambivalent." Later, under the guise of a separate experiment, these subjects were given a questionnaire containing the names of the twenty black and white paired public figures who had been selected previously. The names of these twenty public figures were mixed in the questionnaire with the names of fifty-five other public figures so that they would not be conspicuous. Each public figure in the questionnaire was rated with the now familiar involving "social distance" measure used by Triandis and colleagues (1966) and Allen (1971b). This measure entailed "accept as kin through marriage" and "accept as a neighbor" choices. Of course, only responses to the twenty paired figures were analyzed for this experiment and for other experiments in which the twenty paired figures were used.

The results of this first experiment were exceedingly clear and straightforward. All kinds of subjects, even those who had claimed not to discriminate by race, were significantly more accepting of white than black public figures. To be sure that the results were not peculiar to the particular prejudice test used in the first experiment, a second experiment was done with a new sample of white subjects who were classified by use of a different prejudice test. Again all subjects, including those who had claimed that they did not discriminate by race, showed significantly more acceptance of white than black public figures for the involving social distance relation. To be absolutely sure, subjects in the second experiment were reclassified with the use of yet another prejudice test. For the third time, subjects in all three prejudice categories showed more acceptance of whites than blacks. It didn't matter what prejudice test was used. In every case white subjects were significantly more accepting of white targets for an involving social relation, even those who had claimed not to discriminate by race.

"But It's Not My Fault, They Made Me Do It"

During the course of conducting the experiments just described a few subjects came forward to complain to the experimenters. They said that the questionnaire was unfair. Subjects wanted to assure the experimenters that they were not bigoted persons. They protested that friends and Moms and Dads made them discriminate by race when it came to choices like whom to accept as a member of one's family. In Rokeach's terms, external social pressure was making them discriminate by race and not their own internal dispositions. As a matter of fact some researchers (Mezei, 1971; Silverman and Cochrane, 1972) have claimed to have shown that racial discrimination for involving social relations is due to external pressure. These researchers first had subjects indicate choices for their involving social relations and then asked them whether others put pressure on them to discriminate by race for such relations. Subjects showed racial discrimination in making choices for the involving relations, and also claimed that others pressured them into discriminating by race. But was it that others had pressured them or that they were rationalizing their own racial discrimination by blaming others? The procedures of these experiments do not allow one to decide between these two possibilities.

In spite of the lack of clear experimental support, let's assume for the moment that there is some validity to the claim that "it's not my fault, they made me do it." Let's assume that in general people do pressure other people to discriminate by race in making choices for involving social relations. Does the existence of this external pressure imply that people are not the cause of their own racial discrimination? Does it imply that their internal dispositions are not implicated in their discrimination? This question might be answered by carrying the social pressure notion to its logical conclusion. Let's suppose that a person "A" says "It's not my fault, person 'B' and person 'C' made me discriminate." Suppose further person "B" says "It's not my fault, 'A' and 'C' made me do it." Finally suppose that person "C" says "It's not my fault, 'A' and 'B' made me do it." Wouldn't these conditions exist if it were true that everybody was making everyone else discriminate by race? And if these conditions did exist, wouldn't it be true that each person is not only the target of pressure to discriminate by race, but also the *source* of such pressure? Affirmative answers seem to follow. If a person is the source of pressure to discriminate by race, his internal dispositions are implicated. Any white persons who put pressure on other whites to not accept blacks for involving social relations must harbor negative feelings about blacks, even if they make claims to the contrary.

Reverse Discrimination

The reader probably is aware that white racial liberals (i.e., "unprejudiced" whites) are often accused of "reverse discrimination." "Reverse discrimination" occurs when a white person actually shows more acceptance of blacks than of fellow whites. Actually there is experimental support for the notion of "reverse prejudice." Richard Dienstbier (1970) reported that his white "racially liberal" subjects were more accepting of blacks than whites for some noninvolving social relations such as "admiration" of targets.

Reverse discrimination is perplexing, isn't it? It's hard to understand how racially liberal or unprejudiced whites can show less acceptance of blacks than whites for involving social relations, but *more* acceptance of blacks than whites for noninvolving relations. On the surface it just doesn't seem to fit.

The first question that came to my mind after reading Dienstbier's research report was, Would the reverse discrimination that he reported hold up under replication? There were two reasons why I thought it might not. First Dienstbier merely assumed that his subjects were unprejudiced. He didn't use an independent prejudice test to classify his subjects. Second, he used word persons as targets. Would his results be replicated if public figures served as targets? To find out I attempted to replicate Dienstbier's study with the use of an independent prejudice test and the paired public figures (Allen, 1975).

The experiment to examine "reverse discrimination" was much like the ones just described. The same twenty paired public figures and the fifty-five other public figures were presented to subjects in questionnaire form. This time the figures were rated on the noninvolving "admiration" measure which was used by Triandis and colleagues (1966). Two "dummy" questionnaires which as a whole had no relevance for racial discrimination also were given to subjects. The reason for administering these two questionnaires was to disguise the purpose of the experiment, and more important, to hide a measure of prejudice. Items of a prejudice test were embedded in one of these questionnaires. This procedure was to give subjects the impression that the prejudice test items were relevant to the apparent overall purpose of the questionnaire, "attitudes." Of course, responses to this prejudice test were used as a basis for classifying subjects into the three categories, "prejudiced," "unprejudiced" and "ambivalent." The results closely replicated the results reported by Dienstbier (1970). White subjects who indicated either that they were prejudiced according to prejudice test responses or ambivalent showed more admiration for the white public figures than for the black public figures. However, white subjects who indicated that they were unprejudiced showed more admiration for black than for white public figures. That is, unprejudiced whites showed reverse discrimination for the noninvolving admiration social relation.

Other recent studies report greater favorability for blacks than whites on the part of unprejudiced subjects. Ehor Boyanowsky and Vernon Allen (1973) reported that unprejudiced subjects were more likely to give up their own judgment for that of a black confederate than for that of a white confederate. Likewise, Shirley Weitz (1972), whose sample was generally "liberal," found overfavorability to blacks on both a general and a specific attitudinal measure. Finally, Donald Dutton and Robert Lake (1973) found that unprejudiced subjects who had been threatened by false feedback which indicated that they were prejudiced gave more money to a black panhandler than unprejudiced subjects who were not threatened. This relationship did not hold for a white panhandler.

Reverse Discrimination: Genuine Affinity for the Underdog or an Attempt to Look Like the Champion of the Underdog

But does reverse discrimination mean that unprejudiced whites are genuinely more accepting of blacks than of other whites? On the basis of past research, some of which has been considered in this chapter, it would not be surprising at all to find whites who do not discriminate by race for noninvolving relations. But finding people who accept members of another race more than their own race seems odd. People usually don't show more positive inclination toward that with which they are *not* identified than they do toward that with which

SOCIAL BEHAVIOR

they *are* identified. Also, the people who showed reverse discrimination in the present case were unprejudiced, meaning that they claimed not to discriminate by race one way or the other. These arguments seem unsupportive of the possibility that reverse discrimination is a manifestation of genuine affinity for blacks. Unprejudiced whites may show reverse discrimination for motivational reasons other than stronger positive feelings for blacks than for whites.

There are several possible reasons why unprejudiced whites might display reverse discrimination for noninvolving social relations. First it has been noted by several social psychologists (e.g., Sigall and Page, 1971) that it currently is in vogue to regard racial discrimination as undesirable or "bad," particularly among certain subsets of the population (politicians). This social atmosphere might cause some people to "bend over backwards" not to show that which is no longer approved—racial discrimination. If one wants to be doubly sure of approval, one could display the opposite of what's disapproved.

Second, there is reason to believe that unprejudiced whites have a self-concept which is heavily dependent on being fair-minded (Gaertner, 1974). If one wants to convince oneself that one is fair-minded, one could "bend over backwards" to be fair by doing the opposite of being unfair; instead of discriminating against blacks, discriminate in favor of them.

Finally, how do you think a person who likes to regard himself as fair-minded is going to react to evidence that he sometimes is not fair-minded? If a racial liberal or unprejudiced person recognizes at some level of consciousness that he does discriminate by race for involving relations, he is likely to suffer considerable discomfort. This discomfort may lead to the need to balance the scales by showing the compensatory response of more acceptance of blacks for noninvolving relations. Compensation for displays of discrimination against blacks may be one reason for discrimination in favor of blacks.

What evidence might be accepted as supportive of the thesis that reverse discrimination cannot be interpreted as genuine affinity for blacks on the part of unprejudiced whites, but is instead an attempt to convince oneself and others that one is fair-minded? A person does not necessarily express only one level of acceptance of a target for a social relation. Actually, a person is capable of making several, sometimes conflicting, expressions of acceptance in a social relation toward the same target. These varying expressions toward a target might be classified in several ways, but, minimally, expressions can be cast into two gross categories. These categories are "public expressions"—expressions designed for public consumption—and "private expressions"—expressions one usually makes only to intimates and to oneself. To get an idea of the difference between these two types of expressions, imagine that you are a political liberal (or conservative) talking politics with your conservative (or liberal) boss who is a casual acquaintance. Now compare the expressions that you might make in such a situation with those you might make about politics to a "best friend" in a private conversation.

If unprejudiced whites reflect greater acceptance of blacks than whites not only with public expressions, but also with private expressions, we might interpret the public expressions as indicating genuine affinity for blacks. However, if unprejudiced whites express reverse discrimination in public, but do not show reverse discrimination in private expressions, we may infer that the public expression is motivated by the desire to *appear* fair-minded. Thus the problem of interpreting reverse discrimination reduces to observing unprejudiced whites' public and private expressions of choices for noninvolving social relations.

Assessing public expressions is no problem. To assess public expressions, all one has to do is ask subjects whom they would choose or have them indicate choices through use of questionnaire. Assessing private expressions is a different matter. A stranger approaching a person and asking him to reveal "how you really feel" (i.e., what feelings would be reflected in your private thoughts) probably would elicit a public expression, a lie, or no response. Private expressions must be assessed by unorthodox means. Fortunately, a method for assessing private expressions has been provided by Edward E. Jones and Harold Sigall (1971). The method is called the Bogus Pipeline.

In order to understand how the Bogus Pipeline assesses private expressions and how it was used in an experiment to compare the public and private expressions of unprejudiced whites, the administration of the Bogus Pipeline to a single subject will be outlined (Allen, 1975). Subjects were white male and female college students. Each subject was escorted by the experimenter from a waiting room to an experimental area. The experimental area was a U-shaped hallway bordered by a number of small rooms. Each room was connected

to a central room at the open end of the "U." The subject first was
seated in the hallway and asked to complete a questionnaire containing some innocuous items such as "Are record clubs valuable?" For
each item, the subject could select one of five levels of agreement.
The experimenter collected the questionnaire after it was completed
and led the subject down the hall to the control room. The control
room contained a number of pieces of equipment, most of it electronic equipment. Most prominent in the room was a physiograph.
A physiograph measures physiological responses (e.g., heart rate) and
essentially is the same apparatus used by lie-detector operators. The
physiograph was described to subjects as an "electromyograph" or
EMG. The EMG was said to measure "implicit muscle potentials."
The experimenter pointed out that the EMG apparatus was plugged
into some wall receptacles which were labelled with the room number
of the experimental room. The subject then was led to the experimental room and seated facing a "subject console." The subject console was a cube shaped apparatus having five numbered lights, a dial,
and a switch on its front panel. At a 90° angle to the subject console
was another piece of apparatus which was described as the "EMG
feedback console." This console was a box-like apparatus with five
numbered lights on its front panel. Both pieces of equipment were
plugged into wall receptacles like those in the control room.

The experimenter explained that the EMG actually was a "super-
lie detector." The implicit muscle potentials which were measured by
the EMG unerringly could reveal the *degree* to which a person was
telling the truth, regardless of what he might express outwardly. The
first step in the experiment was to be sure that the EMG was functioning properly and needed no adjustment. To this end the experimenter taped an electrode to the subject's forearm. The electrode was
plugged into a wall receptacle and supposedly was the means by
which the implicit muscle potentials were to be recorded. The subject
was asked to grasp the dial which was mounted under the five lights
of the subject console. Each item of the questionnaire which previously was completed was then read to the subject. For each item the
subject was to concentrate on the particular one of the five levels of
agreement that he would endorse for that item. The subject was cau-
tioned not to actually turn the dial. The EMG would automatically
"read" the muscle potentials and determine which one of the five dial
positions the subject would have selected to indicate degree of agree-

ment if he had actually turned the dial. After concentrating on each item, the subject was to flip the switch which would activate the EMG apparatus in the control room and feed back the subject's "true feelings" about the items. The feedback was accomplished by activation of one of the five lights on the EMG console each of which represented a different level of agreement. The subject assisted the experimenter by turning to the EMG feedback console and recording the number of the light which flashed after he flipped the switch. The subject made the recordings on a fresh copy of the questionnaire. After all questionnaire items had been read, the experimenter retrieved the copy of the questionnaire which the subject had completed in the hallway. A comparison of the two copies revealed that they were identical. The EMG had "read" the subject's feelings about the questionnaire items with perfect accuracy. Needless to say, subjects expressed amazement at the prowess of the EMG. Some gasped and others showed a marked startled reaction.

The experimenter then proceeded to the main part of the experiment. The "main part" was to be some "ratings" of thirty-six public figures. Unbeknownst to the subject, twenty of the figures were the same paired black and white public figures used in the experiments considered above. The electrode remained attached during the main part of the experiment. Using the five point dial, the subject indicated degree of admiration of the public figures. Thus the admiration social relation was again investigated.

During the rating of the public figures, the EMG feedback console was turned so that the experimenter could see it, but not the subject. From the subject's point of view the experimenter could see both the EMG feedback indicating his "true feelings" and the dial-turning responses the subject was told to make. The instruction to turn the dial was given to the subject under the guise of testing the degree of correspondence between dial-turning responses and "true feelings" (i.e., EMG feedback) which were to be simultaneously recorded. The subject was told that he could later examine this correspondence, (or lack thereof, presumably) and was admonished to predict his "true feelings" by dial-turning responses. Since the experimenter could see dial-turning responses *and* EMG feedback and later would examine their correspondence with the subject, the subject was under pressure to make what amounted to private expressions with the dial-turning responses. To do otherwise would lead to being caught in a "lie" or "cover-up" attempt. Therefore dial-turning responses were assumed to be private expressions of admiration of the public figures.

Actually, the super-lie-detector doesn't exist, although some scientists persist in claiming its existence (Woodmansee, 1969). The whole scenario was undertaken in order to convince freshmen who "know" about lie detectors, but not about physiological measurement, that the experimenter actually had access to their private expressions. The "feedback" was accomplished by laying the original questionnaire copy near the experimental room door which was left slightly ajar so that an accomplice could stand behind the partially closed door and copy the subject's original responses. The accomplice secretly was signaled by the experimenter. The signal was to tell the accomplice when to indicate the subject's previous responses by activating the EMG feedback console lights through the use of a hidden control-room apparatus. A hidden button was pressed by the experimenter in order to signal the accomplice. Of course, following their participation, the subjects were offered the opportunity to receive a full explanation of the experiment, its real purpose and the reasons for the deception (see Introduction).

The measurement of public expressions was accomplished by use of the same procedure, with some critical omissions. The EMG apparatus was described to subjects in this second condition as "an efficient and automatic method for recording and analyzing responses." In the experimental room, the EMG feedback console was turned to the wall, the electrode was hidden, and subjects were told that going over the questionnaire was only to familiarize them with the operation of the subject console. In this case Jones and Sigall (1971) had assumed that dial-turning responses were equivalent to questionnaire responses which in turn are equivalent to public expressions. This condition was called the "regular rating" condition, whereas the first condition was called the "bogus pipeline" condition.

All subjects were classified as "unprejudiced," "ambivalent," or "prejudiced" according to their responses to a prejudice test which was given to them at the end of the experiment, but before debriefing. The results for the regular rating condition revealed that unprejudiced subjects, and only unprejudiced subjects, showed strong reverse discrimination. That is, in terms of public expressions, unprejudiced subjects were more accepting of black public figures than of white public figures. However, results were different for the bogus pipeline condition. Unprejudiced subjects failed to show reverse discrimination, and in fact they showed a slight trend in the opposite direction. That is, unprejudiced subjects showed less rather than more acceptance of blacks in terms of their private expressions. Therefore, reverse discrimination appeared to be an attempt on the part of unprejudiced subjects to appear fair-minded, rather than an expression of genuine affinity for blacks. Otherwise, why would reverse discrimination be absent when private expressions were examined?

LIBERAL HYPOCRISY OR THE TWO FACES OF RACIAL LIBERALISM

There has been much talk of "liberal hypocrisy," particularly among conservatives, as one might expect. The most popular example of "liberal hypocrisy" seems to be the observation that liberal congressmen and senators who openly support racial integration and busing, send their own children to all-white private schools. It has probably occurred to the reader that the evidence reported above is consistent with "liberal hypocrisy." On the one hand some racially liberal whites claim not to discriminate by race, but on the other hand they show racial discrimination for involving social relations. Racial liberals reflect greater acceptance of blacks than whites in their public expressions, but it may be only "for show" because this bias in favor of blacks is not present in their private expressions. White racial liberals may express friendliness toward blacks out of one face, but may present a second face out of which quite a different message emanates.

Results of other studies indicate that while unprejudiced subjects show extreme friendliness to blacks with overt behaviors that they can easily control, they show unfriendliness with subtle behaviors that they cannot easily control. In addition, Sam Gaertner (1973) found that liberals claimed that they would be as likely to help a black person as a white person, but, in fact, when younger and older liberals combined were actually given the opportunity to respond to a telephone call for help, they were more likely to help whites than blacks. "Premature hang-ups" as well as help responses were considered. A "premature hang-up" was recorded if a subject listened to a caller long enough to ascertain the caller's race, but not long enough to hear the help request. When the "premature hang-up" responses of younger and older liberals were examined separately, it was revealed that younger liberals actually hung up prematurely on black callers more frequently than they did on white callers. Shirley Weitz (1972) found that while some of her unprejudiced subjects expressed "extreme friendliness" toward blacks in terms of attitudinal expressions, these same subjects were negative toward blacks in terms of voice tone and subtle behaviors. Donald Dutton and Vicki Lennox (1974) gave unprejudiced subjects false feedback which indicated evidence of "prejudice" in them, and found that those who subsequently had an opportunity to compensate by donating to a black panhandler were later less willing than other threatened subjects to volunteer time to civil rights.

WHAT DOES IT ALL MEAN WITH REGARD TO RACISM?

At the beginning of this chapter the question was raised as to whether racism—pervasive antiblack sentiment in American culture—implies that whites always reflect hatred and rejection in all of their social behaviors vis-à-vis blacks. If support for the existence of racism requires that all whites always, regardless of the nature of the social relation in question, reflect rejection of blacks, support is not to be found in the data of experimental social psychology. As we have seen, for noninvolving social relations, race is not a particularly important criterion for acceptance, and racial discrimination is only rarely significant in magnitude.

However, if a more restricted interpretation of racism is adopted, support for the existence of racism can be seen in the data of experimental social psychology. If the charge "antiblack sentiment is pervasive in American culture" is assumed to imply that antiblack sentiment is *clearly and overtly manifested in the behaviors of most white persons for at least one realm of social behavior,* support for the existence of racism is available. Most whites, even those who claim that they do not discriminate by race, show racial discrimination in making choices for involving social relations. In a sense, involving relations might be regarded as the domain for racism.

Given that racism exists, there are a number of predictions

which follow. Among the most prominent of these is that evidence of the effects of culturally dictated antiblack sentiment should be observable early in the developmental process. Just as children learn that males can succeed at many pursuits and females at only a few and that beauty is "good" and ugly is "bad," white children would learn very early that black is "bad" and white is "good." Powerful determinants of social behavior rear their (sometimes) ugly heads early in life. John E. Williams has done many studies over the years that show that white is assumed to be "good" and black is assumed to be "bad," but the most compelling study for these purposes was reported by Williams and Karen Roberson (1967).

The subjects in Williams and Roberson's experiment were white children who were classified into the following age categories: less than three years to less than five years, five to five-and-two-thirds years, more than five-and-two-thirds years to less than seven years. These children were given a story-completion test to assess color meaning. This and all other tests employed pictures of objects or people. An example of a dummy or filler item appearing on the test was a story about a brown and a green airplane which was to be completed by answering the questions "which got caught in the tree?" or "which would fly the fastest?" An example of a critical item was a story about a black and a white dog which was to be completed by answering the questions "which is the clean doggy?" or "which is the bad doggy?" Subjects also were given an analogous story-completion test to assess the meaning of color as applied to people. An example was a story about a black and a white girl which was to be completed by answering the questions "who is the clean little girl?" or "who is the bad little girl?" Dummy items included stories having completions relevant to sex-role knowledge: "who (boy or girl) works after school mowing lawns?" or "who likes to buy new dresses?"

Results indicated that white children attached positive meaning to white objects and negative meaning to black objects with great consistency. This was true even of children as young as three years of age. Subjects showed even greater consistency in attaching positive meaning to white people and negative meaning to black people. In fact, the consistency was so great, even for the youngest age group, that it rivaled the consistency with which subjects assigned so-called male activities to males and so-called female activities to females!

The evidence for the existence of racism is available, but the existence of racism is not generally accepted. As Tom Wicker indicates in the introduction to the *Report of the National Advisory Commission on Civil Rights* (1968) " . . . until the fact of white racism is admitted, it cannot conceivably be expunged" (p. ix). Admitting to racism is not to begin a witch hunt to find "racists" and do them in. It seems that when people "go on a witch hunt" the witch each finds is never himself. Rather we must admit that antiblack sentiment has influenced and continues to influence most of us who are white. Cultures don't change overnight, and the influences of cultures on people are not eliminated within their lifetime. However, white Americans could begin to lessen the effects of racism and to excise it from our culture. Our first step is to monitor our behavior more closely and to teach our children differently than we were taught.

6

Is the
Women's Movement
erasing the mark of oppression from the female psyche?

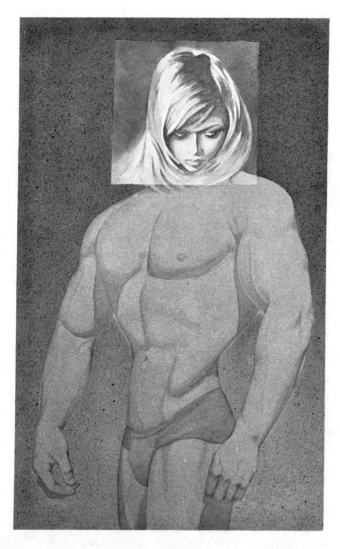

Females are hardier than males. Females live longer than males and are less susceptible to a number of diseases than are males. Recently a friend was trying to obtain some psychological data from some elderly people. He soon discovered that he was going to have to scratch for data from elderly men. There were more elderly women than men among those of both sexes who were available, and more men than women were too senile to respond to questions.

During the nine-hundred-day siege of Leningrad by the Nazis, the order to die was, first to last, the very young, the very old, men, women. Hitler discovered that women were hardy, but unfortunately for him he didn't exploit this discovery very well. In the forced labor camps the women tended to survive the harsh conditions better than men. However, Hitler failed to follow the example of the Allies and use German women in his industries—much to the chagrin of his armaments minister, Albert Speer. Hitler did not want to destroy the tradition of German woman as housewife and mother. The English and Americans employed women in heavy industry and in numerous "male" jobs, to much advantage. Unfortunately, people from both countries promptly forgot at the end of the war that women had proven that they could perform just about every job as well as or better than men.

World War II did allow some males to alter their sexist views. F. W. Winterbotham (1974), coordinator of Ultra, the supersecret cipher program, found himself working among women. The job of deciphering and communicating German intelligence information that could lead to the destruction or salvation of thousands of people was extraordinarily stressful work. Winterbotham made it a point to note that the women he worked with were cool, calm, and collected in the face of intense pressure.

However, it is probably true that males can do some things better than females. If so, for everything that males can do better than females, there is something that females can do better than males. For example, women may make better politicians and public officials than men. There are sex differences, and in this case the differences may favor women. Women may be less aggressive than men, in the hostile sense of the word. If so, they may make more effective—and safer —mediators of international affairs. A good example is the past efforts of Golda Meir to prevent the development of the Middle East war into a world war. It may also be that women are less burdened with need for self-enhancement caused by the voracious "male ego." If so, they may make more selfless public servants. Congresswoman Barbara Jordan provides a good example of selfless dedication to public service.

BUT HOW ARE WOMEN REGARDED?

Unfortunately the above positive characterizations of females are the exception rather than the rule. Women are more frequently characterized in negative terms. Some examples should suffice to make the point.

An adolescent girl who is a friend of our family once proudly presented me with her report card. Her grades were excellent, with one prominent exception. She received a "D" in math. With a show of concern, I queried her about the poor grade. She responded happily, "Oh don't worry. My math teacher says that math is not for girls."

I was not terribly surprised at this incident. By the time it occurred, my wife and I had been repeatedly frustrated in our efforts to keep our preschool-age daughter's mind open concerning what are acceptable pursuits for girls. On several occasions when our daughter was about three, she would come home crying and exclaiming that she had been excluded from "boys' games." By the time she was old enough for the "big wheel" (toy motorcycle) that she had always wanted she had become convinced that it was for boys only. The "big wheel" sat idle for a long time after she finally received it.

If women would make better politicians and public officials than men, why are there so few? Attitudes like the following probably in part account for the paucity of women in government. A friend of a three-time presidential candidate once posed the question "What would happen to the country if the White House were occupied by a menopausal woman at a time when a Bay of Pigs level decision had to be made?" The implication of this question was that "hormonal influences" would make women unfit for high office. By the way, such influences have yet to be proven significant. The irony is great when one realizes that the actual Bay of Pigs decision was a MAN-made disaster.

A popular woman's magazine has a monthly section on real life examples of subtle—and sometimes not so subtle—put-downs on females. One example was taken from an insurance-company pamphlet on careers in forestry. A part of the text informed "a boy" on how to plan a career in forestry. The text of the pamphlet included the suggestion that there were some jobs for women in forestry, in the research laboratory, but "in the main, it is a man's job." The text also indicated that several women had enrolled in a major university's college of forestry. However, only two had ever graduated and neither currently was in forestry. One would find it easy to speculate on why so few had graduated and why no graduates were in forestry. The bottom line was that the two female grads had done the next best thing. They had married foresters.

Another magazine example came from a "thought for the day" calendar. The thought for a day in 1975 was "What is a woman? One of nature's agreeable blunders." The same issue contained a reprint of a pizza-parlor ad. Free pizzas were being offered to parents of newborn children. The lucky Moms and Dads were to get one free pizza for a baby girl and two free pizzas for a baby boy.

Finally, the magazine offered some evidence that it is women who suffer most from being unattractive (see chapter on physical attractiveness). An interview form for a prospective receptionist was reprinted. Would-be receptionists were to be rated on words-typed-per-minute, words of dictation recorded per minute, attractiveness, and willingness to accept a rather meager salary. Below the rating scales were some guidelines for employment action. If the criteria for all four ratings were met, the interviewer was instructed to offer regular employment. However, the interviewer was instructed to "refer the applicant to the typing pool" if she met all but the dictation criterion, and to "refer the applicant to the stenographic pool" if she met all but the attractiveness criterion.

If the anecdotal evidence of bias against females is alarming, the research evidence is downright appalling. A study by Inge Broverman, Susan Vogel, Donald Broverman, Frank Clarkson, and Paul Rosenkrantz (1972) is a good case in point. These researchers first asked a group of males and females to list all the characteristics, attributes, or behaviors on which they thought men and women differed. All of those which were listed at least twice were retained for further study. One-hundred-and-twenty-two characteristics were listed at least twice. Instead of entertaining the usual question of which characteristics applied to males and which applied to females, Broverman and colleagues formed each of the 122 characteristics into bipolar scales in order to determine the degree to which each trait applied to *both* males and females. A bipolar scale is one which has anchors that are opposite in meaning (e.g., good-bad). In this case the scale anchors were separated by 60 points or degrees (see Introduction).

Seventy-four college males and 80 college females were then given the 122 traits and asked to indicate for each scale which pole applied to males and which pole applied to females. Based on this data, scales were located for which one pole was seen by subjects as "masculine" while the other pole was seen as "feminine." The criteria for selection of a scale as able to differentiate between masculine and feminine was 1) 75 percent of both male and female subjects agreed that one pole of the scale was "masculine" and the other pole was "feminine," and 2) there was a statistically significant difference in the tendency for one pole of the scale to be rated as "masculine" and the other to be rated as "feminine." Forty-one scales met these two criteria. Results were replicated across several samples that varied by sex, religious affiliation, and socioeconomic class.

An additional sample of males and females was told which pole of each scale was masculine and which was feminine and was asked to indicate which pole was the most socially desirable. For 29 of the 41 scales (71 percent) the masculine pole was seen as the more socially desirable. Still another sample of males and females was given the same task, but not told which pole of each scale had been rated as masculine and which had been rated as feminine. For the same 29 scales, the masculine pole was seen as more socially desirable. Thus for 71 percent of the scales, the masculine extreme for the characteristic measured by the scales was seen as more socially desirable. The feminine extreme was more desirable on only 12 of the 41 or 29 percent of the scales.

The profundity of these findings can best be appreciated by considering some examples of characterizations of males and females. For the characteristic of "independence" the desirable pole "very independent" was seen as masculine while the undesirable pole "not at all independent" was seen as feminine. On the dominance scale, the desirable end, "dominant," was seen as masculine while the undesirable end, "submissive," was seen as feminine. Further "active" was seen as masculine while "passive" was seen as feminine, "logical" was seen as masculine while "illogical" was seen as feminine, "direct" was seen as masculine while "sneaky" was seen as feminine, "very self-confident" was seen as masculine while "not at all self-confident" was seen as feminine, and "ambitious" was seen as masculine while "unambitious" was seen as feminine. It is interesting that on the "sex superiority" scale, the more *social desirable* pole "thinks men are always superior to women" was seen as masculine while the *undesirable* pole "thinks women are superior to men" was seen as feminine.

In the cases of those twelve scales for which the feminine pole was seen as more desirable, the "desirable" pole in some cases doesn't seem very desirable. For the characteristic "talkativeness," the desirable pole "very talkative" is seen as feminine and the undesirable pole "not at all talkative" was seen as masculine. "Very interested in own appearance" was desirable and feminine while "not at all interested in own appearance" was undesirable and masculine. However, "gentle" was seen as desirable and feminine while "rough" was seen as undesirable and masculine and "very aware of the feelings of others" was seen as desirable and feminine and "not at all aware of the feelings of others" was seen as undesirable and masculine.

To sum it all up, the desirable aspect of a characteristic tends to be seen as masculine while the undesirable aspect tends to be seen as feminine. Males are stereotyped as having mainly desirable characteristics while females are stereotyped as having mainly undesirable characteristics. A girl child is trained to be "feminine" and in the process she is taught to adopt undesirable characteristics.

THE MARK OF OPPRESSION

Women are depreciated by being assigned socially undesirable characteristics, and by the negative feedback that they receive as indicated by the anecdotes considered above. What are the effects of depreciation like that experienced by women? Being an object of discrimination and therefore constantly subject to negative feedback from others tends to undermine one's self-concept. Individuals who are constantly told explicitly and implicitly that they are of less worth than others are likely to begin to *believe* that they are of less worth than others. For example, it has long been known that antisemitism exists among Jews as a result of their persecution (Harding et al., 1954). Black psychologist Kenneth Clark's famous studies (e.g., Clark and Clark,

1947) concerning self-depreciation in black children were even cited during the 1954 Supreme Court hearings on school integration. Clark found that black children preferred white dolls and rejected black dolls when asked to choose which were nice, which looked bad, which they would like to play with, and which were a nice color. Other researchers have replicated Clark's result directly and indirectly over the years, although a recent study (Hraba and Grant, 1970) found some evidence of a reversal of the self-depreciation trend. John E. Williams (1964) found a tendency for black college students to show self-depreciation in 1963. Although this trend was still present in 1969, it was weaker in general and reversed for some black college students (Williams et al., 1971). It seems that self-depreciation is the mark of oppression.

Are Women Oppressed?

The evidence seems to predict that women should, like others who are objects of discrimination and negative feedback, suffer self-depreciation. However, few people seem to expect self-depreciation in women. If one is to suffer the mark of oppression one has to be oppressed. People have had difficulty thinking of American women as oppressed. An "object of oppression" is stereotyped as impoverished, hungry, downtrodden, and struggling to survive. American women, most of whom are white, seem not to fit the stereotype of the oppressed person. That is probably why people were surprised—even shocked—when the research to be reported next was made public.

Women's Evaluation of Women

Philip Goldberg (1968) sought to determine whether women showed self-depreciation. First he had one-hundred college females rate a number of professional areas as to whether they were the domain of males or females. Law and city planning were seen as male professions, elementary school teaching and dietetics were seen as female professions, and linguistics and art history were seen as neither male nor female professions. Professional journals for these six professions were consulted and an article pertaining to each profession was selected. All six articles were edited to 1,500 words. The articles then were assembled into two booklets. If in one booklet a given article was "authored" by a male (e.g., John T. McKay), the author's name which was assigned to the same article in the other booklet was that of a female (e.g., Joan T. McKay). In this way the only thing that varied was the sex of authors of the articles. The content of the articles was held constant.

Forty college females were then given the six articles and told that they were to critically evaluate them. These subjects also were told that they were not expected to be sophisticated in the professions about which the articles were written. Nothing was included in instructions to alert the subjects to the fact that sex of the authors was of interest to the experimenter. The authors' names provided the only sex cue.

Each article was rated on its value, persuasiveness and profundity. Also, the author of each article was rated on writing style, professional competence, professional status, and ability to sway the reader. Results can be summed up in a straightforward manner. Regardless of whether the professional area was "male" or "female" and regardless of rating type, female subjects rated male authors more favorably than female authors. There were some exceptions to this summary statement. Sex of the author made no difference in combined ratings for the art history article. On three of fifty-four possible comparisons between male and female authors (nine rating items times six articles) there was no difference in ratings, and on seven additional comparisons, females were favored. This means that on forty-four of fifty-four possible comparisons, female subjects favored males! Even Goldberg was surprised. College females thought that males were better authors even when they were writing about professions which were considered to be feminine.

Will Success Spoil the Self-Depreciation Effect?

One of Goldberg's colleagues, Gail Pheterson (1969), attempted to replicate Goldberg's original study with the use of middle-aged, non-college females as subjects. Her procedure was identical to that of Goldberg, except for the kinds of articles she employed. Pheterson's articles concerned marriage, child discipline, and special education. Results of Pheterson's study were nil. There was no tendency for the older females to be more favorable to male than to female authors.

In fact, there was a nonsignificant trend for the older females to favor the female authors.

Pheterson's failure to replicate Goldberg's results may have been due to the different articles that she employed or it may have been due to the fact that she used middle-aged, uneducated females as subjects rather than college females. Pheterson, Goldberg, and their colleague Sara Kiesler (1971) opted for the latter explanation. They reasoned that publishing an article was viewed as no great accomplishment by college females, i.e., a published article is not a sign of success for college females. However, for uneducated females the mere fact of a published article may be sufficient to attribute "success" to the author. Females may be viewed as underdogs. When an underdog succeeds against the odds he or she must be exceptional. An exceptional female may be viewed as favorably as a male.

In order to test the notion that success wipes out the tendency for females to depreciate females, Pheterson and colleagues (1971) told 120 college females that they were to participate in an experiment concerning "the artistic judgments of college students." Subjects were shown unknown, abstract, modern paintings via a slide projector. Several different paintings were shown to small groups of subjects. Each painting was attributed to a male artist for half of the subjects and to a female artist for the other half of the subjects. Each painting was described as merely an entry in an art contest for half of the subjects and as a contest winner for the other half of the subjects. In this manner the content of the paintings was held constant while the sex of the artists and the success of their artistic contributions were varied. These manipulations were accomplished by presentation of a written artist-profile with the slide presentation of each painting.

Following the presentation of each painting, subjects were asked the following questions about the artist who had supposedly created the painting: 1) how technically competent is the artist?, 2) how creative is the artist?, 3) what rating would be given to the overall quality and content of the artist's painting?, 4) how great is the emotional impact of the painting?, and 5) what artistic future does the artist have? Subjects answered the questions by responding to rating scales. Answers to the competence question and that of the artist's future produced significant results which confirmed the predictions.

In terms of both competence and artistic future, female subjects
were more favorable to male artists than female artists, but only for
"entry" condition. Female artists were seen as being as competent as
males and as having as bright an artistic future as males if their
paintings and those of the males were contest winners. Females evaluate other females less favorably than males except when those other
females are "successful." According to these results, females have to
be successful in order to be seen by other females as equal to males.
It's to say that only an extraordinary female is as good as a male.

WHATEVER HAPPENED TO THE TENDENCY FOR FEMALES TO DEPRECIATE FEMALES?

The experiment of Pheterson and colleagues (1971) must have been
completed some time in 1969, because it generally takes about two
years for a completed experiment to be written up, go through the
editorial process, and appear in a professional journal. Beginning with
the early 1970s, other people, including some of my students, began
to research the question of whether females depreciate females.

One of my students, Rebecca Wallies (1973), attempted to determine the generality of the finding that successful females are *not*
depreciated by other females. Her experiment was almost identical
to the original Goldberg (1968) experiment. Like Goldberg, Wallies
edited an article from a nursing journal (female profession), an article from an engineering journal (male profession), and an article
from a linguistics journal (neutral profession). Each college female
who performed in the experiment received a booklet containing one
of the articles which was attributed to either a person with a male
name or to a person with a female name, who was described as a
well-known, highly successful and respected member of his or her
profession, or who was only identified by profession. In this way,
profession type, sex of author, and success of author were varied. At
the end of the booklets, subjects found some rating scales for evaluating the authors and their articles.

Wallies found only one significant effect. In overall evaluation
of the authors and their articles, successful authors were evaluated
more favorably than unsuccessful authors. Wallies suggested that the
women's movement was more visible when she did her experiment—

1973—than when Goldberg or Pheterson and colleagues completed their experiments—about 1966 and 1969, respectively. Perhaps the impact of the movement had become significant by 1973 and eliminated the tendency for women to depreciate women.

Shortly after Wallies completed her study, Sarah Higgins (1973) attempted to test Wallies's assumption that the women's movement had influenced female evaluation of females. Higgins reasoned that if the women's movement had lessened the tendency for females to depreciate other females relative to males, the movement's effects should be stronger in college students than in older females. College students are often considered the vanguard of social movements. Also students are still in the process of forming their social philosophy whereas older people are more likely to have developed a static social philosophy thus precluding the incorporation of new and controversial ideas. Therefore, older females should have been less influenced by the women's movement than college females. If so, older females, but not college females, should show depreciation of females.

Higgins's reasoning may seem to be contradicted by the results of Pheterson (1969). Pheterson had found that older females failed to differentially evaluate male and female authors. However, there were several possible causes of Pheterson's failure to detect the depreciation effect. Pheterson's subjects were not only older than college students, but also they were uneducated. More important, Pheterson's subjects evaluated authors of articles which were strongly oriented toward females. In effect, Higgins reasoned that Pheterson's nil results were due to either the education level of her subjects or the female orientation of the articles (or both) rather than to the age of subjects.

Higgins repeated the Goldberg (1968) study with a few variations. The most important variation was that twenty-five of her subjects were female college students while twenty-two were middle-aged females who were college educated. Three art history articles were presented to subjects under the assumption that art history is a sexually neutral profession. Each subject read all three articles and evaluated the competence of the author of each article. Sometimes a given article was "authored" by "Joan Watts," sometimes by "James Burr" and sometimes by the sexually neutral name "Pat Albright." The names were randomly assigned to the articles within each subject's

booklet of three articles. In this way content of the articles was held
constant and sex of the author was varied.

Higgins's results are easy to describe. She didn't have any. Except for a marginally significant tendency for the older females to
evaluate *all* authors more leniently than college students, there were
no significant effects. For a second time the tendency for females to
depreciate females was not replicated.

Another of my students, Alice Robison (1972), adopted a different strategy for investigating female depreciation of females than
had been used by Goldberg (1968). She compared the credibility of
males and females as persuasive communicators. A credible communicator is trusted and considered "expert" by audience members
and, therefore, is more likely to be persuasive than a noncredible
communicator. Robison also employed subjects of both sexes.

Robison subjects were given a persuasive communication which
contained arguments against a "cultural truism." A cultural truism
(McGuire, 1969) is a statement which is known to most members
of a society and which is accepted as true without question. Because
people are not used to hearing attacks on cultural truisms, truisms are
particularly vulnerable to attack by persuasive arguments. Some
examples of cultural truisms are "penicillin is a wonder drug," "one
should brush one's teeth," and "forest fires are harmful and should
be avoided at all costs." Robison employed a communication which
attacked the "forest fires" truism. She used this approach because
maximum persuasive effects leading to change in beliefs and attitudes
tend to occur when truisms are attacked.

The communication against forest-fire prevention was based on
a collection of facts taken from wildlife and forestry magazines.
Among other arguments, the communication suggested that fires
destroy dense undergrowth beneath trees which prevent tree seeds
from sprouting and which smother vegetation needed for animal
nourishment. All subjects read this communication, but for some it
was attributed to "James A. Robinson," for others it was attributed
to "Elizabeth A. Robinson," and for still others it was attributed to
"Pat A. Robinson." After reading the communication subjects responded to various rating scales, most of them aimed at assessing the
question "how credible was the communicator?" These measures
were much like the "favorability of evaluation" measures used in the
other investigations discussed in this chapter, except that they were

more specific. The "credibility measures" assessed perceived trust-worthiness and expertise of communicators.

Once again male and female communicators were not differentially evaluated in terms of credibility by either male or female subjects. Strike-out number three—but hold the presses! Robison had also asked subjects how much they changed their opinions about forest-fire prevention as a result of reading the communication. She found a significant effect which can be summarized as follows: female subjects were more persuaded by male than female or neuter communicators, but male subjects were more persuaded by female than male or neuter communicators. Could it be that by the time Robison did her experiment the women's movement had "sunk in" for males but not for females, so that males were more attentive to the female communicator? It is impossible to say, but Robison's unexpected result was the only case out of three research projects in which my students were able to show differential reactions to males and females.

LI'L ABNER vs. DAISY MAE

My colleague Charles Potkay and his associates have also done research which is relevant to females' tendency to depreciate females. Many commentators have noted that bias against females permeates children's textbooks, story books, children's television and cartoons (e.g., Streicher, 1974). Potkay, along with Catherine Potkay, Greg Boynton, and Julie Klingbeil (1974), attempted to determine whether there is any concrete support for the contention that females are depicted less favorably than males in popular cartoons.

All of the cartoons were investigated which appeared in the newspaper of the town from which subjects were to be drawn. As a first step, some college males and females made familiarity ratings of all of the characters which appeared with regularity in the cartoons. The twenty most familiar characters were selected for use in the main study. The "top twenty" included Li'l Abner, Daisy Mae, Blondie, Mr. Dithers, Linus, Sluggo, Nancy, Beetle Bailey, and Miss Blip. Half of the selected characters were male and half were female.

A representative pose was selected for each character and a picture of each character was made. The pictures were developed as slides for the presentation of characters to subjects. Sixty male and female college students were shown the slides and asked to describe each character using adjectives of their own choosing. They were to think of how each character generally was depicted in its cartoon, rather than how it happened to be depicted in the slide, and generate five adjectives to describe the character. The usual Adjective Generation Technique (AGT) method was used to score the favorability of the adjectives that subjects generated (see chapter on racism).

Results showed that male and female subjects made very similar favorability ratings of cartoon characters. Both male and female subjects showed a very significant tendency to see female characters in a *more* favorable light than male characters. The tendency to depreciate females relative to males was reversed.

Potkay and another associate, Matt Merrens (1975), also were interested in possible bias against females in tests used by psychologists and psychiatrists for assessing the psychological state of individuals. Specifically they wished to determine whether the Thematic Apperception Test (TAT) was biased against women. The TAT is one of many "projective" tests used by clinical psychologists and psychiatrists. In a projective test some ambiguous stimuli (pictures, words, ink blots) are presented to clients or patients who are asked to describe what they see. Because the stimuli have no specific interpretation, it is assumed that clients will project their own feelings, dispositions and thoughts into the stimuli as a way of making interpretations. In the case of the TAT, ambiguous pictures of males and females are shown to clients. For example, included in the test are pictures of a boy with a violin, a man working a field, a man clinging to a rope, a woman holding a man, a girl with a doll, and a woman sitting on a sofa.

Equal numbers of male and female college students served as subjects in five separate experiments, each experiment focusing on a different kind of rating of the male and female figures in the TAT pictures. Each subject performed in only one experiment. TAT pictures were projected onto a screen and each TAT figure was rated by each subject on one of the five measures. Overall, there were seventeen male and seventeen female figures in the TAT pictures.

One of the five measures involved ratings on "cultural favorability." For this measure subjects were asked to rate the favorability of each figure relative to "people living in our society today." On a "mental health" measure subjects were to rate the degree to which they saw each figure as mentally healthy. An "intelligence" measure concerned how intelligent each figure seemed to subjects. An "achievement" measure entailed ratings of the achievement status (perceived success) of each figure. Finally, an "identification" measure involved ratings of "the degree to which [each] figure represents yourself."

The results obtained for the achievement measure will likely seem familiar to the reader. There were nil results on achievement. Male and female subjects rated male and female TAT figures the same. On the mental health measure, both male and female subjects rated female figures as more mentally healthy. There was a difference between ratings of male and female subjects on the cultural favorability measure. Only female subjects rated female figures significantly more favorably than male figures. Male subjects' ratings were in the same direction, but not significant. Male and female subjects disagreed on the intelligence measure also. Male subjects saw no difference between male and female figures on intelligence. However, female subjects rated female figures as higher in intelligence.

Finally, the identification results showed that male subjects identified with male figures and female subjects identified with female figures. It was not surprising to find that males saw themselves as masculine and females saw themselves as feminine. However, another aspect of the identification findings was very interesting. Males were more closely identified with male figures than females were identified with female figures. It may be that females are more flexible in choosing a source of identification than are males. However, an alternative interpretation is possible: it may be that females are more desirous of being the opposite sex than are males. In our society, maleness may be so valued relative to femaleness that, at least to some degree, everyone wants to be male.

Thus far Potkay and his associates have produced results which are consistent with those produced by my student researchers. We have failed to find that females depreciate females. In our research, almost without exception, either there was no difference in evaluations of males and females or females were evaluated more positively than males. Since all the studies by Potkay and his associates and by my student researchers were done at Western Illinois University, it is possible that our results are peculiar to the student population at that university. Perhaps we have a student population that is more liberal in its view of females than students at other universities or than the population in general. However, the opposite seems true. Students at Western Illinois seem more representative of the general population than students elsewhere and thus less liberal in general than students elsewhere. For example, students at Western voted for Nixon in the 1972 election in about the same proportion as the general population whereas students at most universities voted for Mc-Govern. I have other data to suggest that Western students are more like the general population than the U.S. student population. Nonetheless, it is important to know whether what we have found at our Midwestern university has been replicated by other researchers working under different conditions at other universities located in other parts of the country. Let's see what others have found.

EVEN GOLDBERG COULDN'T

Alice Gold completed her doctoral dissertation at a well-known Eastern school in 1972, in which one of her two experiments closely replicated the original Goldberg (1968) experiment. Forty-eight college males and forty-eight college females evaluated four articles in the first experiment. Half of the articles were "authored" by males and half were "authored" by females. Subjects evaluated the author of each article. One of several groups of female subjects did evaluate the male authors more favorably, but the other groups didn't favor one sex over the other. All of the groups of male subjects evaluated the female authors *more* favorably than the male authors. These results paralleled Robison's (1972) opinion change results.

In a second experiment, Gold (1972) essentially did the same experiment as was done by Wallies (1973). Again male and female college students read articles "authored" by males and females. Each author was described as a college freshman (low-skill level) or a scholar (high-skill level) whose article had been a contest winner (success) or a non-winner (no success). Gold's results were similar to those reported by Wallies. There was little evidence of bias against women by either male or female subjects. Regardless of the sex of the authors, contest winners were favored over non-winners.

Hanna Levenson, Brent Burford, Bobbie Bonno, and Loren Davis (1975) did some replications of the Goldberg (1968) study at two different universities in Texas. In a first experiment they replicated Goldberg exactly, except that they employed male as well as female subjects. They used the same kinds of articles as Goldberg: law and city planning (male professions), dietetics and elementary school teaching (female professions), art history and linguistics (neutral professions). As in Goldberg (1968) each subject read each of the six articles. In each subject's booklet of articles, three randomly chosen articles were "authored" by males and three randomly chosen articles were "authored" by females. Levenson and colleagues asked their subjects approximately the same questions about authors as had been asked by Goldberg (1968). Their results, however, were similar to those reported by my students: sex of subject and sex of author made no difference in evaluations. There was a nonsignificant trend, but it was opposite to that expected by the notion of depreciation of females. Females were rated slightly more favorably than males.

In the second experiment, Levenson and colleagues (1975) used a slight variation of the Goldberg (1968) method. Male and female college students were given a task which was more familiar to them than reading professional articles. All subjects were given an essay answer to a "political science quiz question." A grade of A, B, C, D, or F was to be assigned to the "essay answer." For half of the subjects the essay was "authored" by John Thompson and for half it was "authored" by Joan Thompson. Only one significant finding was reported. For female subjects, Joan's essay was given a higher grade than John's.

To top it all, Goldberg and his colleagues replicated the Goldberg (1968) study and reported the results in a paper which was published during 1974. Donna Chobot, Goldberg, Linda Abramson and Paul Abramson (1974) used the same procedure as had been used by Goldberg in his original study. The only differences were that Chobot and colleagues used both female and male subjects and they employed neutral articles. Guess what! They found that sex of subjects and sex of authors made no difference.

Chobot and colleagues do cite a paper which supposedly produced evidence of depreciation of females. However, close examination of the paper reveals little or no support for depreciation of females. The paper in question, by Harriet Mischel (1974), reported several experiments two of which were directly relevant to depreciation of females as originally studied by Goldberg and his colleagues. One experiment was a replication of Goldberg (1968), the only difference being that male and female high school and college students from California were employed as subjects. Mischel did find a tendency for subjects to favor male authors for articles about male professions and female authors for articles about female professions. However, this result was true only for college students. Further, when a separate analysis was done for each article, there were no significant results at all for two of the four articles used in the experiment. Mischel also attempted to replicate Goldberg (1968) in Israel. Although she predicted significant results confirming depreciation of females, none were found. Since the mid to late 1960s when Goldberg and his colleagues did their research there just hasn't seemed to be any unequivocal evidence for depreciation of females by females or males. What happened?

WHAT HATH THE WOMEN'S MOVEMENT WROUGHT?

I suppose that the first thing that comes to mind when one contemplates the many failures to replicate the results of Goldberg and his colleagues is to question whether their results were genuine. Perhaps Goldberg and his colleagues were dealing with a peculiar population of subjects. Perhaps something incidental in Goldberg's instructions to his subjects communicated that antifemale responses were expected (see chapter on hypnotism). Or perhaps their results occurred by chance.

While these possibilities are legitimate, I don't accept them as an explanation of the failure to replicate the tendency for females to depreciate females. I accept the results of Goldberg and his colleagues as genuine. There just are too many reasons to believe that the mark of oppression is self-depreciation. If black Americans and Jewish persons suffer self-depreciation as a result of oppression, shouldn't females also? Females are assigned a set of characteristics which are mostly devalued in our society. Females are limited to only a few professions in terms of our society's expectations of them. Females are in fact underrepresented in almost every prestigious sphere of

American life (Romero, 1969). Isn't this enough to expect self-depreciation? I think so.

But if the female depreciation of females is genuine, why did it disappear during the early 1970s? An obvious possibility is that the women's movement which began to develop during the 1960s became strong enough to have an impact on individuals during the early 1970s. The women's movement may have influenced females and males so that they no longer express negative evaluations of females relative to males. Given that the women's movement has had an influence, the question still remains as to what form the influence has taken.

Does the coincidence of the maturation of the women's movement and the disappearance of depreciatory statements directed toward females mean that people no longer harbor any form of sex bias? Think back on the lifetime of training that you have received concerning what it is to be male and what it is to be female. Doesn't this training go as far back in time as you can remember? Like any training that is strongly introduced early in life, the training to regard males and females in distinctly different ways has become second nature to almost all of us. Further, the ways we have been trained to regard males and females strongly favor males. Can this profound training be reversed by the existence of a social movement of a few years' duration? It doesn't seem possible.

In fact, the reversal of deeply ingrained antiblack sentiments did not occur as a result of the civil rights movement of the 1960s. As discussed in the racism chapter, the tendency to show no racial discrimination, and, particularly, the tendency for whites to show more favorability to blacks than to whites seemed more an attempt by whites to appear egalitarian rather than an indication that antiblack sentiment had been eliminated or reversed. Perhaps something analogous has occurred as a result of the maturity and popularization of the women's movement. Perhaps it no longer is "in" to express negative evaluations of females. Being sexist may have been "cool" during the 1950s, but it may now be unfashionable. In fact, these days, if one is really "with it" one can show that one is in tune with the times by occasionally showing more favorability to females than to males. In other words, the women's movement may have generated lip service to sexual equality rather than genuine change in the deeply ingrained tendency for people to regard females as lesser.

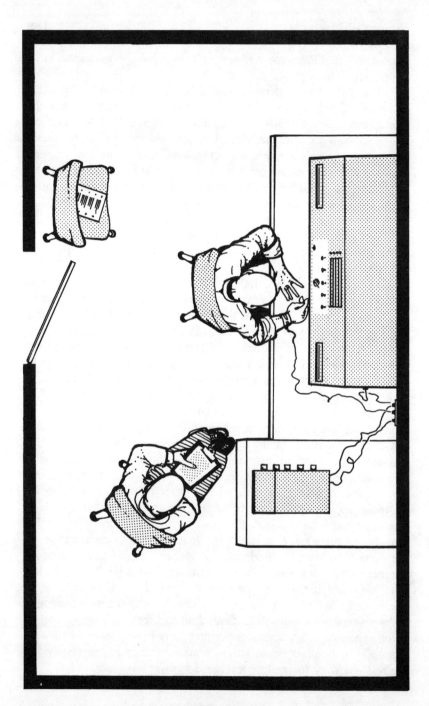

HOOKING WOMEN UP TO THE BOGUS PIPELINE

If the recent tendency for females to be as favorable or more favorable to females than they are to males is superficial or lip service to women's liberation, we should observe public expressions of sexual equality by women, but private expressions of inequality. Recall from the chapter on racism that private expressions are those made to self or intimates in private, while public expressions are those made to strangers or acquaintances in public. Recall also that if there is a discrepancy between public and private expressions, it is assumed that the public expressions are merely for the purpose of appearing fair-minded. Karen Hough and I attempted to determine whether women's public expressions of sexual equality would give way to private expressions favoring males.

Because Hough and Allen (1975) used the same Bogus Pipeline procedure described in the chapter on racism, only a brief reiteration is needed here. One-third of our female college students were brought to the U-shaped hallway of small rooms and first asked to complete the questionnaire of innocuous items. Each subject then was led through the control room and shown the elaborate EMG equipment. After arriving at the experimental room, each subject was told of the prowess of the EMG. The "equipment adjustment" phase then ensued during which each subject was hooked up to the EMG via an electrode. In this phase each subject held the dial on the subject console and concentrated on each of the innocuous items that they had completed previously. Of course, the same answers previously given by each subject were fed back through the EMG feedback console. This was possible because a collaborator had copied each subject's previous responses to the innocuous items. Again subjects were notably startled at the "accuracy" of the EMG and it was assumed that they were convinced that the EMG could "read their true beliefs" (private expressions).

During the main part of the experiment, each subject remained hooked up to the EMG, but the feedback console was turned to the wall so that it could be seen only by the experimenter. Subjects turned the dial to indicate evaluations of male and female targets. Since the experimenter could see both the dial-turning responses and EMG feedback and later would examine the correspondence of the two with the subject, the subject was under pressure to make what amounted to private expressions with the dial turning responses. Thus dial-turning responses were defined as the private expressions of evaluations of male and female targets.

Another third of our college female subjects served in the regular rating condition. Here everything was the same as described above except that there was no reference to the "super lie detector," the electrode was hidden and the feedback console was turned to the wall throughout the procedure. A third condition also was included in which the rating procedures to be described below were instituted in questionnaire form. The remaining third of our subjects served in this condition.

In all conditions, we had subjects rate the capability of a typical male and a typical female to perform in each of twenty-five common professions. The professions were classified as masculine, feminine, or neutral. A pilot study had shown that these three sets of professions fell at appropriate points along the masculine-feminine continuum. Example masculine professions were commercial airplane pilot, doctor, and construction worker. Example feminine professions were florist, librarian, and nurse. Example neutral professions were high school teacher, photographer and singer.

Regardless of the condition in which subjects performed, for each profession subjects were asked to imagine a typical male and female and then judge how well he and she would perform in the professional context. Professions were listed in alphabetical order, and the order of rating the capability of "male" and "female" was randomized. Subjects were asked to make no assumptions about the training or qualifications of the typical male or female being rated. Also, subjects were asked not to make assumptions of the reactions of coworkers to the typical males and females.

For the questionnaire condition we predicted either no difference in competency evaluations of males and females or that females would be favored. This prediction was made because questionnaires are assumed to measure public expressions and we assumed that public expressions about females would be egalitarian. For the regular rating condition we predicted that greater favorability would be shown toward females than males by our college female subjects. Our reasoning was that the regular rating condition essentially was the same as a questionnaire condition and that the presence of a female experimenter (Karen) who would be watching the responses as these occurred would sensitize our subjects to "being in tune with the women's movement." In a sense we expected that female subjects would "bend over backwards" to show the female experimenter that they favored females. For the Bogus Pipeline condition where private expressions are assumed to occur, we expected that female subjects would show greater favorability to males. This result would indicate that the tendency for females to depreciate females still was present despite public expressions to the contrary.

The prediction for the questionnaire condition was confirmed. Regardless of professional category, female subjects rated females more favorably than males. The "typical female" was rated as being more capable in the professions than the "typical male." Unfortunately the other predictions were not confirmed. Although males were rated as more capable than females in *both* the Bogus Pipeline and regular rating conditions, the differences were trivial and non-significant.

I now believe that whenever one reveals that he or she is interested in assessing "sex prejudice" in some sense or another, individuals are very careful to show no prejudice. In all conditions of the present study the words "male" and "female" were used repeatedly. Subjects must have believed that we were interested in comparing males and females with the intent of drawing conclusions concerning which sex is "better." In the questionnaire condition this cuing as to our interest probably spurred subjects to put on a show of sexual egalitarianism. After all, marks on a questionnaire provide no clue as to the motivation behind the marks.

However, in the Bogus Pipeline and regular rating conditions all of the fancy equipment, the elaborate procedure along with the vague statement of purpose may have alarmed and confused subjects. Probably they really didn't know what our purpose was, but it must have been clear to them that a comparison of the sexes was in some way related to our purpose. Being unsure of our purpose, but knowing that a comparison of the sexes was being made, subjects may have opted for the safest response: rate all targets the same, thus being sure to reveal no bias at all.

The reader should note the difference between the conditions which prevailed in this study and those which prevailed in the Allen (1975) Bogus Pipeline Study. In Allen (1975) subjects probably were not alarmed and confused. My experimenters told these subjects to do something that was probably quite familiar to them: to rate some public figures. Most people are aware that public figures are periodically evaluated in national public opinion polls. Furthermore, in that study subjects were probably not aware that we were interested in differences in reactions to blacks and whites. The list of public figures that was read to subjects contained persons who varied not only in race, but also in sphere of fame, life-style, ideology, attractiveness, sex, and in other less apparent ways. Blacks also constituted a minority of persons on the list.

Partly in view of the data of the Hough and Allen (1975) experiment, I now believe that sexism is so "out of fashion" that individuals, especially college students, will almost always show no bias when they know a sex comparison is being made. Alternatively, they may even show a bias in favor of females if they perceive (1) that it will be well-received, (2) will place them in a favorable light, and (3) if they are sure that they cannot be accused of distortion. It seems that depreciation of females has become largely an underground phenomenon. The only way to detect it may be to employ very subtle methods so that subjects are not alerted to an experimenter's interest in comparing the sexes. I turn next to the use of such subtle methods.

SOME INDIRECT EVIDENCE THAT SUBTLE METHODS REVEAL BIAS AGAINST WOMEN

Although research by Kay Deaux is only indirectly related to the line of research initiated by Goldberg, she has conducted some studies that revealed bias against women. The probable reason why she has had some success in demonstrating bias against women where others have experienced mostly failure is that she employed subtle methods of research in examining public expressions.

One subtle aspect of the methods used by Deaux was that her subjects evaluated only a male or a female target person, rather than both. Most of the studies done by Goldberg and by those who have replicated his research entailed having subjects evaluate both male and female targets. Being exposed to targets of both sexes may have cued subjects that the experimenter was interested in comparing the sexes.

A second aspect of the subtle methods used by Deaux was that her technique for evaluating targets made it difficult for subjects to determine the experimenter's purpose and made it difficult for subjects to distort their evaluations so as to look fair-minded. In this way the evaluation techniques used by Deaux and her colleagues were like the AGT (see the chapter on racism).

In a study done by Deaux and Janet Taynor (1973), male and female college students evaluated either a male or a female target. Evaluations were based on audiotape recordings of interviews with target persons who supposedly were being considered for a "scholarship abroad." Some subjects heard an interview with a male target who showed high competence, while other subjects heard an interview with a female target who showed high competence. Still other subjects heard either a low-competent male or a low-competent female. After hearing the interview, each subject evaluated his or her target person on intelligence and general competence.

Results showed that both male and female subjects regarded the high-competent male target as more intelligent and competent than the high-competent female target. However, for low-competent targets, the results showed bias in favor of females. Low-competent females were seen as more intelligent and competent than low competent males.

Deaux and Tim Emswiller (1974) did another experiment which entailed having male and female college students evaluate the performance of target persons on a "perceptual discrimination" task. Small groups of subjects were assembled for each experimental session. They were told that half of them would evaluate the remaining subjects on the perceptual discrimination task. Actually, all subjects were evaluators. This ruse was accomplished by placing each subject in an isolation booth, presenting him or her with an audiotape recording, and leading each subject to believe that he or she was hearing another subject actually performing on the discrimination task.

The perceptual discrimination task that subjects "overheard" involved presenting the target with a list of objects such as "mop" or "wrench." For each consecutive object on the list, the target was asked to look at a complex picture and determine whether the object was embedded in the picture. Each subject was provided with a score sheet which indicated the correct response for each object and picture. In this way the subject could tell how the supposed "other subject" was doing on the task. Subjects were told in advance that the average person made 12.3 correct responses out of 25. All targets made 16 correct responses out of 25. Thus subjects were led to believe that the target they overheard had performed well.

Each subject overheard either a male or a female target who was to identify either male oriented objects (e.g., wrench) or female oriented objects (e.g., mop). Targets were evaluated on several scales. One of them was a skill-luck scale. A word implying "Skill" was written at one end of the scale and "Luck" was written at the other end (see the Introduction). A mark near the "Luck" end of the scale indicated that the subject thought that the target was lucky to perform so well. A mark near the "Skill" end of the scale indicated that the subject thought that the target performed so well because he or she was skilled. Other scales measured general performance, general intelligence, and expectations of the subjects about their own performance an a similar task.

On the Skill-Luck scale results also showed that good performance by male targets identifying male-oriented objects was attributed to skill, while the same good performance by female targets identifying the same male-oriented objects was attributed to luck. For the female-oriented objects Skill-Luck attributions to male and female targets did not differ.

On the "expectations about own performance" measure, male subjects expected to do better than did female subjects. However, on the general performance measure, subjects regardless of sex saw no significant difference in the performances of male and female targets. Also, on the general intelligence scale, there was no significant difference between the intelligence evaluations given male and female targets by either male or female subjects.

In still another experiment, Deaux, Leonard White, and Elizabeth Farris (1975) had male and female college students play an electronic dart-throwing game. Some subjects performed in a "skill game" condition. These subjects were told that dart-throwing performance was determined by skill. Other subjects were told that luck determined dart-throwing performance. These subjects performed in the "luck game" condition. Some subjects were able to choose the "luck game" or the "skill game," while other subjects were randomly assigned to either the "luck game" or the "skill game." The actual dart-throwing results were rigged so that male and female subjects performed equally well, overall.

When subjects were allowed to choose either the "luck game" or the "skill game," male subjects chose the "skill game" over the "luck game" by a four to one margin. Female subjects chose the "luck game" over the "skill game" by a two to one margin. The remainder of the results reported by Deaux and her colleagues pertained only to subjects who had no choice in whether they played the skill or the luck game. Before they tried their hand at electronic dart throwing, all of these subjects were asked to indicate how well they expected to perform in the "game" to which they were assigned. Results showed that male subjects anticipated a better performance than did female subjects. However, a further analysis indicated that this sex difference in performance expectations held only for the "skill game" condition.

Subjects were allowed to "throw the darts" as many times as they wanted. The number of tries at dart throwing attempted by a subject was a measure of that subject's persistence at his or her assigned "game." Male subjects were more persistent at the "skill game" than female subjects, and female subjects were more persistent at the "luck game" than male subjects. However, when subjects were asked to evaluate how well they did at dart throwing, male and female subjects did not differ significantly in their evaluations. Female subjects saw themselves as performing as well as male subjects.

In summary, Deaux's research indicates the following: 1) given that male and female targets perform well and equally so, males are seen as more competent and skillful, 2) males have more confidence in themselves in that they expect to perform better than females, 3) females prefer and persist at "luck games" whereas males prefer and persist at "skill games." The latter could be interpreted to mean that females assume that they lack skills and depend on luck. However, some of Deaux's findings don't appear to be consistent with the notion that females as well as males depreciate females. Apparently even more subtle research methods may be needed to consistently uncover depreciation of females.

EXPRESSIONS TO FRIENDS AND STRANGERS

One of my students, Melissa Roberts (1977), attempted to develop a more subtle method than the methods that had been used by previous researchers. Part of the method that she devised was suggested by the Bogus Pipeline. In order to exploit the ability of the Bogus Pipeline to reveal "private expressions" while avoiding its tendency to arouse apprehension, she used an adaptation of the Bogus Pipeline, without the plumbing. Instead of using elaborate but bogus electrical equipment, she obtained private expressions of subjects by employing close friends of subjects as collaborators.

Twelve male and fourteen female college students volunteered to serve as collaborators. These people were not privy to the purpose of the study and were not compensated for their services. Each collaborator chose a close friend to be a subject. The only restriction on choices was that collaborators had to choose friends of their own sex. Thus fourteen female and twelve male subjects participated in the experiment.

To obtain private expressions, collaborators were told to engage subjects in a conversation about the "typical male" or the "typical female" in our society today. Half of the student subjects were assigned to the typical female condition and half to the typical male condition. To make the conversations seem spontaneous, collaborators said that their psychology instructor had lectured that day on the role of "females in our society" (or "males in our society") and that "it has caused me to consider how I really feel." Collaborators went on to say that a psychology classroom discussion on the same subject was to take place at the next class meeting and that he or she was unsure "about my own feelings." "What do you think?" was then asked of the subject. At this point the subject was encouraged to freely express his or her own feelings about the typical male or the typical female. The collaborators jotted down some notes under the guise of preparing themselves for the next day's classroom discussion. Actually each collaborator only recorded the adjectives that the subject used to describe the typical male or the typical female. In other words the Adjective Generation Technique (AGT) was used once again so that the adjectives could be scored for favorability of expressions directed toward males or females (see the chapter on racism).

The AGT seems particularly appropriate for this purpose because of its subtlety. With the AGT subjects are not provided with rating scale anchors such as "good-bad" or "attractive-unattractive." Therefore, subjects are in the dark as to whether the adjectives are to be scored on "favorability" or some other dimension such as "anxiety," "racial prejudice," "intelligence," "admiration," "masculinity-feminity," or "acceptance as a friend." In fact, subjects have no way of knowing *whether* the adjectives are to be scored in some way or simply examined by the researcher without being scored.

One week before or one week after subjects conversed with collaborators, each subject received a telephone call from a stranger for the purpose of obtaining public expressions. The caller indicated that a survey was being conducted in order to compare two different methods of assessing "how people feel and think about a number of social phenomena." One method was like the bipolar adjective scales described in the Introduction, while the other method was the AGT. First, subjects were to make expressions about organized religion, competitive sports, and marriage, using the bipolar adjective method, and then they were asked to make expressions about factory workers, marijuana, and females (or males) in our society using the AGT. Finally, subjects were asked some questions about the two methods. Of course, the only information of interest was the AGT expressions about males or females. All of the other questions were used simply to disguise the purpose of the call.

Approximately two months after subjects had given their public and private expressions, they received a final telephone call. The caller indicated that he or she was working for the experimenters and was calling to provide them with details concerning the experiment. A thorough debriefing followed as well as an offer to provide subjects with a description of results when analysis of the data was completed.

It was expected that subjects' public expressions about the typical male and about the typical female would be equally favorable or the typical female would be regarded more favorably. However, it was expected that subject's private expressions would reflect greater favorability for the typical male. Thus it was expected that subjects who were asked to describe the typical female would make expressions at a lower favorability level in the private condition than in the public condition. On the other hand subjects who were asked to describe the typical male were expected to make expressions at the same level of favorability in the public and private conditions. These outcomes were expected to be shown by both male and female subjects.

Results were as predicted. Regardless of sex of subject, the typical female was rated at the same level of favorability as the typical male in the public condition. Also, in the private condition, regardless of sex of subject, the typical male was described significantly more favorably than the typical female. Subjects who described the typical female made significantly less favorable expressions in the private condition than in the public condition, but their counterparts who described the typical male made expressions at the same favorability level in the two conditions.

At last some evidence that depreciation of females is an underground phenomenon! Both male and female subjects were less favorable to females in a private conversation with a close friend than they were when they publicly discussed females with a stranger. Thus the public display of equality must have been for "show," because it lapsed into a display of inequality in private.

HAS THE MARK OF OPPRESSION BEEN REMOVED?

There is an idea implicit in all that has been considered above. It is that the tendency for females to show self-depreciation and for males to depreciate females has not been eliminated in spite of the coming of age of the women's movement. In other words I have argued that the answer to the question which was posed as the title of this chapter is negative. I have contended that the women's movement has not erased the mark of oppression from the female psyche, at least not yet. The women's movement has limited "depreciation of females" to private expressions instead of causing it to be eliminated.

Such a conclusion may sound pessimistic. I wish to correct that possible impression. That females (and males) are merely giving lip service to sexual equality is not all bad. Lip service to equality is better than the open derogation that was typical prior to this decade. Further, lip service eventually can lead to positive effects. It is known that mouthing a point of view that one doesn't accept (i.e., one doesn't say the same thing in private) eventually can lead to acceptance (McGuire, 1969). If people continue to give lip service to sexual equality, in time they may come to believe themselves. The women's movement may not have succeeded in generating positive perceptions of females in the past, but it may succeed in the future.

WHAT FUTURE FOR FEMALES?

Even if the image of females really has not changed as a result of ten years of public debate over the status of females, there have been some important and positive practical changes. Almost on a daily basis, women are, so to speak, "cracking career barriers": finding positions in professions or life pursuits which were once considered for men only. Each time a woman gets a position in a setting which was once an exclusively male domain, she increases the likelihood that other women who follow her will be able to get a similar position. And each time a woman is observed succeeding in a previously "men only" setting, the expectations of the observers change a little so that the next woman to try to function in that setting may find the path to success easier. Babe Zaharias was the first notable woman golfer. After Babe there were many women golfers of note. Her struggles to succeed made it easier for the women who followed in her footsteps.

Success breeds success and the increasing success that females are having in previously all-male domains virtually guarantees that parity of the sexes eventually will become a reality. It likely will not happen in our lifetime and there will be regressions, but it will happen. With each passing year it will be more and more true that males and females will be regarded as equals in terms of general capability.

Does sexual equality mean that males and females will become the same and that all differences will disappear? Will we no longer be able to distinguish between the sexes as some people fear? If the answers to these questions were affirmative, there might be cause for many individuals to despair. "Vive la différence" is a positive statement to most individuals.

Well, don't worry, if you are one of those who are fearful that the sexes will become almost indistinguishable. There are certain biological differences between males and females which cannot be denied. These biological differences as well as some socially determined differences between males and females virtually guarantee that the sexes will always be different in some ways. What we can look forward to in the future is not that sex differences will disappear. Rather we may expect that in the future people will no longer assume that the observation of a sex difference on some psychological, physical, or social dimension means necessarily that one sex must be regarded as "superior" to the other sex on that dimension. People can be different from one another without the necessity of some being regarded as "superior" to others.

WHAT FUTURE FOR MALES?

Will the gains of females be the losses of males? A yes answer is justified to some degree. Males will have to give up at least some of the powers and privileges that they have traditionally enjoyed. Men will face stronger competition for jobs which, in good times, were to be had for the asking. Men may have to take more direct responsibility for rearing and caring for children and for running their household. Also, there could be some temporary loss of self-esteem. Men will no longer be able to claim that they alone are the "breadwinners" and "heads" of their house. It will no longer be *his* house and *his* car and so forth.

But the news is not all bad by any means. If men have had most of the power, they also have had most of the accompanying responsibility. If men have been responsible for "winning most of the bread" and for making most of the family decisions, they have suffered most of the stress that accompanies the assumption of these responsibilities. If men have claimed the house and the car, they have had to tolerate the stress which comes with the responsibility for acquiring them. Bearing heavy responsibility may have its rewards, but it also has its drawbacks. Sharing some of the responsibility with women means that some of the male burden is lifted.

The male social role is becoming more and more difficult to play because of the increased complexity of modern life. It is difficult to be stoic in the face of crisis when modern life provides an ever increasing number of crises. It is difficult to be willing "to die for one's country" when wars are becoming more and more frequent and the weapons of war more and more diabolical. It is difficult to play the "success game" when it seems that once one reaches the next highest rung on the ladder of success, a still higher rung beckons. With equality of the sexes will come the expectation that females will share in playing some of the more difficult parts of what has traditionally been the male role. If females share in coping with crises, providing physical security, and obtaining "success," the expectations directed toward males will be less demanding. Life will be easier and less stressful for them.

Of course, males will begin to play some of the more difficult parts of the female role, such as child care. Males will very likely discover that many aspects of the female role can be very rewarding. For example, if men begin to participate more significantly in child care, they may enjoy the experience. At the same time they may help to relieve the burden of almost total responsibility for child care that has traditionally been borne by women.

References

Introduction

Aronson, E., & Carlsmith, J. Cognitive consequences of forced compliance. *Journal of Abnormal and Social Psychology*, 1963, *66*, 584–88.

Cohen, A. R. An experiment on small rewards for discrepant compliance and attitude change. In J. Brehm and A. R. Cohen, *Explorations in Cognitive Dissonance*. New York: John Wiley and Sons, 1962.

Festinger, L. *A theory of cognitive dissonance*. Stanford: Stanford Univ. Press, 1957.

Festinger, L., & Carlsmith, J. Cognitive consequences of forced compliance. *Journal of Abnormal and Social Psychology*, 1959, *58*, 203–210.

Gibson, J. J., Purdy, J., & Lawrence, L. A method of controlling stimulation for the study of space perception: the optical tunnel. *Journal of Experimental Psychology*, 1955, *50*, 1–14.

Leventhal, H., Singer, R. P., & Jones, S. Effect of fear and specificity of recommendation upon attitudes and behavior. *Journal of Personality and Social Psychology*, 1965, *2*, 20–29.

Linder, D. E., Cooper, J., & Jones, E. E. Decision freedom as a determinant of the role of incentive magnitude in attitude change. *Journal of Personality and Social Psychology*, 1967, *6*, 245–254.

McGuire, W. J. The nature of attitudes and attitude change. In G. Lind-
    zey and E. Aronson (Eds.), *The Handbook of Social Psychology*
    (Vol. 3, 2nd ed.), pp. 136–314. Reading, Mass: Addison-Wesley,
    1969.

1   Hypnotism

Allport, G. W. The historical background of modern social psychology.
    In G. Lindzey (Ed.), *The Handbook of Social Psychology*, Vol. 1.
    New York: Addison-Wesley, 1954, 3–56.
Barber, T. X. *Hypnosis: a scientific approach*. New York: Van Nostrand
    Reinhold Co., 1969.
Barber, T. X. Who believes in hypnosis? *Psychology Today*, July 1970,
    20.
Barber, T. X., & Calverley, D. S. The relative effectiveness of task moti-
    vating instructions and trance induction procedure in the production
    of "hypnotic-like" behaviors. *Journal of Nervous and Mental Dis-
    orders*, 1963, *137*, 107–116.
Barber, T. X., & Calverley, D. S. Effect of *E*'s tone of voice on "hypnotic-
    like" suggestibility. *Psychological Reports*, 1964a, *15*, 139–144.
Barber T. X., & Calverley, D. S. The definition of the situation as a vari-
    able affecting "hypnotic-like" suggestibility. *Journal of Clinical Psy-
    chology*, 1964b, *20*, 438–440.
Barber, T. X., & Calverley, D. S. Experimental studies in hypnotic behav-
    ior: Suggested deafness evaluated by delayed auditory feedback.
    British Journal of Psychology, 1964c, *55*, 439–446.
Barber, T. X., & Calverley, D. S. Empirical evidence for a theory of "hyp-
    notic" behavior: Effects of suggestibility of five variables typically
    included in hypnotic induction procedures. *Journal of Consulting
    Psychology*, 1965, *29*, 98–107.
Boring, E. G. *A history of experimental psychology*. New York: Apple-
    ton-Century-Crofts, 1957.
Chaves, J. F., & Barber, T. X. Hypnotic procedures and surgery: A criti-
    cal analysis with applications to "acupuncture analgesia." *The
    American Journal of Clinical Hypnosis*, 1976, *18*, 217–236.
Levitt, E. E., & Overly, T. M. A comparison of the performance of hyp-
    notic subjects and simulators on a variety of measures: A pilot
    study. *The International Journal of Clinical and Experimental Hyp-
    nosis*, 1971, *19*, 234–242.
McDonald, R. M., & Smith, J. R. Trance logic in tranceable and simulat-
    ing subjects. *The International Journal of Clinical and Experimental
    Hypnosis*, 1975, *23*, 80–89.
Orne, M. T. The simulation of hypnosis: Why, how and what it means.
    The International Journal of Clinical and Experimental Hypnosis,
    1971, *19*, 183–210.
Orne, M. T., & Evans, F. J. Social control in the psychological experi-
    ment: Antisocial behavior and hypnosis. *Journal of Personality and
    Social Psychology*, 1965, *1*, 189–200.

Patten, E. F. Does post-hypnotic amnesia apply to practice effects? *Journal of General Psychology*, 1932, *7*, 196–201.

Pattie, F. A. A report of attempts to produce uniocular blindness by hypnotic suggestion. *British Journal of Medical Psychology*, 1935, 230–241.

Sarbin, T. R., & Farberow, N. L. Contributions to role-taking theory: A clinical study of self and role. *Journal of Abnormal and Social Psychology*, 1952, *47*, 117–125.

Wickramasekera, I. Effects of "hypnosis" and task motivational instructions in attempting to influence "voluntary" self-deprivation of money. *Journal of Personality and Social Psychology*, 1971, *19*, 311–314.

FILM

Upjohn Company. Hypnosis as Sole Anesthesia for Cesarean Section. Kalamazoo, Mich.

2 Obedience

Cox, J. Compellingness of commands, authoritarianism, and obedience to authority. Unpublished paper, Western Illinois University, 1971.

Elms, A., & Milgram, S. Personality characteristics associated with obedience and defiance toward authoritative command. *Journal of Experimental Research in Personality*, 1966, *1*, 282–289.

Kelman, H., & Lawrence, L. American response to the trial of Lt. Calley. *Psychology Today*, 1972, *6*, 41.

Kilham, W., & Mann, L. Level of destructive obedience as a function of transmitter and executant roles in the Milgram obedience paradigm. *Journal of Personality and Social Psychology*, 1974, *29*, 696–702.

Meyer, P. If Hitler asked you to electrocute a stranger, would you? *Esquire*, February, 1970.

Milgram, S. Some conditions of obedience and disobedience to authority. *Human Relations*, 1965, *18*, 57–76.

Milgram, S. *Obedience to authority*. New York: Harper & Row, 1974.

Sheridan C. L., & King, R. G. Obedience to authority with an authentic victim. Paper presented at the American Psychological Association convention, 1972.

Smith, G. Sex and obedience to authority. Unpublished paper, Western Illinois University, 1973.

West, S. G., Gunn, S. P., & Chernicky, P. Ubiquitous Watergate: An attributional analysis. *Journal of Personality and Social Psychology*, 1975, *32*, 55–65.

FILM

Milgram, S. "Obedience" (a filmed experiment). Distributed by the New York University film library. Copyright, 1965.

3   Good Samaritan

Alender, M. The influence of expertise on the bystander effect. Unpublished paper, Department of Psychology, Western Illinois University, 1972.

Borofsky, G. L., Stollak, G. E., & Messe, L. A. Sex differences in bystander reactions to physical assault. *Journal of Experimental Social Psychology*, 1971, *7*, 269–279.

Clark, R. D., & Word, L. E. Why don't bystanders help? Because of ambiguity. *Journal of Personality and Social Psychology*, 1972, *24*, 392–400.

Darley, J. M., & Latané, B. When will people help in a crisis. *Psychology Today*, 1968a, December.

Darley, J. M., & Latané, B. Bystander intervention in emergencies: Diffusion of responsibility. *Journal of Personality and Social Psychology*, 1968b, *8*, 377–383.

Darley, J. M., Teger, I., & Lewis, L. D. Do groups inhibit individuals' responses to potential emergencies? *Journal of Personality and Social Psychology*, 1973, *26*, 395–399.

Hurley, D., & Allen, B. P. The effect of the number of people present in a nonemergency situation. *Journal of Social Psychology*, 1974, *92*, 27–29.

Latané, B., & Darley, J. M. Group inhibition of bystander intervention in emergencies. *Journal of Personality and Social Psychology*, 1968, *10*, 215–221.

Latané, B., & Darley, J. M. *The unresponsive bystander: why doesn't he help*. New York: Appleton-Century-Crofts, 1970.

Latané, B., & Rodin, J. A lady in distress: inhibiting effects of friends and strangers on bystander intervention. *Journal of Experimental Social Psychology*, 1969, *5*, 189–202.

Levy, P., Lundgren, D., Ansel, M., Fell, D., Fink, B., & McGrath, J. E. Bystander effect in a demand without threat situation. *Journal of Personality and Social Psychology*, 1972, *24*, 166–171.

Mason, D., & Allen, B. P. The bystander effect as a function of ambiguity and emergency character. *Journal of Social Psychology*, 1976, *100*, 145–146.

Piliavin, J. A., & Piliavin, I. M. The effect of blood on reactions to a victim. *Journal of Personality and Social Psychology*, 1972, *23*, 353–361.

Piliavin, I. M., Piliavin, J. A., & Rodin, J. Costs, diffusion, and the stigmatized victim. *Journal of Personality and Social Psychology*, 1975, *32*, 429–438.

Piliavin, I. M., Rodin, J., & Piliavin, J. A. Good Samaritanism: An underground phenomenon? *Journal of Personality and Social Psychology*, 1969, *13*, 289–299.

References   **209**

Schwartz, S. H., & Clausen, G. T. Responsibility, norms, and helping in an emergency. *Journal of Personality and Social Psychology,* 1970, *16,* 299–310.

Seedman, A. A., & Hellman, P. *Chief.* New York: Arthur Fields Books, Inc., 1974.

4 Beauty and the Beast

Allen, B. P. Race and physical attractiveness as criteria for white subjects' dating choices. *Social Behavior and Personality,* 1976, *4,* 289–296.

Allen, B. P., and Wroble, S. Attractive people like themselves better than unattractive people—most of the time: Self-descriptions employing the AGT. Paper presented at the Midwestern Psychological Association Convention, 1975.

Berscheid, E., Dion, K., Walster, E., and Walster, W. G. Physical attractiveness and dating choice: A test of the matching hypothesis. *Journal of Experimental Social Psychology,* 1971, *7,* 173–189.

Berscheid, E., & Walster, E. Beauty and the best. *Psychology Today,* 1972, *24,* 207–213.

Cavior, N., & Boblett, P. Physical attractiveness of dating vs. married couples. Paper presented at the American Psychological Association Convention, 1972.

Clifford, M., & Walster, E. The effect of physical attractiveness on teacher expectations. *Sociology of Education,* 1973, *46,* 248–258.

Dermer, M., & Thiel, D. When beauty may fail. *Journal of Personality and Social Psychology,* 1975, *31,* 1168–1176.

Dion, K. Physical attractiveness and evaluations of children's transgressions. *Journal of Personality and Social Psychology,* 1972, *24,* 207–213.

Dion, K. Young children's stereotyping of facial attractiveness. *Developmental Psychology,* 1973, *9,* 183–188.

Dion, K. Children's physical attractiveness and sex as determinants of adult punitiveness. *Developmental Psychology,* 1974, *10,* 772–778.

Dion, K., & Berscheid, E. Physical attractiveness and peer perception among children. *Sociometry,* 1974, *37,* 1–12.

Dion, K., Berscheid, E., & Walster, E. What is beautiful is good. *Journal of Personality and Social Personality,* 1972, *24,* 285–290.

Donley, B., & Allen, B. P. Influences of experimenter attractiveness and egoinvolvement on paired associates learning. *Journal of Social Psychology,* 1977, *101,* 151–152.

Hartnett, J. J., Gottlieb, J., and Hayes, R. L. Social facilitation theory and experimenter attractiveness, *Journal of Social Psychology,* 1976, *99,* 293–294.

Hudson, J. W., & Henze, L. Campus values in mate selection: a replication. *Journal of Marriage and The Family,* 1969, *31,* 772–775.

Krebs, D., & Adinolfi, A. Physical attractiveness, social relations, and personal life-style. *Journal of Personality and Social Psychology,* 1975, *31,* 245–253.

Landy, D., & Sigall, H. Beauty is talent. *Journal of Personality and Social Psychology,* 1974, *29,* 299–304.

Mathes, E. W. The effects of physical attractiveness and anxiety on heterosexual attraction over a series of five encounters. *Journal of Marriage and the Family,* 1975, November, 769–773.

Mathes, E., & Kahn, A. Physical attractiveness, happiness, neuroticism, and self-esteem. *The Journal of Psychology,* 1975, *90,* 27–30.

Meredith, M. The influence of physical attractiveness, independence and honesty on date selection. Unpublished paper, Western Illinois University, 1972.

Murstein, B. I., & Christy, P. Physical attractiveness and marriage adjustment in middle-aged couples. *Journal of Personality and Social Psychology,* 1976, *34,* 537–542.

Nowak, C. A. Youthfulness, attractiveness and the midlife woman: Analysis of the appearance signal in adult development. Paper presented at the Midwestern Psychological Association Convention, 1976.

Potkay, C. R. *The Rorschach Clinician.* New York: Gruen & Stratton, 1971.

Renninger, C. A., & Williams, J. E. Black-white color connotations and racial awareness in preschool children. *Perceptual & Motor Skills,* 1966, *22,* 771–785.

Rosenthal, R. *Experimenter effects in behavioral research.* New York: Appleton-Century-Crofts, 1966.

Shepard, M. The effects of physical attractiveness and trustworthiness in long- and short-term dating selection. Unpublished paper, Western Illinois University. 1973.

Sigall, H., & Landy, D. Radiating beauty: effects of having a physically attractive partner on person perception. *Journal of Personality and Social Psychology,* 1973, *28,* 214–224.

Singer, J. E. The use of manipulative strategies: Machiavellianism and attractiveness. *Sociometry,* 1964, *27,* 128–150.

Tinken, P. L. Testing for a reality basis to the "beautiful-is-good" stereotype. Unpublished Master's thesis, Western Illinois University, 1976.

Vreeland, R. S. Is it true what they say about Harvard boys? *Psychology Today,* 1972, *5,* 65–68.

Walster, E., Aronson, V., Abrahams, D., & Rottmann, L., Importance of physical attractiveness in dating behavior. *Journal of Personality and Social Psychology,* 1966, *4,* 508–516.

5   Racism in America?

Allen, B. P. The importance of race in the rating of stimulus persons attributed with beliefs that are highly congruent with the beliefs of raters: A test of a belief congruence hypothesis. Paper presented at the Southwestern Psychological Association Convention, 1970.

Allen, B. P. Impressions of persuasive communicators: a test of a belief congruence hypothesis. *Journal of Social Psychology*, 1971a, *85*, 145–146.

Allen, B. P. Social distance and admiration reactions of "unprejudiced" whites. *Journal of Personality*, 1975, *43*, 709–726.

Allen, B. P. Social distance reactions to black and white communicators: A replication of an investigation in support of belief congruence theory. *Psychonomic Science*, 1971b, *22*, 344.

Allen, B. P., & Potkay, C. R. Misunderstanding the Adjective Generation Technique (AGT): Comments on Bem's Rejoinder. *Journal of Personality*, 1977b, in press.

Allen, B. P., & Potkay, C. R. The relationship between AGT self-description and significant life events: A longitudinal study. *Journal of Personality*, 1977a, *45*, 207–219.

Allen, B. P., & Potkay, C. R. Variability of self-description on a day-to-day basis; Longitudinal use of the adjective generation technique. *Journal of Personality*, 1973, *41*, 638–652.

Boyanowsky, E. O., & Allen, V. L. Ingroup norms and self identity as determinants of discriminatory behavior. *Journal of Personality and Social Psychology*, 1973, *25*, 408–418.

Dientsbier, R. A. Positive and negative prejudice: Interactions of prejudice with race and social desirability. *Journal of Personality*, 1970, *38*, 198–215.

Dutton, D. G., & Lake, R. A. Threat of own prejudice and reverse discrimination in interracial situations. *Journal of Personality and Social Psychology*, 1973, *28*, 94–100.

Dutton, D. G., & Lennox, V. L. Effect of prior "token" compliance on subsequent interracial behavior. *Journal of Personality and Social Psychology*, 1974, *29*, 65–71.

Gaertner, S. L. Helping behavior and racial discrimination among racial liberals and conservatives. *Journal of Personality and Social Psychology*, 1973, *25*, 335–341.

Gaertner, S. L. Racial attitudes of liberals. Paper presented at the American Psychological Association convention, 1974.

Goldschmid, M. L. (Ed.). *Black Americans and White Racism*. New York: Holt, Rinehart and Winston, 1970.

Goldstein, M., & Davis, E. E. Race and belief: A further analysis of the social determinants of behavioral intentions. *Journal of Personality and Social Psychology*, 1972, *22*, 346–355.

Harding, J., Kutner, B., Proshansky, H., & Chein, I. Prejudice and ethnic relations. In G. Lindzey (Ed.), *Handbook of Social Psychology*, Vol. 2. Reading, Mass.: Addison-Wesley Publishing Co., Inc., 1954, pp. 1021–1061.

Jones, E. E., & Sigall, H. The bogus pipeline: A new paradigm for measuring affect and attitude. *Psychological Bulletin*, 1971, *76*, 349–364.

Life. The search for a black past. Vol. 65, Numbers 21, 22, 23, & 24, 1968 (Nov. 22–Dec. 13).

Malcolm X (with Alex Haley). *The Autobiography of Malcolm X.* New York: Grove Press, 1964.

Mezei, L. Perceived social pressure as an explanation of shifts in the relative influence of race and belief on prejudice across social interactions. *Journal of Personality and Social Psychology,* 1971, *19,* 69–81.

Osgood, C. E., Suci, G. J., & Tannenbaum, P. H. *The measurement of meaning.* Urbana: University of Illinois Press, 1957.

Quarles, B. *The negro in the making of America.* New York: Collier Books, 1964.

Report of National Advisory Commission on Civil Rights. New York: Bantam Books, 1968.

Rokeach, M. Belief versus race as determinants of social distance: Comment on Triandis' paper. *Journal of Abnormal & Social Psychology,* 1961, *62,* 187–188.

Rokeach, M., & Mezei, L. Race & shared belief as factors in social choice. *Science,* 1966, *151,* 167–172.

Rokeach, M., & Rothman, G. The principle of belief congruence and the congruity principle as models of cognitive interaction. *Psychological Review,* 1965, *72,* 128–142.

Rokeach, M., Smith, P., & Evans, R. I. Two kinds of prejudice or one? In M. Rokeach (Ed.), *Open and Closed Mind.* New York: Basic Books, 1960, 132–168.

Schwartz, B. N., & Disch, R. (Eds.). *White racism.* New York: Dell, 1970.

Sigall, H., & Page, R. Current stereotypes: a little fading, a little faking. *Journal of Personality and Social Psychology,* 1971, *18,* 247–255.

Silverman, B. I., & Cochrane, R. Effect of social context on the principle of belief congruence. *Journal of Personality and Social Psychology,* 1972, *22,* 259–268.

Tannenbaum, F. *Slave and citizen: The negro in America.* New York: Knopf, 1947.

Triandis, H. C. A note on Rokeach's theory of prejudice. *Journal of Abnormal and Social Psychology,* 1961, *62,* 184–186.

Triandis, H. C., Loh, W. D., & Levin, L. A. Race, status, quality of spoken English, and opinion about civil rights as determinants of interpersonal attitudes. *Journal of Personality and Social Psychology,* 1966, *3,* 468–472.

Weitz, S. Attitude, voice, and behavior: A repressed affect model of interaction. *Journal of Personality and Social Psychology,* 1972, *24,* 14–21.

Williams, J. E. Connotations of color names among Negroes and Caucasians. *Perceptual and Motor Skills,* 1964, *18,* 721–731.

Williams, J. E., & Edwards, C. D. An exploratory study of the modification of color concepts and racial attitudes in preschool children. *Child Development,* 1969, *40,* 737–750.

Williams, J. E., & Roberson, K. A method for assessing racial attitudes in preschool children. *Educational and Psychological Measurement*, 1967, *27*, 671–689.

Woodmansee, J. J. The pupil response as a measure of social attitudes. In G. Summers (Ed.), *Attitude Measurement*. New York: Rand McNally, 1969.

6   Women's Movement

Allen, B. P. Social distance and admiration reactions of "unprejudiced" whites. *Journal of Personality*, 1975, *43*, 709–726.

Broverman, I. K., Vogel, S. R., Broverman, D., Clarkson, F. E., & Rosenkrantz, P. S. Sex-role stereotypes: a current appraisal. *Journal of Social Issues*, 1972, *28*, 59–78.

Chobot, D. S., Goldberg, P. A., Abramson, L. M., & Abramson, P. R. Prejudice against women: A replication and extension. *Psychological Reports*, 1974, *35*, 478.

Clark, K. B., & Clark, M. P. Racial identification and preference in Negro children. In T. Newcomb & E. Hartley (Eds.), *Readings in Social Psychology*. New York: Holt, Rinehart, and Winston, 1947.

Deaux, K., & Emswiller, T. Explanations of successful performance on sex-linked tasks: What is skill is luck for the female. *Journal of Personality and Social Psychology*, 1974, *29*, 80–85.

Deaux, K., & Taynor, J. Evaluation of male and female ability: Bias works two ways. *Psychological Reports*, 1973, *32*, 261–262.

Deaux, K., White, L., & Farris, E. Skill vs. Luck: Field and laboratory studies of male and female preferences. *Journal of Personality and Social Psychology*, 1975, *32*, 629–636.

Gold, A. R. Reactions to work by authors differing in sex and achievement. Unpublished dissertation, Department of Psychology, Columbia University, New York, New York, 1972.

Goldberg, P. Are women prejudiced against women? *Trans-Action*, 1968, *5* (April), 28–30.

Harding, J., Kutner, B., Proshansky, H., & Chein, I. Prejudice and ethnic relations. In G. Lindzey (Ed.), *Handbook of Social Psychology* (Vol. 2, 1st ed.), pp. 1021–1061. Reading, Mass.: Addison-Wesley, 1954.

Higgins, S. Subject age as a factor in female prejudice against females. Unpublished paper, Dept. of Psychology, Western Illinois University, 1973.

Hough, K. S., & Allen, B. P. Is the "women's movement" erasing the mark of oppression from the female psyche? *The Journal of Psychology*, 1975, *89*, 249–258.

Hraba, J., & Grant, G. Black is beautiful: A reexamination of racial preference and identification. *Journal of Personality and Social Psychology*, 1970, *16*, 398–402.

Levenson, H., Burford, B., Bonno, B., & Davis, L. Are women still prejudiced against women? A replication and extension of Goldberg's study. *Journal of Psychology*, 1975, *89*, 67–71.

McGuire, W. J. The nature of attitudes and attitude change. In G. Lindzey and E. Aronson (Eds.), *The Handbook of Social Psychology* (Vol. 3, 2nd ed.), pp. 136–314. Reading, Mass: Addison-Wesley, 1969.

Mischel, H. N. Sex bias in the evaluation of professional achievements. *Journal of Educational Psychology*, 1974, *66*, 175–166.

Pheterson, G. I. Female prejudice against men, Unpublished paper, Dept. of Psychology, Connecticut College, 1969.

Pheterson, G., Kiesler, S., & Goldberg, P. Evaluation of the performance of women as a function of their sex, achievement, and personal history. *Journal of Personality and Social Psychology*, 1971, *19*, 114–118.

Potkay, C. R., & Merrens, M. R. Sources of male chauvinism in the TAT. *Journal of Personality Assessment*, 1975, *39*, 471–479.

Potkay, C. R., Potkay, C. E., Boynton, G. J., & Klingbeil, J. A. Adjective Generation Technique descriptions of male and female comic strip characters. Unpublished paper, Department of Psychology, Western Illinois University, 1974.

Roberts, M. J. The cultural favorability of being female. Unpublished paper, Department of Psychology, Western Illinois University, 1977.

Robison, A. J. Opinion change as a function of the communicator's sex. Unpublished paper, Dept. of Psychology, Western Illinois University, 1972.

Romero, P. W. (Ed.) *In black America*. Washington: Pioneer Paperback, 1969.

Streicher, H. W. The girls in the cartoons. *The Journal of Communication*, 1974, *42*, 125–129.

Wallies, R. V. Success information as a factor in female evaluation of males and females, Unpublished paper, Dept. of Psychology. Western Illinois University, 1973.

Williams, J. E. Connotations of color names among Negroes and Caucasians. *Perceptual and Motor Skills*, 1964, *18*, 721–731.

Williams, J. E., Tucker, R., & Dunham, F. Changes in the connotations of color names among Negroes and Caucasians: 1963-1969. *Journal of Personality and Social Psychology*, 1971, *19*, 222–228.

Winterbotham, F. W. *The ultra secret*. New York: Dell, 1974.

Author Index

Subject Index

Academic grade, and males and
females, 187
Academic performance and
attractiveness, 108–9, 117
Adjective Generation Technique
(AGT)
advantages of, 153–54, 184,
198–99
in use, 153, 184, 198–200
Admiration measure, 146–47,
160, 165–67
Age regression, suggested, 4, 21–23
Ambiguity, and the bystander effect
research, 74–76, 79–81
real life examples of, 69, 76
80–81, 85–88, 91
Ambivalent prejudice, 158
Amnesia, suggested, 21
Analgesia, suggested, 4, 19–21

Animal magnetism, 2
Anti-female prejudice and
sterotypes
examples, 173–76
experimental evidence, 177–80,
195–200
when predicted, 188–89, 194,
200
Anxiety, 99
Apathy, 66, 70
Apparent racial discrimination,
135–36
Armed forces, and obedience, 55
Attractiveness
anti-social act and, 106–7
association with an attractive
person, 113–16
attractives and unattractives,
116–17